Predictive Modeling Using Logistic Regression

Course Notes

Predictive Modeling Using Logistic Regression Course Notes was developed by Mike Patetta. Additional contributions were made by Dan Kelly, Danny Modlin, Rich Perline, and Chip Wells. Editing and production support was provided by the Curriculum Development and Support Department.

Predictive Modeling Using Logistic Regression Course Notes

Book code E2171, course code LWPMLR93/PMLR93, prepared date 21May2012. LWPMLR93_001

ISBN 978-1-61290-253-1

Table of Contents

Course Description

This course covers predictive modeling using SAS/STAT software with emphasis on the LOGISTIC procedure. This course also discusses selecting variables, assessing models, treating missing values, and using efficiency techniques for massive data sets.

To learn more…

For information about other courses in the curriculum, contact the SAS Education Division at 1-800-333-7660, or send e-mail to training@sas.com. You can also find this information on the Web at support.sas.com/training/ as well as in the Training Course Catalog.

For a list of other SAS books that relate to the topics covered in this Course Notes, USA customers can contact our SAS Publishing Department at 1-800-727-3228 or send e-mail to sasbook@sas.com. Customers outside the USA, please contact your local SAS office.

Also, see the Publications Catalog on the Web at support.sas.com/pubs for a complete list of books and a convenient order form.

Prerequisites

Before attending this course, you should

- have experience executing SAS programs and creating SAS data sets, which you can gain from the SAS Programming I: Essentials course
- have experience building statistical models using SAS software
- have completed a statistics course that covers linear regression and logistic regression, such as the Statistics I: Introduction to ANOVA, Regression, and Logistic Regression course.

Chapter 1 Predictive Modeling

1.1 Introduction

Objectives

- Describe the predictive modeling nomenclature.
- Identify the applications for predictive modeling.
- Illustrate the variable annuity data set.

3

Supervised Classification

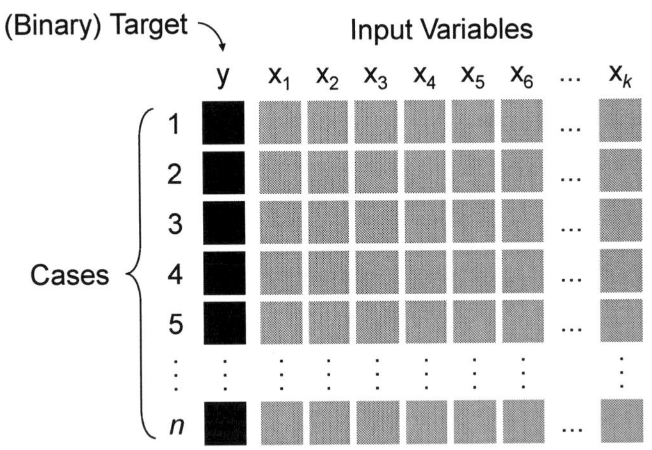

4

The data used to develop a predictive model consist of a set of *cases* (*observations, examples*). Associated with each case is a vector of *input variables* (*predictors, explanatory variables, features*) and a *target variable* (*outcome, response*). A predictive model maps the vector of input variables to the target. The target is the outcome to be predicted. The cases are the units on which the prediction is made.

In *supervised classification* (Hand 1997), the target is a class label. A predictive model assigns, to each case, a score (or a set of scores) that measures the propensity that the case belongs to a particular class. When there are only two possible classes of outcomes, you refer to the target as *binary*. Often, you think of one class in terms of the occurrence of a particular event (such as response to an offer) and the other class is the complement (not responding to the offer).

The term *supervised* is used when the class label is known for each case. If the label is known, then why build a prediction model?

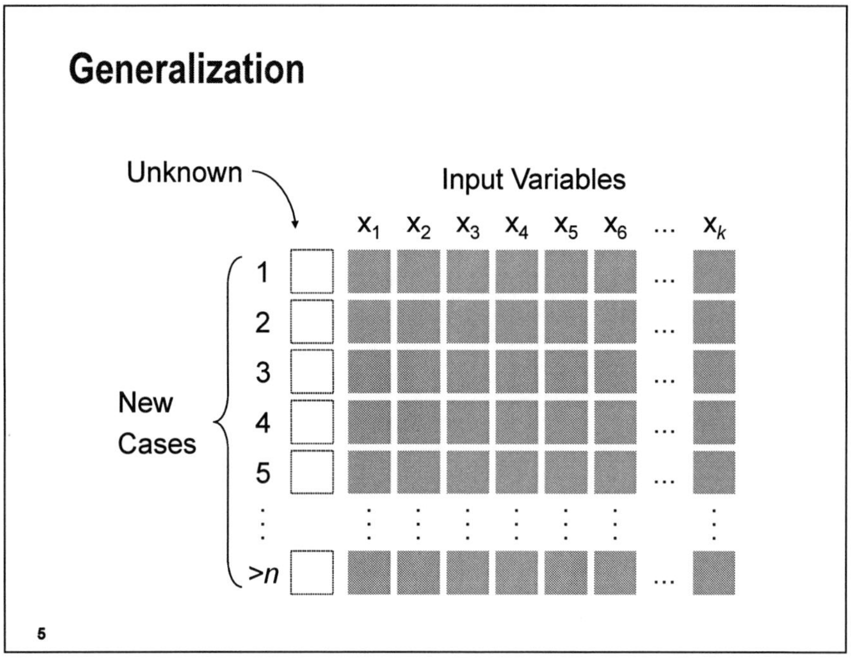

The prediction model is used on new cases where the values of the input variables are known, but the class labels are unknown. The principal aim of predictive modeling is generalization. *Generalization* means the ability to predict the outcome on novel cases.

In contrast, the principal aim of traditional statistical analysis is inference. Confidence intervals, hypothesis tests, and *p*-values are the common inferential tools. Similar methods used by predictive modelers (such as logistic regression) may be used to infer how input variables affect the target. The validity of the inference relies on understanding the statistical properties of methods and applying them correctly.

Understanding the relationships between variables can be important in predictive modeling as well. However, in many practical settings, the discovery of structure is informal and exploratory. The validity of predictive modeling methods is assessed empirically. If a model generalizes well, then this may be all that is considered important. Indeed, some predictive modeling methods (such as neural nets) are essentially impossible to interpret and are not estimated using formal inferential methods, but they are still found to be highly useful.

Applications

Target Marketing

Attrition Prediction

Credit Scoring

Fraud Detection

6

There are many business applications of predictive modeling. *Database marketing* uses customer databases to improve sales promotions and product loyalty. In target marketing, the cases are customers, the inputs are attributes such as previous purchase history and demographics, and the target is often a binary variable indicating a response to a past promotion. The aim is to find segments of customers that are likely to respond to some offer so they can be targeted. Historic customer databases can also be used to predict who is likely to switch brands or cancel services (churn). Loyalty promotions can then be targeted at new cases that are at risk.

Credit scoring (Hand and Henley 1997) is used to decide whether to extend credit to applicants. The cases are past applicants. Most input variables come from the credit application or credit reports. A relevant binary target is whether the case defaulted (charged-off) or paid-off the debt. The aim is to reduce defaults and serious delinquencies on new applicants for credit.

In fraud detection, the cases are transactions (for example, telephone calls, credit card purchases) or insurance claims. The inputs are the particulars and circumstances of the transaction. The binary target is whether that case was fraudulent. The aim is to anticipate fraud or abuse on new transactions or claims so that they can be investigated or impeded.

Supervised classification also has less business-oriented uses. Image classification has applications in areas such as astronomy, nuclear medicine, and molecular genetics (McLachlan 1992; Ripley 1996; Hand 1997).

Variable Annuity Data Set

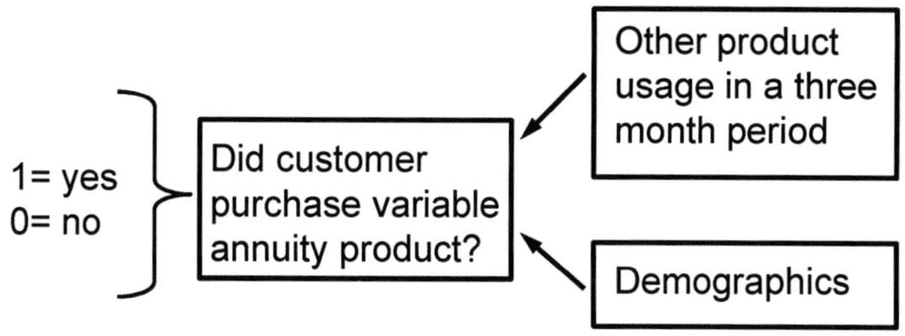

7

Example: A target marketing campaign for a bank was undertaken to identify segments of customers who are likely to respond to a variable annuity (insurance product) marketing campaign. A data set was created with 32,264 cases (banking customers) and 47 input variables. The binary target variable, **Ins**, indicates whether the customer bought the variable annuity product. The 47 input variables represent other product usage in a three month period and demographics. Two of the inputs are nominally scaled; the others are interval or binary. The data are in a SAS data set called **develop**.

These are the variables in the data set:

Ins	purchase variable annuity account (`1`=`yes`, `0`=`no`)
AcctAge	age of oldest account in years
DDA	checking account (`1`=`yes`, `0`=`no`)
DDABal	checking account balance
Dep	number of checking deposits
DepAmt	amount deposited
CashBk	number of times customer received cash back
Checks	number of checks
DirDep	direct deposit (`1`=`yes`, `0`=`no`)
NSF	occurrence of insufficient funds (`1`=`yes`, `0`=`no`)
NSFAmt	amount of insufficient funds
Phone	number of times customer used telephone banking

Teller	number of teller visits
Sav	saving account (`1`=`yes`, `0`=`no`)
SavBal	saving balance
ATM	used ATM service (`1`=`yes`, `0`=`no`)
ATMAmt	ATM withdrawal amount
POS	number of point of sale transactions
POSAmt	amount in point of sale transactions
CD	has certificate of deposit (`1`=`yes`, `0`=`no`)
CDBal	certificate of deposit balance
IRA	has retirement account (`1`=`yes`, `0`=`no`)
IRABal	retirement account balance
LOC	has line of credit (`1`=`yes`, `0`=`no`)
LOCBal	line of credit balance
Inv	has investment account (`1`=`yes`, `0`=`no`)
InvBal	investment account balance
ILS	has installment loan (`1`=`yes`, `0`=`no`)
ILSBal	installment loan balance
MM	has money market account (`1`=`yes`, `0`=`no`)
MMBal	money market balance
MMCred	number of money market credits
MTG	has mortgage account (`1`=`yes`, `0`=`no`)
MTGBal	mortgage balance
CC	has credit card account (`1`=`yes`, `0`=`no`)
CCBal	credit card balance
CCPurc	number of credit card purchases
SDB	has a safety deposit box (`1`=`yes`, `0`=`no`)
Income	income in thousands of dollars
HMOwn	owns home (`1`=`yes`, `0`=`no`)
LORes	length of residence in years

HMVal	home value in thousands of dollars
Age	age of customer in years
CRScore	credit score
Moved	recent address change (**1**=**yes**, **0**=**no**)
InArea	local address (**1**=**yes**, **0**=**no**)

Exploring the Data

Example: Examine the **develop** data set by generating descriptive statistics and frequency tables.

The DATA step reads in the original data and creates a data set in the work library. This prevents writing over the original data.

```
/* pmlr01d01.sas */
libname pmlr 'SAS-data-library';
data develop;
   set pmlr.develop;
run;
```

The %LET statement enables you to define a macro variable and assign it a value. The statement below creates a macro variable named **inputs** and assigns it a string that contains all the numeric input variable names. This reduces the amount of text you need to enter in other programs.

```
%let inputs=acctage dda ddabal dep depamt cashbk checks
            dirdep nsf nsfamt phone teller atm atmamt pos posamt
            cd cdbal ira irabal loc locbal inv invbal ils ilsbal
            mm mmbal mmcred mtg mtgbal sav savbal cc ccbal
            ccpurc sdb income hmown lores hmval age crscore
            moved inarea;
```

The MEANS procedure generates descriptive statistics for the numeric variables. The statistics requested below are the number of observations, the number of missing values, the mean, the minimum value, and the maximum value. The macro variable, **inputs**, is referenced in the VAR statement by prefixing an ampersand (&) to the macro variable name. The FREQ procedure examines the values of the target variable and the nominal input variables.

```
proc means data=develop n nmiss mean min max;
   var &inputs;
run;

proc freq data=develop;
   tables ins branch res;
run;
```

Variable	Label	N	N Miss	Mean	Minimum	Maximum
AcctAge	Age of Oldest Account	30194	2070	5.9086772	0.3000000	61.5000000
DDA	Checking Account	32264	0	0.8156459	0	1.0000000
DDABal	Checking Balance	32264	0	2170.02	-774.8300000	278093.83
Dep	Checking Deposits	32264	0	2.1346082	0	28.0000000
DepAmt	Amount Deposited	32264	0	2232.76	0	484893.67
CashBk	Number Cash Back	32264	0	0.0159621	0	4.0000000
Checks	Number of Checks	32264	0	4.2599182	0	49.0000000
DirDep	Direct Deposit	32264	0	0.2955616	0	1.0000000
NSF	Number Insufficient Fund	32264	0	0.0870630	0	1.0000000
NSFAmt	Amount NSF	32264	0	2.2905464	0	666.8500000
Phone	Number Telephone Banking	28131	4133	0.4056024	0	30.0000000
Teller	Teller Visits	32264	0	1.3652678	0	27.0000000
Sav	Saving Account	32264	0	0.4668981	0	1.0000000
SavBal	Saving Balance	32264	0	3170.60	0	700026.94
ATM	ATM	32264	0	0.6099368	0	1.0000000
ATMAmt	ATM Withdrawal Amount	32264	0	1235.41	0	427731.26
POS	Number Point of Sale	28131	4133	1.0756816	0	54.0000000
POSAmt	Amount Point of Sale	28131	4133	48.9261782	0	3293.49
CD	Certificate of Deposit	32264	0	0.1258368	0	1.0000000
CDBal	CD Balance	32264	0	2530.71	0	1053900.00
IRA	Retirement Account	32264	0	0.0532792	0	1.0000000
IRABal	IRA Balance	32264	0	617.5704550	0	596497.60
LOC	Line of Credit	32264	0	0.0633833	0	1.0000000
LOCBal	Line of Credit Balance	32264	0	1175.22	-613.0000000	523147.24
Inv	Investment	28131	4133	0.0296826	0	1.0000000
InvBal	Investment Balance	28131	4133	1599.17	-2214.92	8323796.02
ILS	Installment Loan	32264	0	0.0495909	0	1.0000000
ILSBal	Loan Balance	32264	0	517.5692344	0	29162.79
MM	Money Market	32264	0	0.1148959	0	1.0000000
MMBal	Money Market Balance	32264	0	1875.76	0	120801.11
MMCred	Money Market Credits	32264	0	0.0563786	0	5.0000000
MTG	Mortgage	32264	0	0.0493429	0	1.0000000
MTGBal	Mortgage Balance	32264	0	8081.74	0	10887573.28
CC	Credit Card	28131	4133	0.4830969	0	1.0000000
CCBal	Credit Card Balance	28131	4133	9586.55	-2060.51	10641354.78

CCPurc	Credit Card Purchases	28131	4133	0.1541716	0	5.0000000
SDB	Safety Deposit Box	32264	0	0.1086660	0	1.0000000
Income	Income	26482	5782	40.5889283	0	233.0000000
HMOwn	Owns Home	26731	5533	0.5418802	0	1.0000000
LORes	Length of Residence	26482	5782	7.0056642	0.5000000	19.5000000
HMVal	Home Value	26482	5782	110.9121290	67.0000000	754.0000000
Age	Age	25907	6357	47.9283205	16.0000000	94.0000000
CRScore	Credit Score	31557	707	666.4935197	509.0000000	820.0000000
Moved	Recent Address Change	32264	0	0.0296305	0	1.0000000
InArea	Local Address	32264	0	0.9602963	0	1.0000000

The results of PROC MEANS show that several variables have missing values and several variables are binary.

Ins	Frequency	Percent	Cumulative Frequency	Cumulative Percent
0	21089	65.36	21089	65.36
1	11175	34.64	32264	100.00

Branch of Bank				
Branch	Frequency	Percent	Cumulative Frequency	Cumulative Percent
B1	2819	8.74	2819	8.74
B10	273	0.85	3092	9.58
B11	247	0.77	3339	10.35
B12	549	1.70	3888	12.05
B13	535	1.66	4423	13.71
B14	1072	3.32	5495	17.03
B15	2235	6.93	7730	23.96
B16	1534	4.75	9264	28.71
B17	850	2.63	10114	31.35
B18	541	1.68	10655	33.02
B19	285	0.88	10940	33.91
B2	5345	16.57	16285	50.47
B3	2844	8.81	19129	59.29
B4	5633	17.46	24762	76.75
B5	2752	8.53	27514	85.28
B6	1438	4.46	28952	89.73
B7	1413	4.38	30365	94.11
B8	1341	4.16	31706	98.27
B9	558	1.73	32264	100.00

Area Classification				
Res	Frequency	Percent	Cumulative Frequency	Cumulative Percent
R	8077	25.03	8077	25.03
S	11506	35.66	19583	60.70
U	12681	39.30	32264	100.00

The results of PROC FREQ show that 34.6 percent of the observations have acquired the insurance product. There are 19 levels of **Branch** and 3 levels under **Res** (`R`=rural, `S`=suburb, `U`=urban).

1.2 Analytical Challenges

Objectives

- Describe the analytical challenges that predictive modelers face.
- Offer some solutions to these challenges.

11

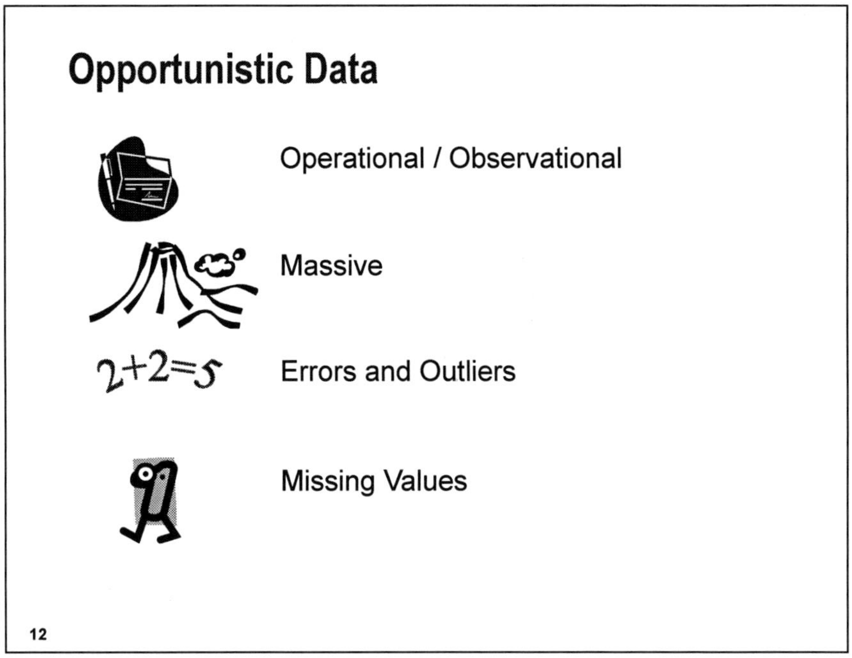

The data that are typically used to develop predictive models can be characterized as *opportunistic*. The data were collected for operational purposes unrelated to statistical analysis (Huber 1997). Such data are usually massive, dynamic, and dirty. Preparing data for predictive modeling is often very difficult. For example, the parts of the data that are relevant to the analysis need to be acquired. Furthermore, the relevant inputs usually need to be created from the raw operational fields. Many statistical methods do not scale well to massive data sets because most methods were developed for small data sets generated from designed experiments.

Mixed Measurement Scales

sales, executive, homemaker, ...

88.60, 3.92, 34890.50, 45.01, ...

F, D, C, B, A

0, 1, 2, 3, 4, 5, 6, ...

M, F

27513, 21737, 92614, 10043, ...

13

When there are large numbers of input variables, there is usually a variety of measurement scales represented. The input variable may be intervally scaled (amounts), binary, nominally scaled (names), ordinally scaled (grades), or counts. Nominal input variables with a large number of levels (such as ZIP code) are commonplace and present complications for regression analysis.

High Dimensionality

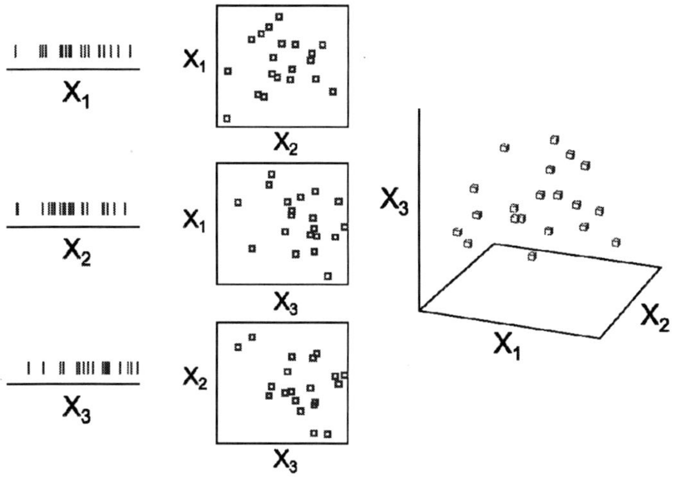

14

The *dimension* refers to the number of input variables (actually input degrees of freedom). Predictive modelers consider large numbers (hundreds) of input variables. The number of variables often has a greater effect on computational performance than the number of cases. High dimensionality limits the ability to explore and model the relationships among the variables. This is known as the *curse of dimensionality*, which was distilled by Breiman et al. (1984) as:

> *The complexity of a data set increases rapidly with increasing dimensionality.*

The remedy is dimension reduction; ignore irrelevant and redundant dimensions without inadvertently ignoring important ones.

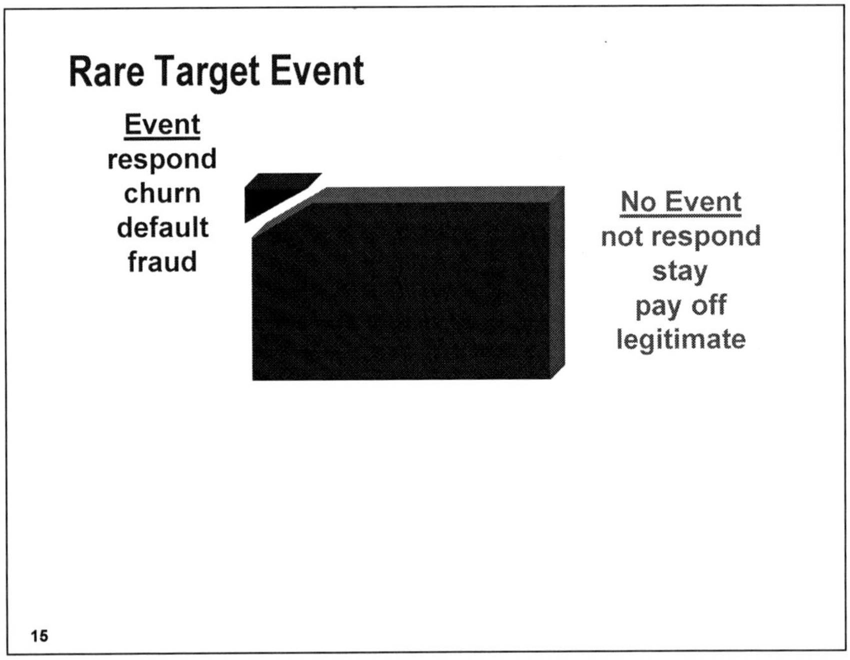

In predictive modeling, the event of interest is often rare. With rare events, the effective sample size for building a reliable prediction model is closer to 3 times the number of event cases than to the nominal size of the data set (Harrell 1997). A seemingly massive data set might have the predictive potential of one that is much smaller.

One widespread strategy for predicting rare events is to build a model on a sample that disproportionally over-represents the event cases (for example, an equal number of events and nonevents). Such an analysis introduces biases that need to be corrected so that the results are applicable to the population.

Nonlinearities and Interactions

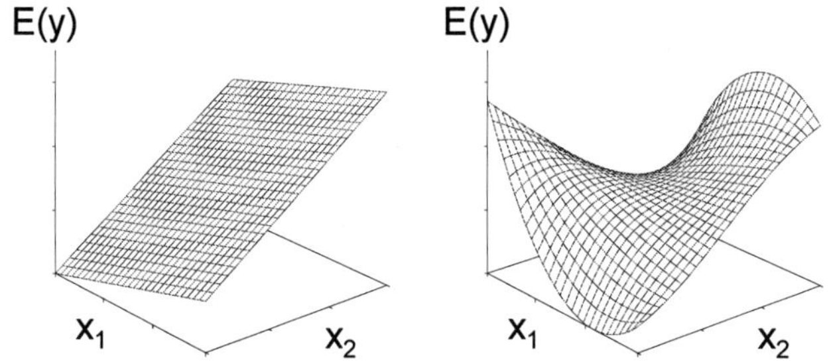

Linear
Additive

Nonlinear
Nonadditive

16

Predictive modeling is a multivariate problem. Each important dimension might affect the target in complicated ways. Moreover, the effect of each input variable might depend on the values of other input variables. The curse of dimensionality makes this difficult to untangle. Many classical modeling methods (including standard logistic regression) were developed for inputs with effects that have a constant rate of change and do not depend on any other inputs.

Model Selection

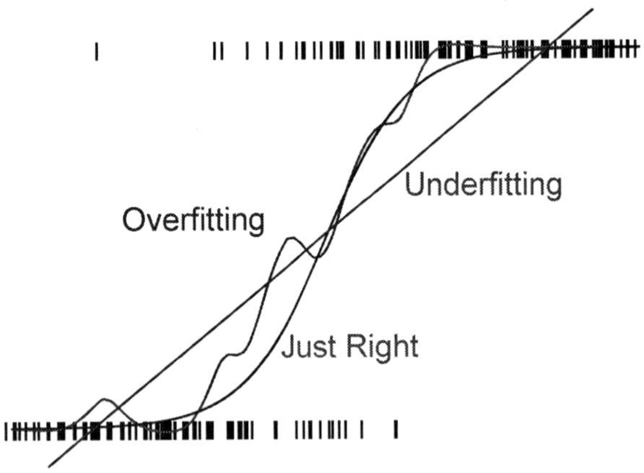

17

Predictive modeling typically involves choices from among a set of models. These might be different types of models. These might be different complexities of models of the same type. A common pitfall is to overfit the data (to use too complex a model). An overly complex model might be too sensitive to peculiarities in the sample data set and not generalize well to new data. However, using too simple a model can lead to *underfitting,* where true features are disregarded.

1.01 Multiple Choice Poll

Which situation poses the biggest analytical challenge in your job as a predictive modeler?

a. Large number of missing values
b. Nominal variables with a large number of levels
c. Large number of predictor variables
d. Rare target events
e. None of the above

18

1.3 Chapter Summary

The principal objective of predictive modeling is to predict the outcome on new cases. Some of the business applications include target marketing, attrition prediction, credit scoring, and fraud detection. One challenge in building a predictive model is that the data usually were not collected for purposes of data analysis. Therefore, the data are usually massive, dynamic, and dirty. For example, the data usually have large numbers of input variables. This limits the ability to explore and model the relationships among the variables. Thus, detecting interactions and nonlinearities becomes a cumbersome problem.

When the target is rare, a widespread strategy is to build a model on a sample that disproportionally over-represents the events. The results will be biased, but they can be easily corrected to represent the population.

A common pitfall in building a predictive model is to overfit the data. An overfitted model will be too sensitive to the nuances in the data and will not generalize well to new data. However, a model that underfits the data will systematically miss the true features in the data.

Chapter 2 Fitting the Model

2.1 The Model

Objectives

- Define the concepts of logistic regression.
- Fit a logistic regression model in the LOGISTIC procedure.
- Score new cases in PROC LOGISTIC.

3

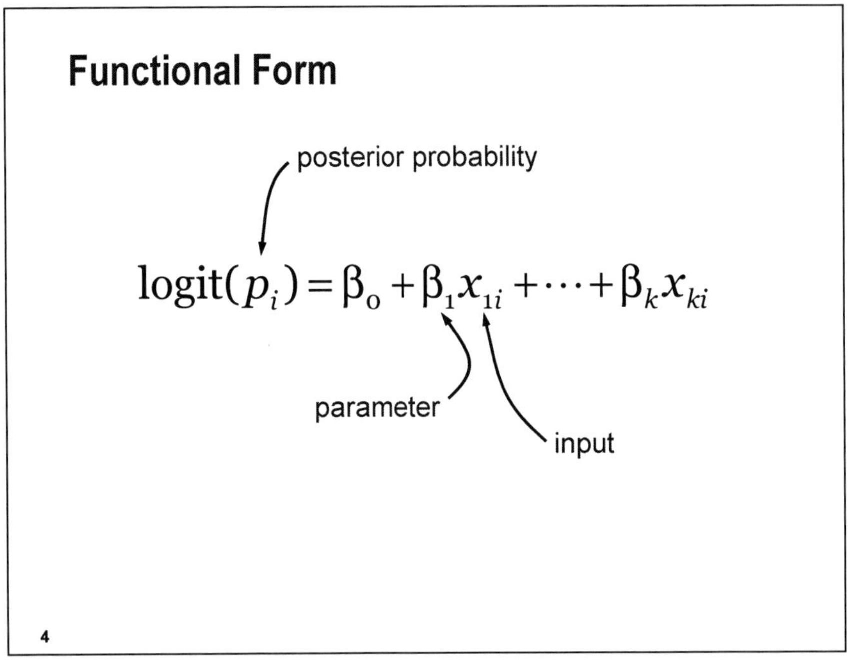

The data set consists of i=1,2,…,n cases. Each case belongs to one of two classes. A binary indicator variable represents the class label for each case

$$y_i = \begin{cases} 1 & \text{target event for case } i \\ 0 & \text{no target event for case } i \end{cases}$$

Associated with each case is k-vector of input variables

$$\mathbf{x}_i = (x_{1i}, x_{2i}, \ldots, x_{ki})$$

The posterior probability of the target event given the inputs is

$$p_i = E(y_i \mid \mathbf{x}_i) = \Pr(y_i = 1 \mid \mathbf{x}_i)$$

The standard logistic regression model assumes that the logit of the posterior probability is a linear combination of the input variables. The parameters, $\beta_0,\ldots,\beta_k$, are unknown constants that must be estimated from the data.

The Logit Link Function

$$\text{logit}(p_i) = \ln\left(\frac{p_i}{1-p_i}\right) = \eta \quad \Leftrightarrow \quad p_i = \frac{1}{1+e^{-\eta}}$$

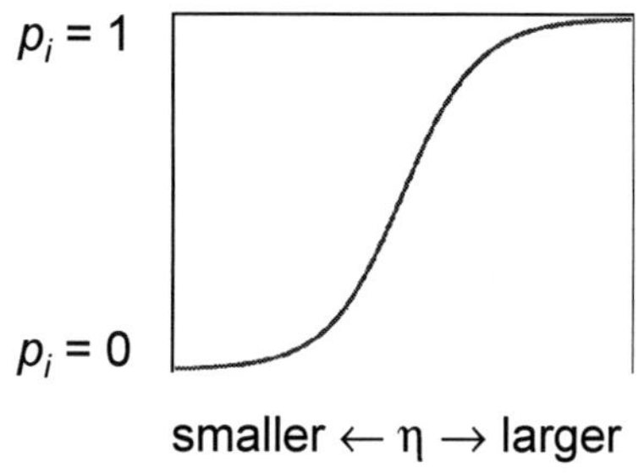

5

A linear combination can take any value. Probability must be between zero and one. The logit transformation (which is the log of the odds) is a device for constraining the posterior probability to be between zero and one. The logit function transforms the probability scale to the real line $(-\infty, +\infty)$. Therefore, modeling the logit with a linear combination gives estimated probabilities that are constrained to be between zero and one.

Logistic regression is a special case of the *generalized linear model*

$$g(E(y\,|\,\mathbf{x})) = \beta_0 + \beta_1 x_1 + \cdots + \beta_k x_k$$

where the expected value of the target is linked to the linear predictor by the function $g(\bullet)$. The link function depends on the scale of the target.

The Fitted Surface

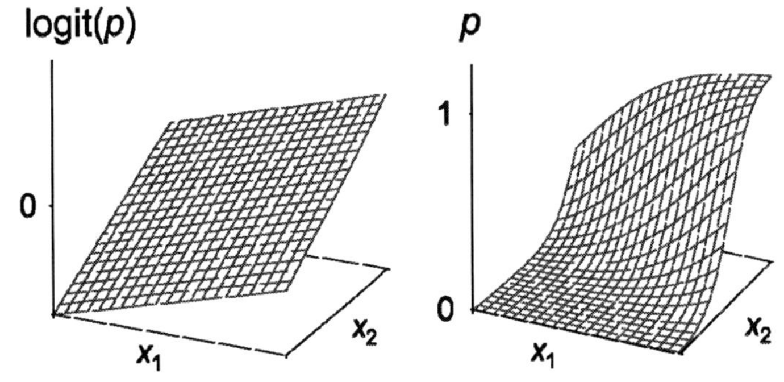

6

The graph of a linear combination on the logit scale is a (hyper)plane. On the probability scale, it becomes a sigmoidal surface. Different parameter values give different surfaces with different slopes and different orientations. The nonlinearity is solely due to the constrained scale of the target. The nonlinearity only appears when the fitted values are close to the limits of their sensible range (>.8 or <.2).

Interpretation

Unit change in $x_2 \Rightarrow$

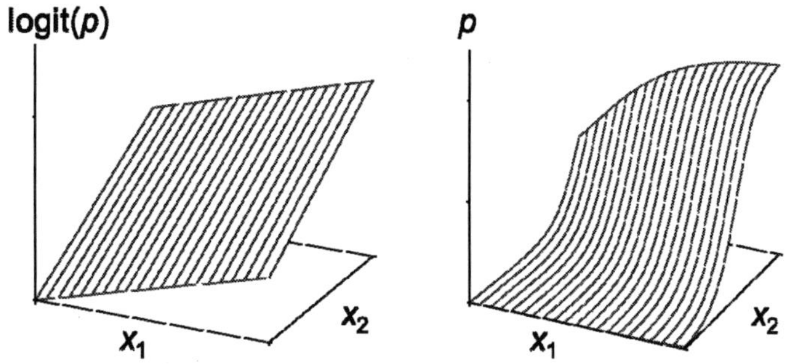

β_2 change in logit

100(exp(β_2)-1)% change in the odds

7

A linear-additive model is particularly easy to interpret since each input variable affects the logit linearly. The coefficients are the slopes. Exponentiating each parameter estimate gives the odds ratios, which compares the odds of the event in one group to the odds of the event in another group.

Odds Ratio from a Logistic Regression Model

Estimated logistic regression model:

logit(p) = –.7567 + .4373*(**gender**)

where females are coded 1 and males are coded 0

Estimated odds ratio (Females to Males):

odds ratio = $(e^{-.7567+.4373})/(e^{-.7567})$ = 1.55

8

The slide above shows how odds ratios are simple functions of the parameters. For example, suppose you want to examine the relationship between **gender** and the target variable. The odds ratio for **gender** compares the predicted odds of females to have the outcome to the predicted odds of males. If **gender** is coded 1 for females and 0 for males, the odds ratio is simply the exponentiation of the parameter estimate for **gender**. An odds ratio of 1.55 means that females have 1.55 times the odds of having the outcome compared to males.

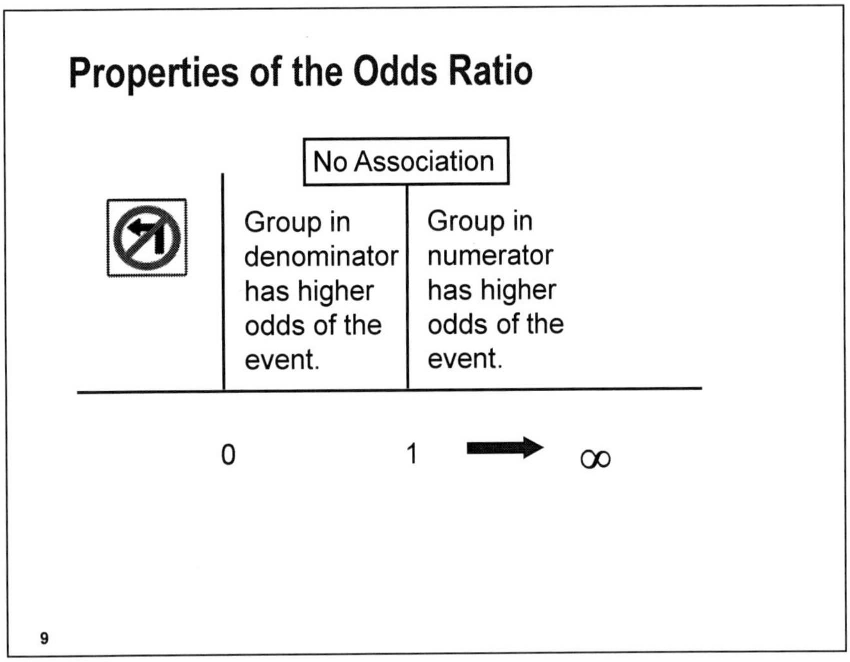

The odds ratio shows the strength of the association between the predictor variable and the response variable. If the odds ratio is 1, then there is no association between the predictor variable and the response. If the odds ratio is greater than 1, then the group in the numerator has higher odds of having the event. If the odds ratio is less than 1, then the group in the denominator has higher odds of having the event. For example, an odds ratio of 3 indicates that the odds of getting the event in the group in the numerator are 3 times that in the group in the denominator.

The odds ratio represents the multiplicative effect of each input variable. Moreover, the effect of each input variable does not depend on the values of the other inputs (additivity).

However, this simple interpretation depends on the model being correctly specified. In predictive modeling, you should not presume that the true posterior probability has such a simple form. Think of the model as an approximating (hyper)plane. Consequently, you can determine the extent that the inputs are important in representing the approximating plane.

Logistic Discrimination

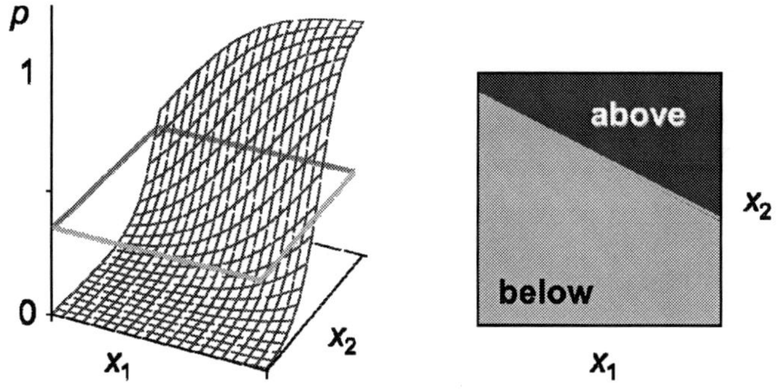

10

In supervised classification, the ultimate use of logistic regression is to allocate cases to classes. This is more correctly termed logistic discrimination (McClachlan 1989). An allocation rule is merely an assignment of a cutoff probability, where cases above the cutoff are allocated to class 1 and cases below the cutoff are allocated to class 0. The standard logistic discrimination model separates the classes by a linear surface ((hyper)plane). The decision boundary is always linear. Determining the best cutoff is a fundamental concern in logistic discrimination.

Maximum Likelihood Estimation

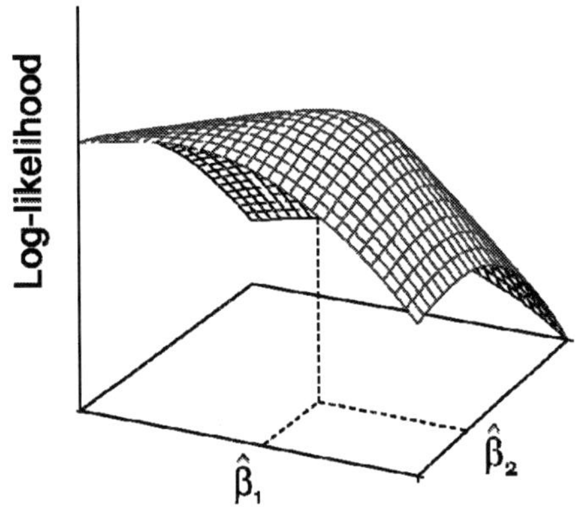

11

The method of maximum likelihood (ML) is usually used to estimate the unknown parameters in the logistic regression model. The likelihood function is the joint probability density function of the data treated as a function of the parameters. The maximum likelihood estimates are the values of the parameters that maximize the probability of obtaining the sample data.

It is usually computationally more convenient to work with the log of the likelihood rather than the likelihood itself. The parameter estimates that maximize the log of the likelihood will also maximize the likelihood. Then if you assume that the y_i independently have Bernoulli distributions with probability p_i (which is a function of the parameters), then the log of the likelihood is given by

$$\sum_{i=1}^{n}\left(y_i \ln(p_i)+(1-y_i)\ln(1-p_i)\right) \quad = \quad \sum_{i|y=1}^{n_1}\ln(p_i)+\sum_{i|y=0}^{n_0}\ln(1-p_i)$$

where n_0 and n_1 are the numbers of class 0 and class 1, respectively. The form of the log-likelihood shows the intuitively appealing result that the ML estimates be chosen so that p_i is large when y_i=1 and small when y_i=0.

In ML estimation the combination of parameter values that maximize the likelihood (or log-likelihood) are pursued. There is, in general, no closed form analytical solution for the ML estimates as there is for linear regression on a normally distributed response. They must be determined using an iterative optimization algorithm. Consequently, logistic regression is considerably more computationally expensive than linear regression.

Software for ML estimation of the logistic model is commonplace. Many SAS procedures can be used; most notable are the LOGISTIC, GENMOD, CATMOD, and DMREG procedures (SAS Enterprise Miner).

Concordant versus Discordant

	Customer Bought Variable Annuity Product		
Customer Did Not Buy Variable Annuity Product	Predicted Outcome Probability	High	Low
	High	Tie	Discordant Pair
	Low	Concordant Pair	Tie

12

In logistic regression, several measures that assess the predictive accuracy of the model are reported. These measures are calculated from the percent concordant, discordant, and tied pairs. For all possible pairs of observations with different outcomes (in this example, buying variable annuity account products), a comparison is made of the predicted outcome probabilities. If the observation with the outcome has a higher predicted outcome probability compared to an observation without the outcome, the pair is *concordant*. However, if the observation with the outcome has a lower predicted outcome probability compared to the predicted outcome probability of an observation without the outcome, the pair is *discordant*. If the predicted outcome probabilities are the same, the pair is *tied*.

LOGISTIC Procedure

```
PROC LOGISTIC <options>;
     CLASS variable</v-options>;
     MODEL response=<effects></options>;
     ODDSRATIO <'label'> variable </ options>;
     ROC <'label'> <specification> </ options>;
     ROCCONTRAST <'label'><contrast></ options>;
     SCORE <options>;
     UNITS predictor1=list1 </option>;
     OUTPUT <OUT=SAS-data-set> keyword=name...
               keyword=name></option>;
RUN;
```

13

The LOGISTIC procedure fits logistic regression models for binary, ordinal, or nominal response data.

Selected LOGISTIC procedure statements:

CLASS	specifies the classification variables to be used in the analysis. The CLASS statement must precede the MODEL statement.
MODEL	specifies the response variable and the predictor variables (which can be character or numeric). The MODEL statement is required, and only one is allowed with each invocation of PROC LOGISTIC.
ODDSRATIO	produces odds ratios for variables even when the variables are involved in interactions with other covariates, and for classification variables that use any parameterization. You can specify several ODDSRATIO statements.
ROC	specifies models to be used in the ROC comparisons. You can specify more than one ROC statement. ROC statements are identified by their label.
ROCCONTRAST	compares the different ROC models. You can specify only one ROCCONTRAST statement.
SCORE	creates a data set that contains all the data in the DATA= data set together with posterior probabilities and, optionally, prediction confidence intervals. You can specify several SCORE statements.
UNITS	enables you to obtain an odds ratio estimate for a specified change in a predictor variable. The unit of change can be a number, standard deviation (SD) or a number times the standard deviation (2*SD).

2.01 Multiple Choice Poll

The odds ratio for a $1000-increase in income is 1.074. What does this mean for every $1000-increase in income?

a. The probability of the event increases 7.4%.
b. The logit increases 7.4%.
c. The odds of the event increases 7.4%.
d. The log of the odds of the event increases 7.4%.

14

Introduction to the LOGISTIC Procedure

Example: Fit a logistic regression model to the **develop** data set. Specify **Ins** as the target variable and **DDA**, **DDABal**, **Dep**, **DepAmt**, **CashBk**, **Checks**, and **Res** as the input variables. Use the EVENT=option to model the probability of buying the variable annuity product. Specify **Res** as a CLASS variable using reference cell coding and S as the reference cell. Use the UNITS statement to obtain an odds ratio estimate for a 1000-unit change in **DDABal** and **DepAmt**. Create an effect plot for **DDABal**, **DepAmt**, **Checks**, and **Res** with confidence bands and an odds ratio plot with a horizontal orientation and the statistics displayed. Use the ODDSRATIO statement to compute the odds ratios for all the pairwise comparisons in **Res**. Specify profile likelihood confidence intervals, and request standardized estimates for the parameters for the continuous input variables.

```
/* pmlr02d01.sas */
proc logistic data=develop plots(only)=(effect(clband x=(ddabal depamt
             checks res)) oddsratio (type=horizontalstat));
   class res (param=ref ref='S');
   model ins(event='1')=dda ddabal dep depamt cashbk checks res
             / stb clodds=pl;
   units ddabal=1000 depamt=1000 / default=1;
   oddsratio 'Comparisons of Residential Classification' res
             / diff=all cl=pl;
run;
```

Selected PROC LOGISTIC statement option:

PLOTS= controls the plots produced through ODS Statistical Graphics.

Selected global plot option:

ONLY suppresses the default plots. Only specifically requested plot-requests are displayed.

Selected plot requests:

EFFECT displays and enhances the effect plots for the model.

ODDSRATIO displays and enhances the odds ratio plots for the model when the CLODDS= option or ODDSRATIO statements are also specified.

Selected effect plot options:

CLBAND displays confidence limits on the plots.

X= specifies effects to be used on the X-axis of the effect plots. You can specify several different X-axes: continuous variables must be specified as main effects, while CLASS variables can be crossed.

Selected ODDSRATIO plot option:

TYPE	controls the look of the graphic. The default TYPE=HORIZONTAL option places the odds ratio values on the X-axis, while the TYPE=HORIZONTALSTAT option also displays the values of the odds ratios and their confidence limits on the right side of the graphic. The TYPE=VERTICAL option places the odds ratio values on the Y-axis, while the TYPE=VERTICALBLOCK option (available only with the CLODDS= option) places the odds ratio values on the Y-axis and puts boxes around the labels.

Selected CLASS statement option:

PARAM=	specifies the parameterization method for the classification variable or variables. The default is PARAM=EFFECT.
REF=*'level'* | *keyword*	specifies the reference level for PARAM=EFFECT, PARAM=REF, and their orthogonalizations. For an individual variable, you can specify the level of the variable to use as the reference level. For a global or individual variable, you can use one of the following keywords: FIRST designates the first ordered level as the reference. LAST designates the last ordered level as the reference. This is the default.

Selected MODEL statement options:

EVENT=*'category'* | *keyword*	specifies the event category for the binary response model. PROC LOGISTIC models the probability of the event category. The EVENT= option has no effect when there are more than two response categories. You can specify the value (formatted if a format is applied) of the event category in quotation marks or you can specify one of the following keywords: FIRST designates the first ordered category as the event. This is the default. LAST designates the last ordered category as the event.
CLODDS=	request confidence intervals for the odds ratios. Computation of these confidence intervals is based on the profile likelihood (CLODDS=PL, which is desirable for small sample sizes) or based on individual Wald tests (CLODDS=WALD). By specifying CLODDS=BOTH, the procedure computes two sets of confidence intervals for the odds ratios, one based on the profile likelihood and the other based on the Wald tests.
STB	requests that standardized estimates for the parameters be printed for each continuous predictor variable.

Selected UNITS statement option:

DEFAULT= gives a list of units of change for all predictor variables that are not specified in the UNITS statement. If the DEFAULT= option is not specified, PROC LOGISTIC does not produce customized odds ratio estimates for any predictor variable that is not listed in the UNITS statement.

Selected ODDSRATIO statement options:

CL specifies whether to create Wald or profile-likelihood confidence limits, or both. By default, Wald confidence limits are produced.

DIFF= specifies whether the odds ratios for a classification *variable* are computed against the reference level, or all pairs of *variable* are compared. By default, DIFF=ALL. The DIFF= option is ignored when *variable* is continuous.

The LOGISTIC Procedure

Model Information	
Data Set	WORK.DEVELOP
Response Variable	Ins
Number of Response Levels	2
Model	binary logit
Optimization Technique	Fisher's scoring

Number of Observations Read	32264
Number of Observations Used	32264

Response Profile		
Ordered Value	**Ins**	**Total Frequency**
1	0	21089
2	1	11175

Probability modeled is Ins=1.

The results consist of a number of tables. The Response Profile table shows the target variable values listed according to their ordered values. By default, the target-variable values are ordered alphanumerically and PROC LOGISTIC always models the probability of the first ordered value. Because you used the EVENT= option, in this example, the model is based on the probability of buying the variable annuity product (**Ins**=1).

Class Level Information			
Class	**Value**	**Design Variables**	
Res	R	1	0
	S	0	0
	U	0	1

The Class Level Information table shows the **Res** variable was dummy coded into two design variables using reference cell coding and the level S as the reference level.

Model Convergence Status
Convergence criterion (GCONV=1E-8) satisfied.

Model Fit Statistics		
Criterion	**Intercept Only**	**Intercept and Covariates**
AIC	41633.206	39565.329
SC	41641.587	39640.765
-2 Log L	41631.206	39547.329

The Model Fit Statistics table contains the Akaike information criteria (AIC) and the Schwarz criterion (SC). These are goodness-of-fit measures that you can use to compare one model to another.

Testing Global Null Hypothesis: BETA=0			
Test	**Chi-Square**	**DF**	**Pr > ChiSq**
Likelihood Ratio	2083.8761	8	<.0001
Score	1843.2388	8	<.0001
Wald	1768.0578	8	<.0001

The Likelihood Ratio, Wald, and Score tests all test the null hypothesis that all regression coefficients of the model other than the intercept are 0.

Type 3 Analysis of Effects			
Effect	DF	Wald Chi-Square	Pr > ChiSq
DDA	1	633.6092	<.0001
DDABal	1	448.5968	<.0001
Dep	1	42.8222	<.0001
DepAmt	1	30.6227	<.0001
CashBk	1	24.1615	<.0001
Checks	1	1.6168	0.2035
Res	2	2.7655	0.2509

The Type 3 Analysis of Effects table shows which input variables are statistically significant controlling for all of the other input variables in the model.

Analysis of Maximum Likelihood Estimates							
Parameter		DF	Estimate	Standard Error	Wald Chi-Square	Pr > ChiSq	Standardized Estimate
Intercept		1	0.1519	0.0304	24.8969	<.0001	
DDA		1	-0.9699	0.0385	633.6092	<.0001	-0.2074
DDABal		1	0.000072	3.39E-6	448.5968	<.0001	0.2883
Dep		1	-0.0714	0.0109	42.8222	<.0001	-0.0678
DepAmt		1	0.000018	3.225E-6	30.6227	<.0001	0.0660
CashBk		1	-0.5629	0.1145	24.1615	<.0001	-0.0408
Checks		1	-0.00402	0.00317	1.6168	0.2035	-0.0114
Res	R	1	-0.0467	0.0316	2.1907	0.1388	
Res	U	1	-0.0379	0.0280	1.8375	0.1752	

The parameter estimates measure the rate of change in the logit (log odds) corresponding to a one-unit change in input variable, adjusted for the effects of the other inputs. The parameter estimates are difficult to compare because they depend on the units in which the variables are measured. The standardized estimates convert them to standard deviation units. The absolute value of the standardized estimates can be used to give an approximate ranking of the relative importance of the input variables on the fitted logistic model. The variable **Res** has no standardized estimate because it is a class variable.

Association of Predicted Probabilities and Observed Responses			
Percent Concordant	66.4	Somers' D	0.350
Percent Discordant	31.4	Gamma	0.358
Percent Tied	2.2	Tau-a	0.158
Pairs	235669575	c	0.675

The Association of Predicted Probabilities and Observed Responses table lists several measures that assess the predictive ability of the model. Recall that for all pairs of observations with different values of the target variable, a pair is concordant if the observation with the outcome has a higher predicted outcome probability (based on the model) than the observation without the outcome. A pair is discordant if the observation with the outcome has a lower predicted outcome probability than the observation without the outcome.

The four rank correlation indexes (Somer's D, Gamma, Tau-a, and c) are computed from the numbers of concordant and discordant pairs of observations. In general, a model with higher values for these indexes (the maximum value is 1) has better predictive ability than a model with lower values for these indexes.

Odds Ratio Estimates and Profile-Likelihood Confidence Intervals				
	Label	Estimate	95% Confidence Limits	
Comparisons of Residential Classification	Res R vs S	0.954	0.897	1.015
Comparisons of Residential Classification 2	Res R vs U	0.991	0.933	1.053
Comparisons of Residential Classification 3	Res S vs U	1.039	0.983	1.097

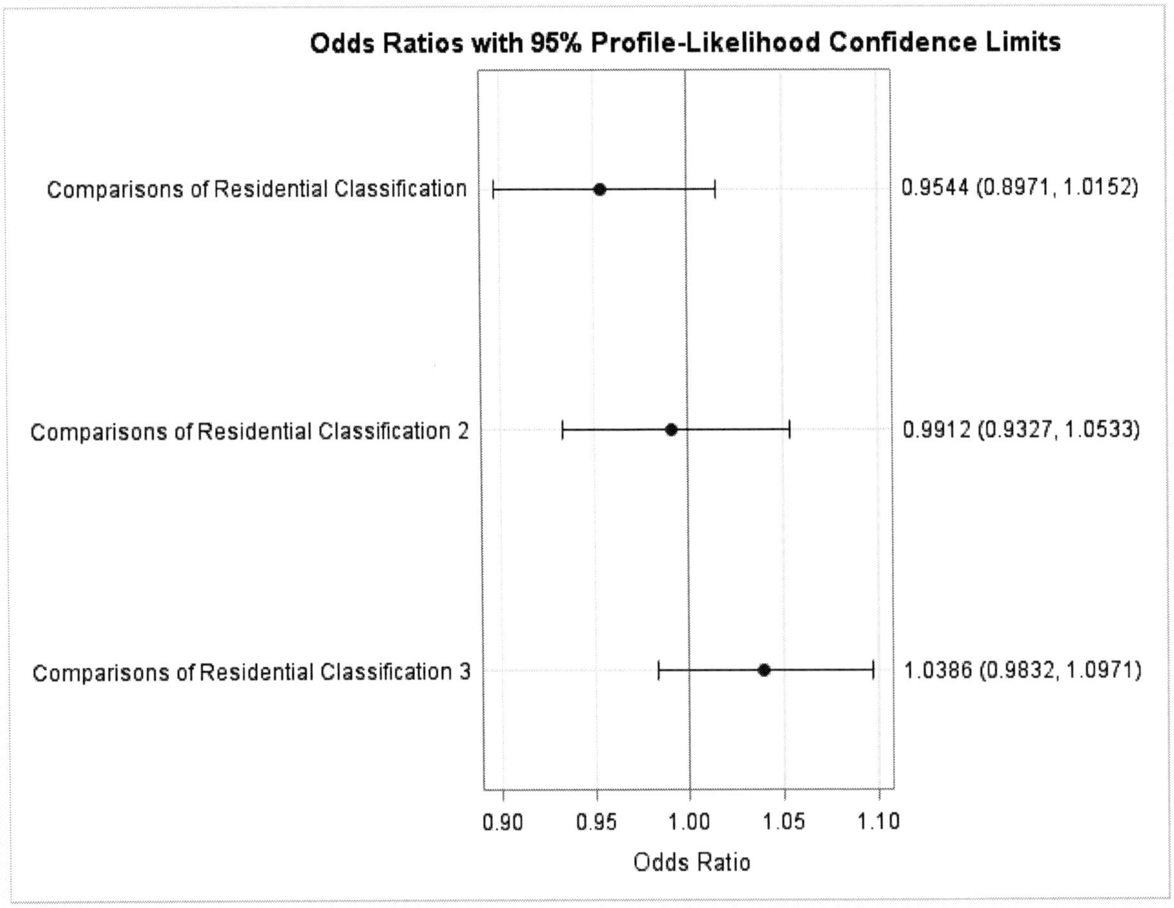

The table produced from the ODDSRATIO statement shows the odds ratios that compare rural residence to suburb residence, rural residence to urban residence, and suburb residence to urban residence. The 95% confidence limits show that none of the comparisons are statistically significant at the 0.05 level.

The odds ratio plot that corresponds to the ODDSRATIO statement shows the odds ratios that compares rural residence to suburb residence (0.9544), rural residence to urban residence (0.9912), and suburb residence to urban residence (1.0386).

Odds Ratio Estimates and Profile-Likelihood Confidence Intervals				
Effect	**Unit**	**Estimate**	**95% Confidence Limits**	
DDA	1.0000	0.379	0.352	0.409
DDABal	1000.0	1.074	1.067	1.082
Dep	1.0000	0.931	0.911	0.951
DepAmt	1000.0	1.018	1.012	1.025
CashBk	1.0000	0.570	0.452	0.709
Checks	1.0000	0.996	0.990	1.002
Res R vs S	1.0000	0.954	0.897	1.015
Res U vs S	1.0000	0.963	0.911	1.017

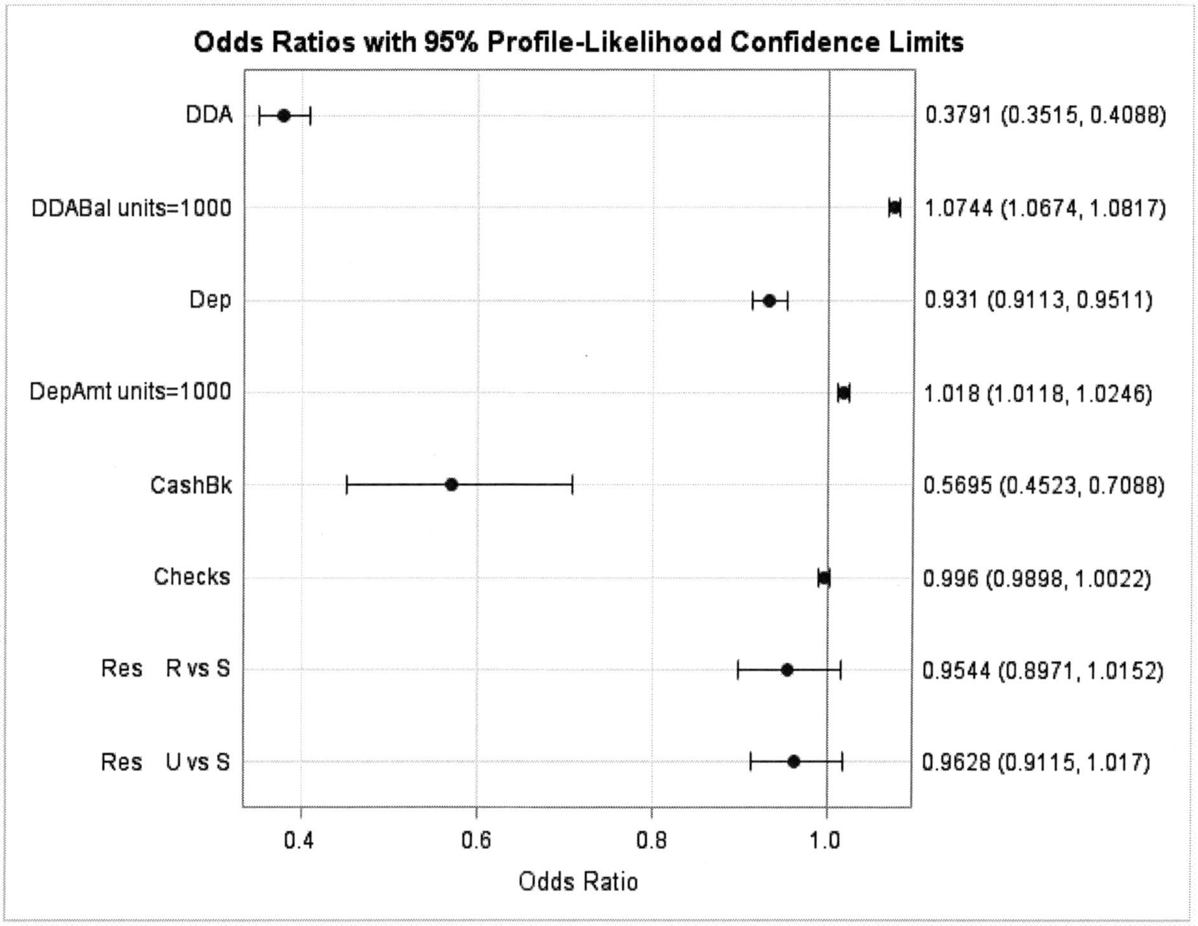

The odds ratio measures the effect of the input variable on the target adjusted for the effect of the other input variables. For example, the odds of acquiring an insurance product for **DDA** (checking account) customers are .379 times the odds for non-**DDA** customers. Equivalently, the odds of acquiring an insurance product are 1/.379 or 2.64 times more likely for non-**DDA** customers compared to **DDA** customers.

For continuous variables, it might be useful to convert the odds ratio to a percentage increase or decrease in odds. For example, the odds ratio for a 1000-unit change in **DDABal** is 1.074. Consequently, the odds of acquiring the insurance product increase 7.4% (calculated as 100(1.074–1)) for every thousand-dollar increase in the checking balance, assuming that the other variables do not change.

The odds ratio plot incorporates the information from the Profile Likelihood Confidence Interval for Odds Ratio table.

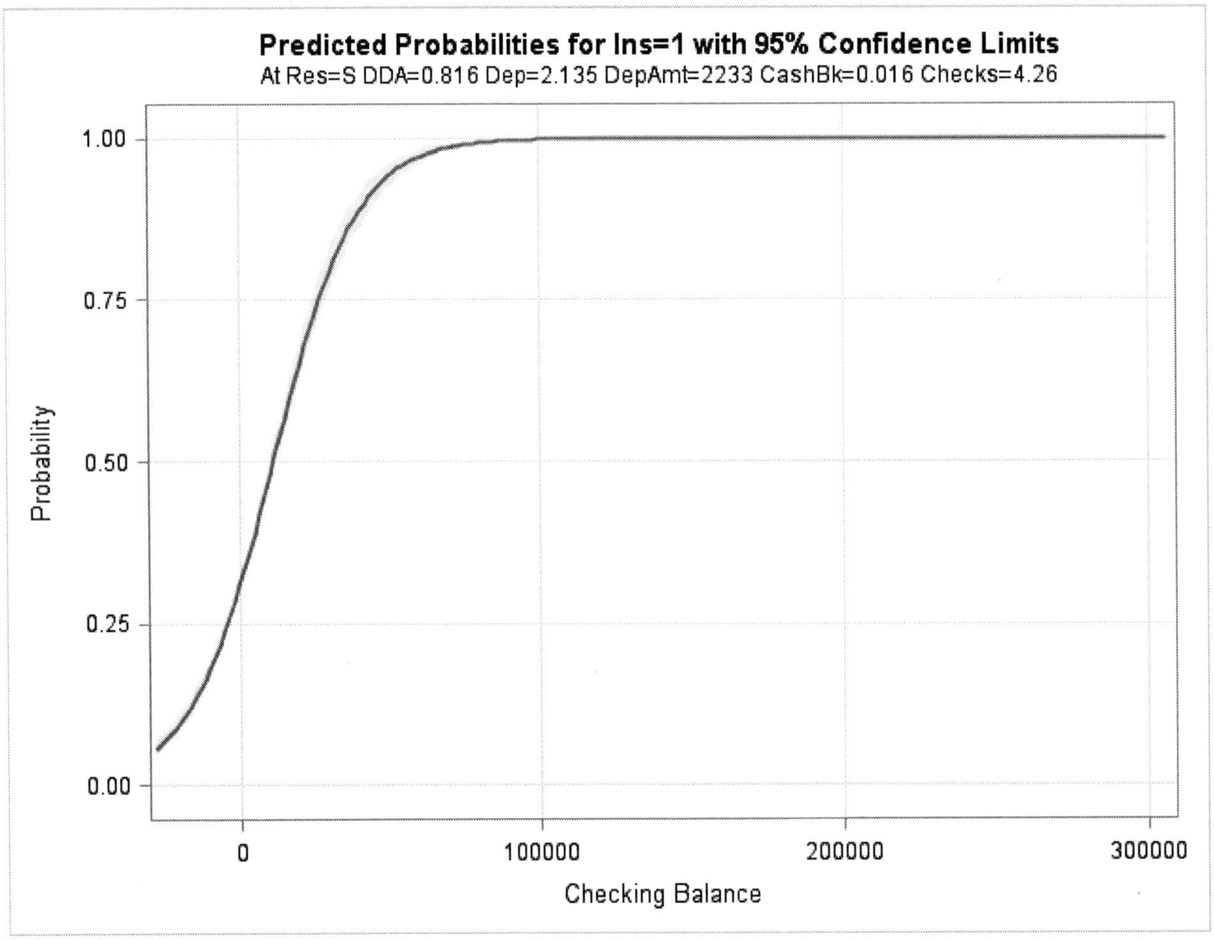

The effect plot for checking account balance shows the predicted probabilities of the event by the values of checking account balance setting the other continuous predictor variables at their means and the categorical predictor variable (**Res**) at its reference level. The plot shows a strong positive relationship between the probability of buying the variable annuity product and checking account balance.

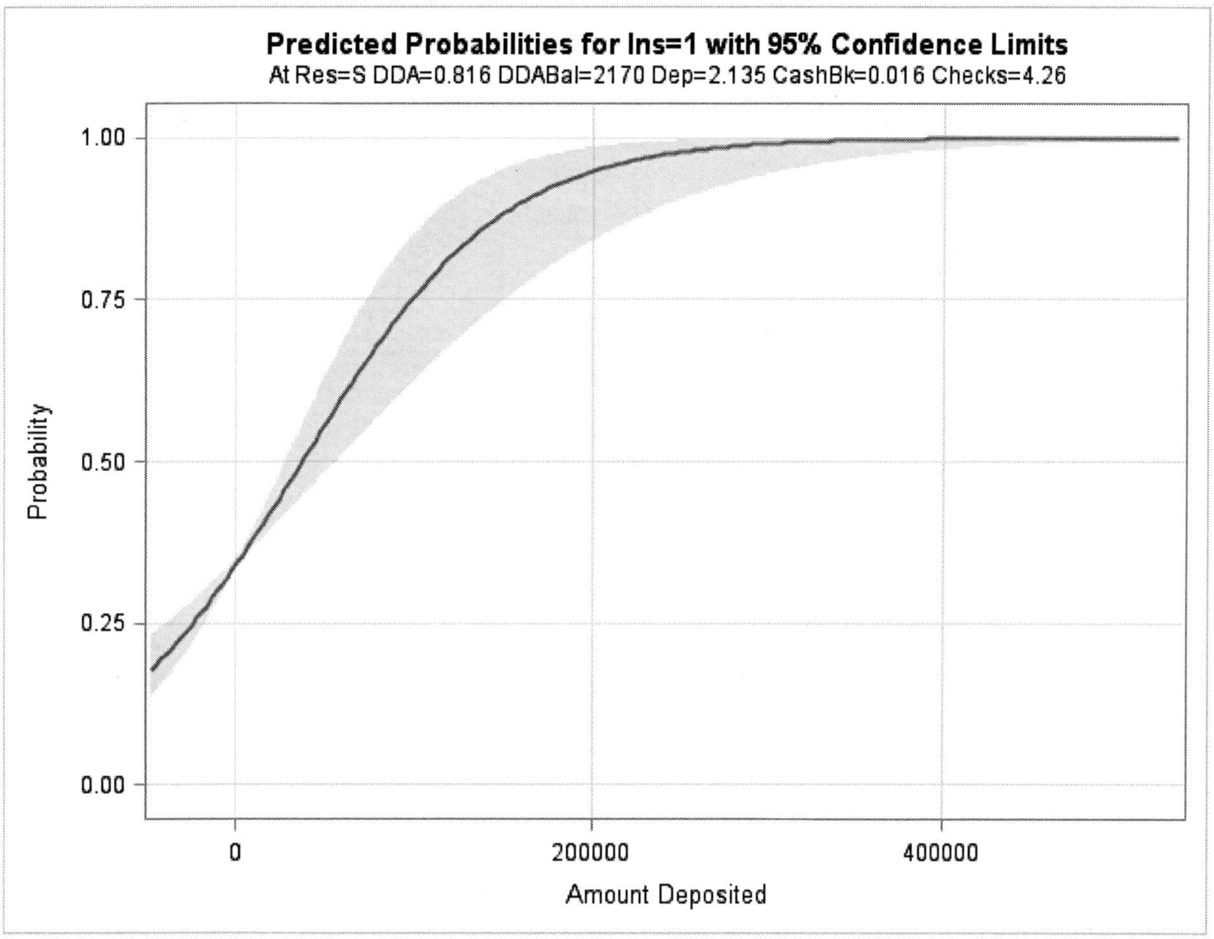

The effect plot for amount deposited shows a strong positive relationship between the probability of buying the variable annuity product and the amount deposited. Confidence bands around the regression line show that the precision of the predicted probabilities decreases as you move farther away from the mean probability and the mean of amount deposited.

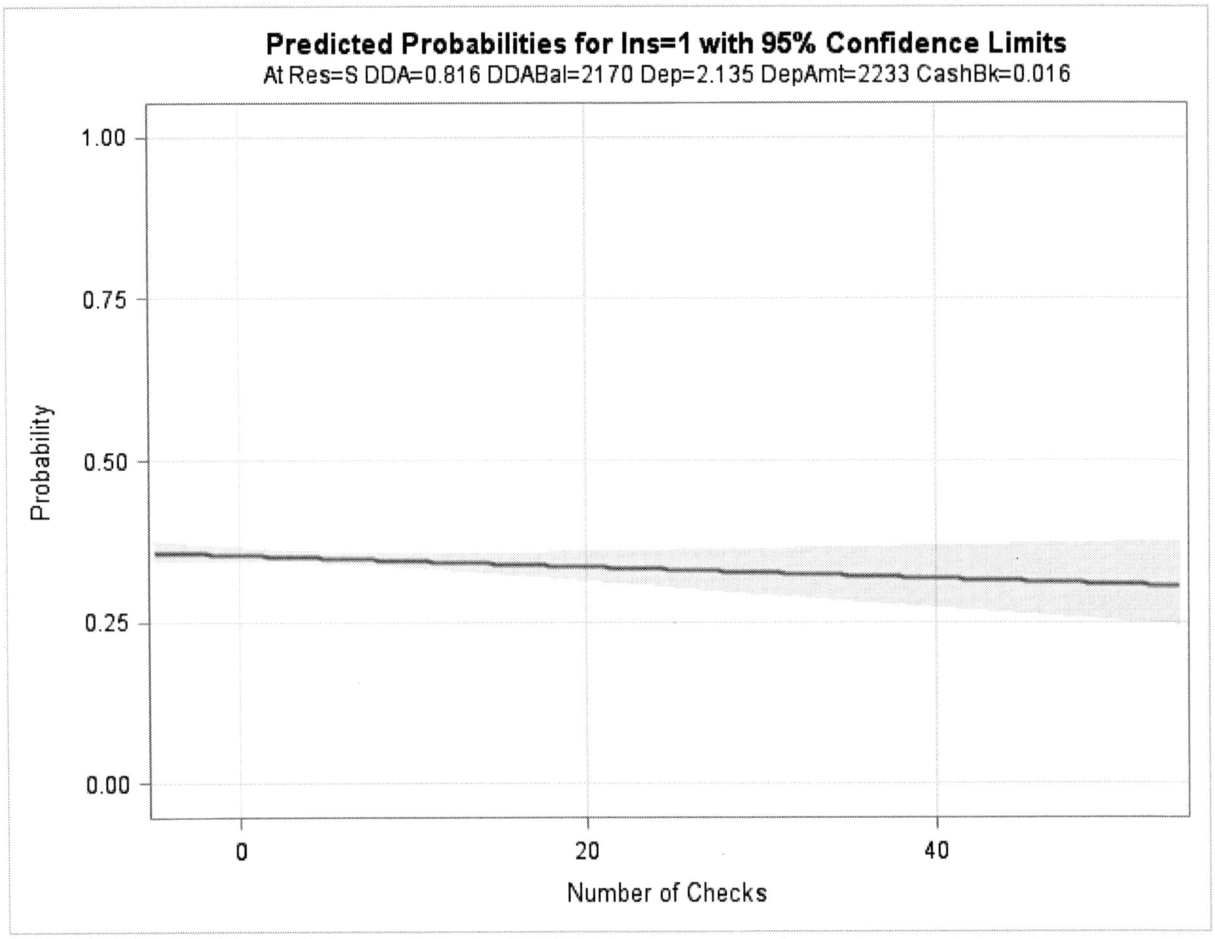

The effect plot for number of checks shows a weak negative relationship between the probability of buying the variable annuity product and number of checks.

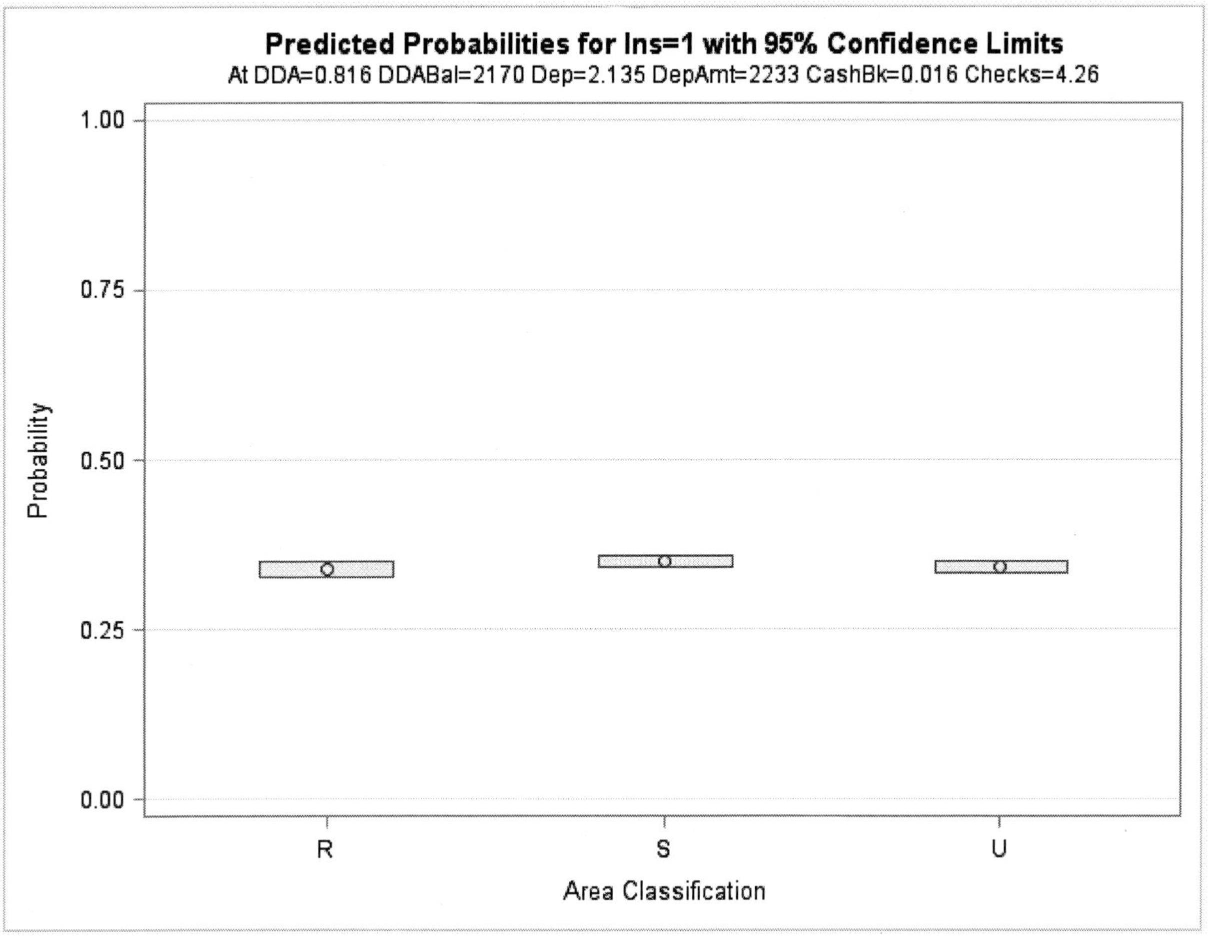

The effect plot for area classification shows no relationship between the probability of buying the variable annuity product and the residential area of the customer.

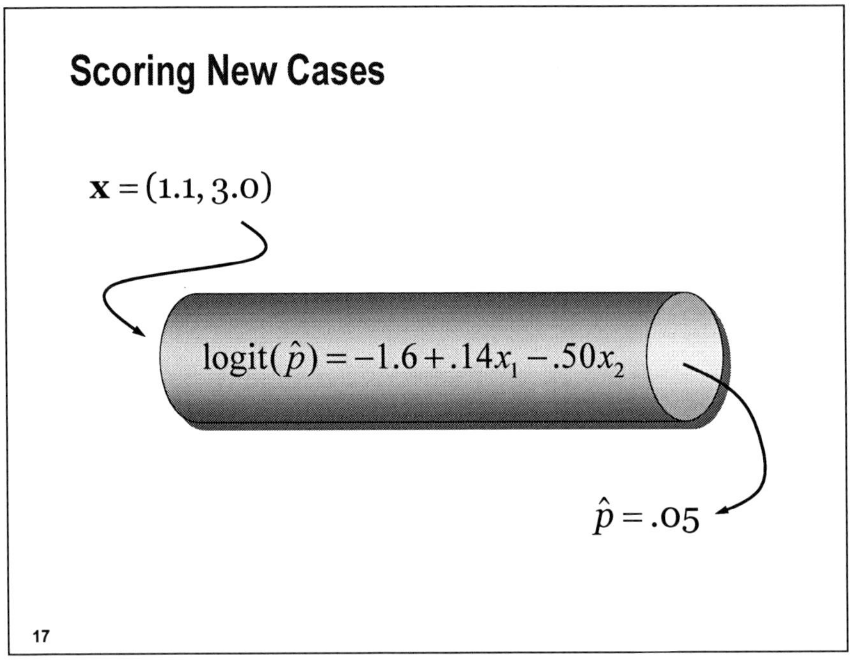

The overriding purpose of predictive modeling is to score new cases. Predictions can be made by simply plugging in the new values of the inputs.

Scoring New Cases

Example: Use the SCORE statement in PROC LOGISTIC to score the **pmlr.new** data set.

```
/* pmlr02d02.sas */
proc logistic data=develop;
   model ins(event='1')= dda ddabal dep depamt cashbk checks;
   score data=pmlr.new out=scored;
run;
```

Selected SCORE statement options:

DATA= names the data set you want to score. It is not necessary for the data set to contain the target variable unless you are specifying the FITSTAT or OUTROC= option.

OUT= names the data set that contains all the information in the DATA= data set together with the posterior probabilities and, optionally, prediction confidence intervals.

```
proc print data=scored(obs=10);
   var p_1 dda ddabal dep depamt cashbk checks;
run;
```

Obs	P_1	DDA	DDABal	Dep	DepAmt	CashBk	Checks
1	0.27476	1	56.29	2	955.51	0	1
2	0.32343	1	3292.17	2	961.60	0	1
3	0.30275	1	1723.86	2	2108.65	0	2
4	0.53144	0	0.00	0	0.00	0	0
5	0.27180	1	67.91	2	519.24	0	3
6	0.32482	1	2554.58	1	501.36	0	2
7	0.27205	1	0.00	2	2883.08	0	12
8	0.30558	1	2641.33	3	4521.61	0	8
9	0.53144	0	0.00	0	0.00	0	0
10	0.28679	1	52.22	1	75.59	0	0

The predicted probability that **Ins** is 1 is named **P_1**.

2.2 Adjustments for Oversampling

Objectives

- Explain the concept of oversampling.
- Illustrate the offset method.
- Adjust the model for oversampling in PROC LOGISTIC.

21

Sampling Designs

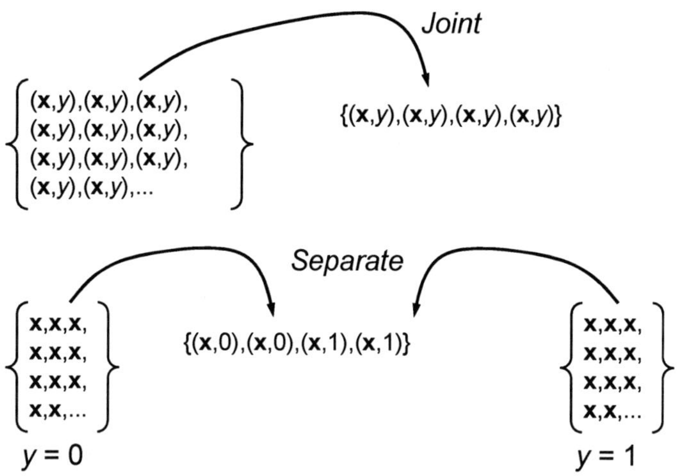

22

In *joint* (mixture) sampling, the input-target pairs are randomly selected from their joint distribution. In *separate* sampling, the inputs are randomly selected from their distributions within each target class.

Separate sampling is standard practice in supervised classification. When the target event is rare, it is common to oversample the rare event, that is, take a disproportionately large number of event cases. Oversampling rare events is generally done for data efficiency purposes.

Separate sampling is also known as

- case-control sampling
- choice-based sampling
- stratified sampling on the target, not necessarily taken with proportional allocation
- biased sampling
- y-conditional sampling
- outcome-dependent sampling
- oversampling.

The *priors*, π_0 and π_1, represent the population proportions of class 0 and 1, respectively. The proportions of the target classes in the sample are denoted ρ_0 and ρ_1. In separate sampling (nonproportional) $\pi_0 \neq \rho_0$ and $\pi_1 \neq \rho_1$, the adjustments for oversampling require the priors be known a priori. Notice that if $\pi_1=\rho_1$, then $\pi_0=\rho_0$ and the offset will be 0, as you would expect since the sample proportions and population proportions of responders and non-responders are the same.

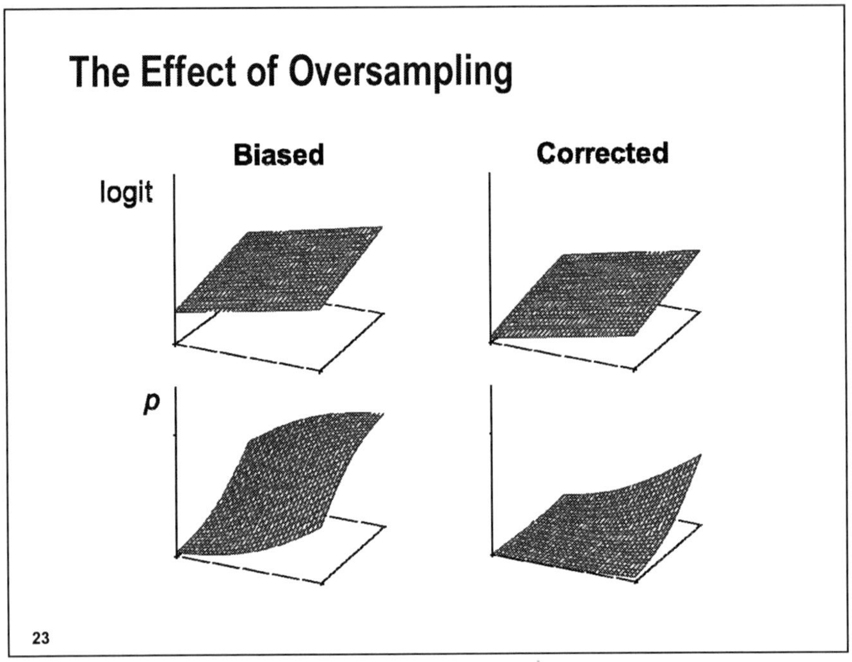

The maximum likelihood estimates were derived under the assumption that y_i have independent Bernoulli distributions. This assumption is appropriate for joint sampling but not for separate sampling. However, the effects of violating this assumption can be easily corrected. In logistic regression, only the estimate of the intercept, β_0, is affected by using Bernoulli ML on data from a separate sampling design (Prentice and Pike 1979). If the standard model

$$\text{logit}(p_i) = \beta_0 + \beta_1 x_1 + \cdots + \beta_k x_k$$

is appropriate for joint sampling, then ML estimates of the parameters under separate sampling can be determined by fitting the *pseudo model* (Scott and Wild 1986, 1997)

$$\text{logit}(p_i^*) = \ln\left(\frac{\rho_1 \pi_0}{\rho_0 \pi_1}\right) + \beta_0 + \beta_1 x_1 + \cdots + \beta_k x_k$$

where p^* is the posterior probability corresponding to the biased sample. Consequently, the effect of oversampling is to shift the logits by a constant amount – the *offset*

$$\ln\left(\frac{\rho_1 \pi_0}{\rho_0 \pi_1}\right)$$

When rare events have been oversampled $\pi_0 > \rho_0$ and $\pi_1 < \rho_1$, the offset is positive (the logit is too large). This vertical shift of the logit affects the posterior probability in a corresponding fashion.

Offset

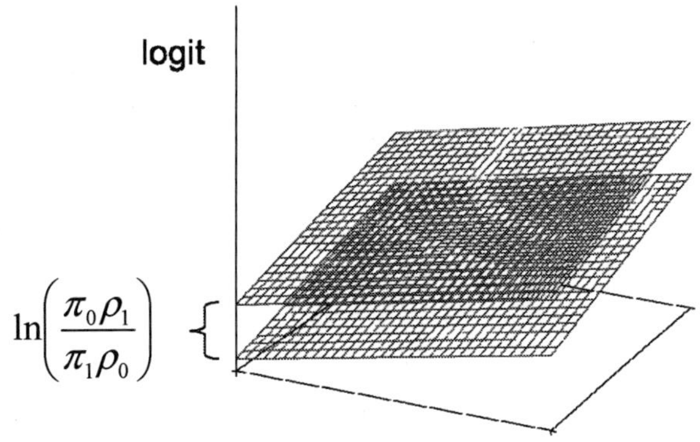

24

The pseudo model can be fitted directly by incorporating the offset into the model. Alternatively, the offset could be applied *after* the standard model is fitted. Subtracting the offset from the predicted values and solving for the posterior probability gives

$$\hat{p}_i = \frac{\hat{p}_i^* \rho_0 \pi_1}{(1-\hat{p}_i^*)\rho_1\pi_0 + \hat{p}_i^* \rho_0 \pi_1}$$

where $\hat{p}_i^*$ is the unadjusted estimate of the posterior probability. Both approaches give identical results. For both types of adjustments, the population priors, π_0 and π_1, need to be known a priori while the sample priors, ρ_0 and ρ_1, can be estimated from the data.

Because only the intercept is affected, the adjustments might not be necessary. If the goal of the analysis is to understand the relationships between the inputs and the target, or to rank order the population, then the adjustment is not critical. If the predicted probabilities are important, and not just necessary for rank ordering or classification, then the correction for oversampling is necessary.

Correcting for Oversampling

Example: Separate sampling was used to create the **develop** data set. The proportion of the target event in the population was .02, not .346 as appears in the sample. First use the %LET statement to define the macro variable **pi1** for the population prior for class 1 (**Ins**=1).
Then use the SCORE statement and the PRIOREVENT= option to correct the predicted probabilities back to the population scale.

```
/* pmlr02d03.sas */
%let pi1=.02;            /* supply the prior for class 1 */

proc logistic data=develop;
   model ins(event='1')=dda ddabal dep depamt cashbk checks;
   score data=pmlr.new out=scored priorevent=&pi1;
run;
```

Selected SCORE statement option:

PRIOREVENT= specifies the prior event probability for a binary response model.

```
proc print data=scored(obs=10);
   var p_1 dda ddabal dep depamt cashbk checks;
run;
```

Obs	P_1	DDA	DDABal	Dep	DepAmt	CashBk	Checks
1	0.014381	1	56.29	2	955.51	0	1
2	0.018078	1	3292.17	2	961.60	0	1
3	0.016447	1	1723.86	2	2108.65	0	2
4	0.041854	0	0.00	0	0.00	0	0
5	0.014171	1	67.91	2	519.24	0	3
6	0.018191	1	2554.58	1	501.36	0	2
7	0.014189	1	0.00	2	2883.08	0	12
8	0.016665	1	2641.33	3	4521.61	0	8
9	0.041854	0	0.00	0	0.00	0	0
10	0.015250	1	52.22	1	75.59	0	0

The average of the predicted probabilities is 0.02 rather than 0.346.

2.02 Multiple Choice Poll

If the value for the offset is 3.2567, then the model corrected for oversampling will have which of the following?

a. An intercept that is 3.2567 lower in value compared to the model fitted to the biased sample
b. Probabilities that are 3.2567% higher than the probabilities from the model fitted to the biased sample
c. Probabilities that are 3.2567% lower than the probabilities from the model fitted to the biased sample
d. Parameter estimates that are 3.2567% lower than the parameter estimates from the model fitted to the biased sample

26

Exercises

A national veterans' organization seeks to better target its solicitations for donation. By only soliciting the most likely donors, less money will be spent on solicitation efforts and more money will be available for charitable concerns. Solicitations involve sending a small gift to an individual together with a request for donation. Gifts include mailing labels and greeting cards.

The organization has more than 3.5 million individuals in its mailing database. These individuals have been classified by their response behavior to previous solicitation efforts. Of particular interest is the class of individuals identified as lapsing donors. These individuals made their most recent donation between 12 and 24 months ago. The organization found that by predicting the response behavior of this group, they could use the model to rank all 3.5 million individuals in their database. With this ranking, a decision can be made to either solicit or ignore an individual in the current solicitation campaign. The current campaign refers to a greeting card mailing sent in June of 1997. It is identified in the raw data as the 97NK campaign.

The raw analysis data have been reduced for the purpose of this course. A subset of slightly more than 19,000 records has been selected for modeling. As will be seen, this subset was not chosen arbitrarily. In addition, the 481 fields have been reduced to 47. Some of the fields were eliminated when their potential association with the analysis objective was considered (for example, it is doubtful that CD player ownership is strongly correlated with donation potential). Other fields were combined to form summaries of a particular customer behavior. In general, if the variable has **PROM** in its name, then the variable is related to the number of items the organization sent to the customer. However, if the variable has **GIFT** in its name, then the variable is related to the amount of money the customer sent to the organization.

The data are in a data set called **pva_raw_data**. The following table details the variables and descriptions:

Variable	Description
CARD_PROM_12	Count of card promotions in the last 12 months
CLUSTER_CODE	Socio-Economic Cluster Code
CONTROL_NUMBER	ID
DONOR_AGE	Donor Age
DONOR_GENDER	Donor Gender
FREQUENCY_STATUS_97NK	Count of Donations between June 1995 and June 1996 (capped at 4)
HOME_OWNER	Home Owner flag
INCOME_GROUP	Income Bracket, from 1 to 7
IN_HOUSE	Flag for *In-House* donor program
LAST_GIFT_AMT	Amount of most recent donation

LIFETIME_AVG_GIFT_AMT	Average donation amount, ever
LIFETIME_CARD_PROM	Number of card promotions, ever
LIFETIME_GIFT_AMOUNT	Total donation amount, ever
LIFETIME_GIFT_COUNT	Total number of donations, ever
LIFETIME_GIFT_RANGE	Maximum gift amount less minimum gift amount
LIFETIME_MAX_GIFT_AMT	Maximum gift amount, ever
LIFETIME_MIN_GIFT_AMT	Minimum gift amount, ever
LIFETIME_PROM	Count of solicitations ever sent
MEDIAN_HOME_VALUE	Census data
MEDIAN_HOUSEHOLD_INCOME	Census data
MONTHS_SINCE_FIRST_GIFT	Months since first donation
MONTHS_SINCE_LAST_GIFT	Months since most recent donation
MONTHS_SINCE_ORIGIN	Months since entry onto the file
MOR_HIT_RATE	Data recorded by a third party-Mail Order Response rate
NUMBER_PROM_12	Count of promotions in the last 12 months
OVERLAY_SOURCE	Source of Demographic overlay
PCT_MALE_MILITARY	Census data
PCT_MALE_VETERANS	Census data
PCT_OWNER_OCCUPIED	Census data
PCT_VIETNAM_VETERANS	Census data
PCT_WWII_VETERANS	Census data
PEP_STAR	Flag to identify consecutive donors
PER_CAPITA_INCOME	Census data
PUBLISHED_PHONE	Flag
RECENCY_STATUS_96NK	Categorization of donation patterns
RECENT_AVG_CARD_GIFT_AMT	Average donation amount to card promotions since June 1994

RECENT_AVG_GIFT_AMT	Average donation amount to promotions since June 1994
RECENT_CARD_RESPONSE_COUNT	Count of responses to card promotions since June 1994
RECENT_CARD_RESPONSE_PROP	Proportion of responses to card promotions since June 1994
RECENT_RESPONSE_COUNT	Count of responses to promotions since June 1994
RECENT_RESPONSE_PROP	Proportion of responses to promotions since June 1994
RECENT_STAR_STATUS	STAR status flag, since June 1994
SES	A clustering of the levels of **CLUSTER_CODE**
TARGET_B	B=Binary, flag for response to 97NK—Target Variable
TARGET_D	Dollar amount of response to 97NK
URBANICITY	Categorization of residency
WEALTH_RATING	Measures wealth relative to others within state

1. **Fitting a Logistic Regression Model**

   a. Submit the program **pmlr00d01.sas**. Create a macro variable to store π_1, the proportion of responders in the population. This value is 0.05. Then fit a logistic regression model using the **pva** data set with **TARGET_B** as the target variable and **PEP_STAR**, **RECENT_AVG_GIFT_AMT**, and **FREQUENCY_STATUS_97NK** as the input variables. Model the probability that the target variable equals 1 and request 95% profile likelihood confidence intervals for the odds ratio. Use the SCORE statement to append the predicted probability to the data, correcting for oversampling. Create effect plots with confidence bands for the three input variables and create an odds ratio plot with a horizontal orientation and display the statistics.

      1) Interpret the c statistic.

      2) Interpret the odds ratio for **PEP_STAR**.

      3) Interpret the effect plot for **RECENT_AVG_GIFT_AMT**.

2.03 Multiple Choice Poll

The c statistic was 0.601. This can be interpreted as the probability of which of the following?

a. A customer donating to the national veterans' organization
b. A customer not donating to the national veterans' organization
c. If one person is randomly selected from the group of donors and another person is randomly selected from the non-donors, 60.1% of the time the donor will have the higher predicted probability of the target event as given by this model

29

2.3 Chapter Summary

The standard logistic regression model assumes that the logit of the posterior probability is a linear combination of the input variables. The logit transformation is used to constrain the posterior probability to be between zero and one. The parameter estimates are estimated using the method of maximum likelihood. This method finds the parameter estimates that are most likely given the data. When you exponentiate the parameter estimates, you obtain the odds ratio, which compares the odds of the event in one group to the odds of the event in another group.

When you oversample rare events, you can use the SCORE statement and the PRIOREVENT= option to adjust the model so that the posterior probabilities reflect the population.

General form of the LOGISTIC procedure:

```
PROC LOGISTIC <options>;
      CLASS variable</v-options>;
      MODEL response=<effects></options>;
      ODDSRATIO <'label'> variable </ options>;
      ROC <'label'> <specification> </ options>;
      ROCCONTRAST <'label'><contrast>
                         </ options>;
      SCORE <options>;
      UNITS predictor1=list1 </option>;
      OUTPUT <OUT=SAS-data-set> keyword=name...
                  keyword=name></option>;
RUN;
```

2.4 Solutions

Solutions to Exercises

1. **Fitting a Logistic Regression Model**

   a. Submit the program **pmlr00d01.sas**. Create a macro variable to store π_1, the proportion of responders in the population. This value is 0.05. Then fit a logistic regression model using the **pva** data set with **TARGET_B** as the target variable and **PEP_STAR**, **RECENT_AVG_GIFT_AMT**, and **FREQUENCY_STATUS_97NK** as the input variables. Model the probability that the target variable equals 1 and request 95% profile likelihood confidence intervals for the odds ratio. Use the SCORE statement to append the predicted probability to the data, correcting for oversampling. Create effect plots with confidence bands for the three input variables and create an odds ratio plot with a horizontal orientation and display the statistics.

An electronic copy of the solution program is in **pmlr02s01.sas**.

```
%let ex_pi1=0.05;

proc logistic data=pva plots(only)=(effect(clband x=(pep_star
          recent_avg_gift_amt frequency_status_97nk))
          oddsratio (type=horizontalstat));
   model target_b(event='1')=pep_star recent_avg_gift_amt
                    frequency_status_97nk / clodds=pl;
   score data=pva out=scopva priorevent=&ex_pi1;
run;
```

The LOGISTIC Procedure

Model Information	
Data Set	WORK.PVA
Response Variable	TARGET_B
Number of Response Levels	2
Model	binary logit
Optimization Technique	Fisher's scoring

Number of Observations Read	19372
Number of Observations Used	19372

Response Profile		
Ordered Value	TARGET_B	Total Frequency
1	0	14529
2	1	4843

Probability modeled is TARGET_B=1.

Model Convergence Status
Convergence criterion (GCONV=1E-8) satisfied.

Model Fit Statistics		
Criterion	Intercept Only	Intercept and Covariates
AIC	21789.113	21351.668
SC	21796.984	21383.154
-2 Log L	21787.113	21343.668

Testing Global Null Hypothesis: BETA=0			
Test	Chi-Square	DF	Pr > ChiSq
Likelihood Ratio	443.4451	3	<.0001
Score	448.9127	3	<.0001
Wald	439.1624	3	<.0001

Analysis of Maximum Likelihood Estimates					
Parameter	DF	Estimate	Standard Error	Wald Chi-Square	Pr > ChiSq
Intercept	1	-1.6241	0.0584	773.5119	<.0001
PEP_STAR	1	0.3078	0.0361	72.8485	<.0001
RECENT_AVG_GIFT_AMT	1	-0.00555	0.00204	7.3829	0.0066
FREQUENCY_STATUS_97N	1	0.2147	0.0168	163.3538	<.0001

Association of Predicted Probabilities and Observed Responses			
Percent Concordant	58.9	Somers' D	0.201
Percent Discordant	38.8	Gamma	0.206
Percent Tied	2.3	Tau-a	0.075
Pairs	70363947	c	0.601

1) The c statistic of 0.601 can be interpreted as the probability of a customer who donated to the national veterans' organization having a higher predicted probability (of donating to the organization) compared to a customer who did not donate.

Odds Ratio Estimates and Profile-Likelihood Confidence Intervals				
Effect	Unit	Estimate	95% Confidence Limits	
PEP_STAR	1.0000	1.360	1.268	1.460
RECENT_AVG_GIFT_AMT	1.0000	0.994	0.990	0.998
FREQUENCY_STATUS_97N	1.0000	1.239	1.199	1.281

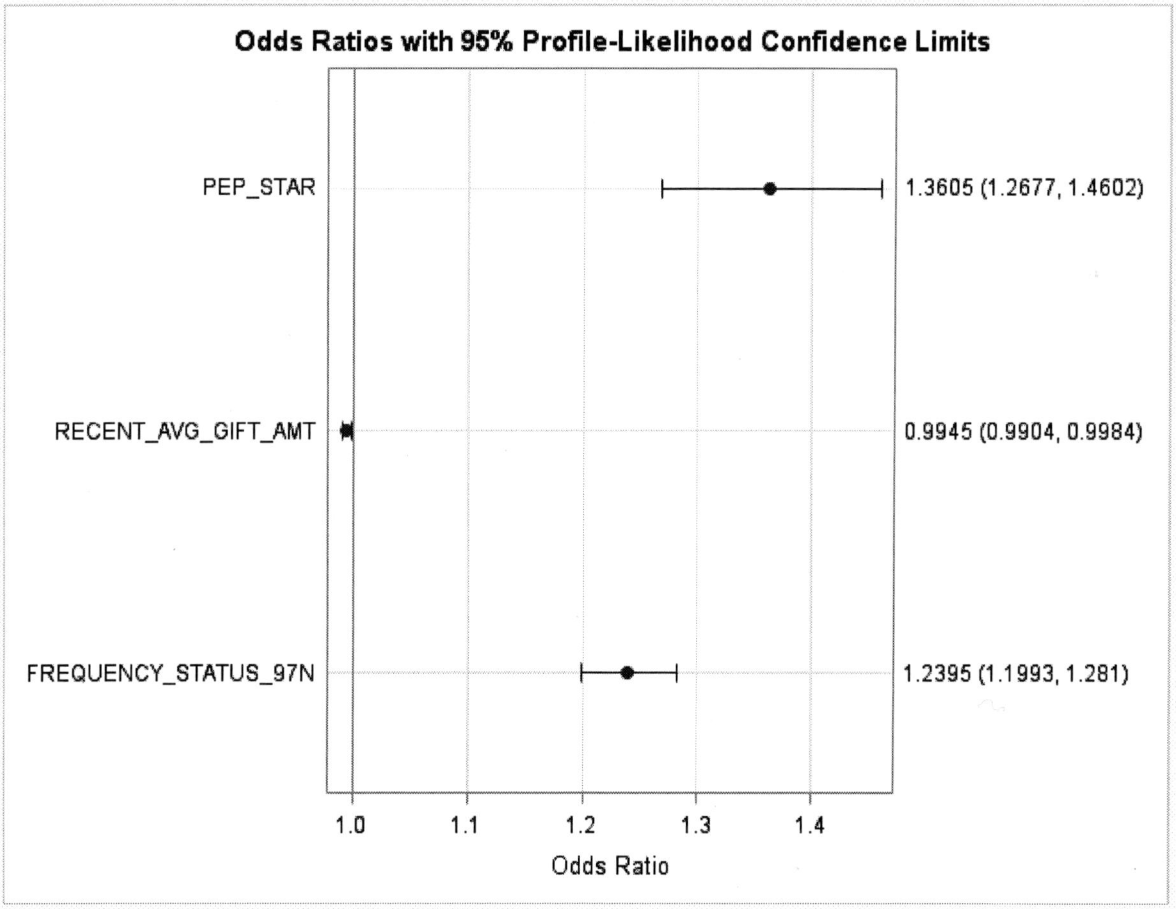

2) The odds ratio for **PEP_STAR** indicates that customers who are consecutive donors have 1.36 times the odds of responding to a solicitation compared to customers who are not consecutive donors.

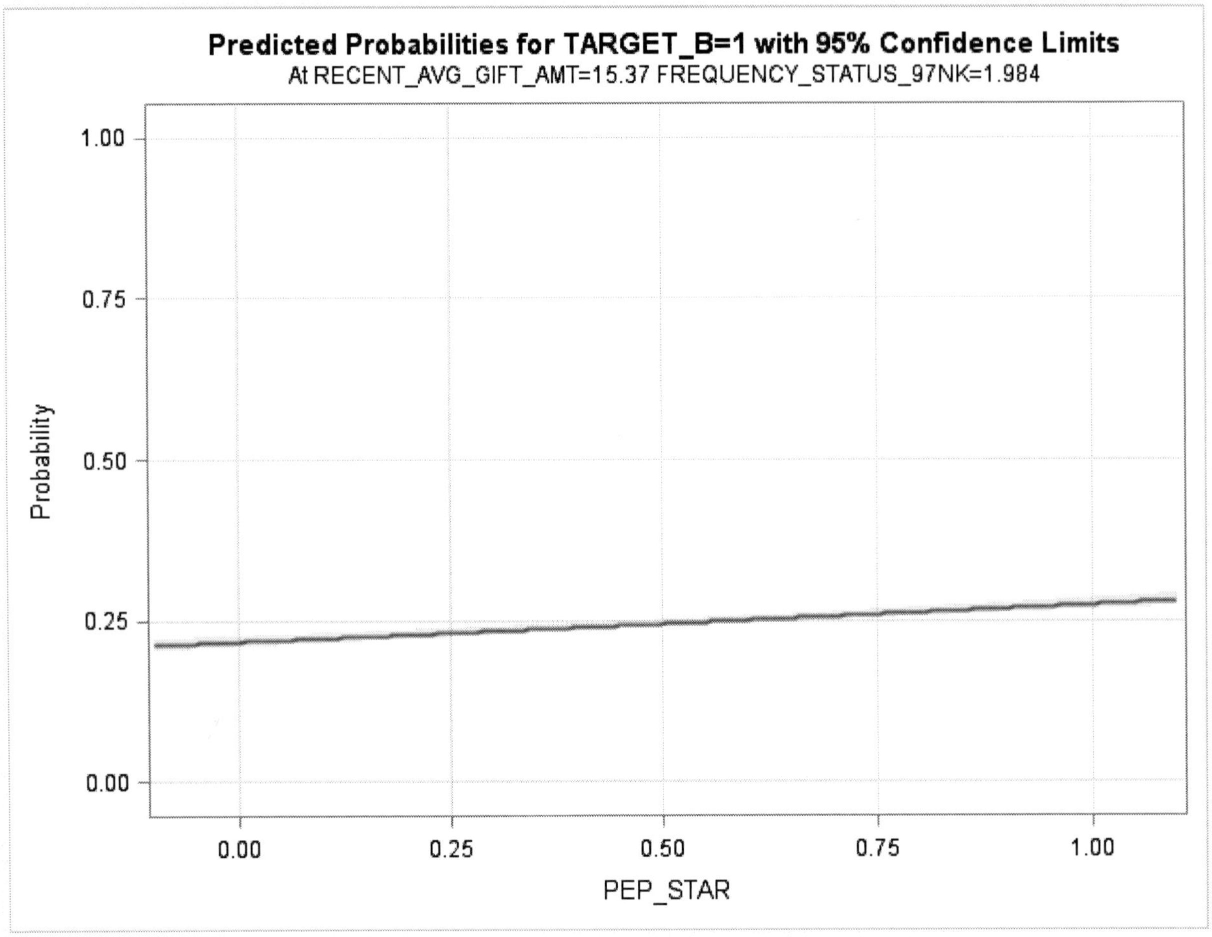

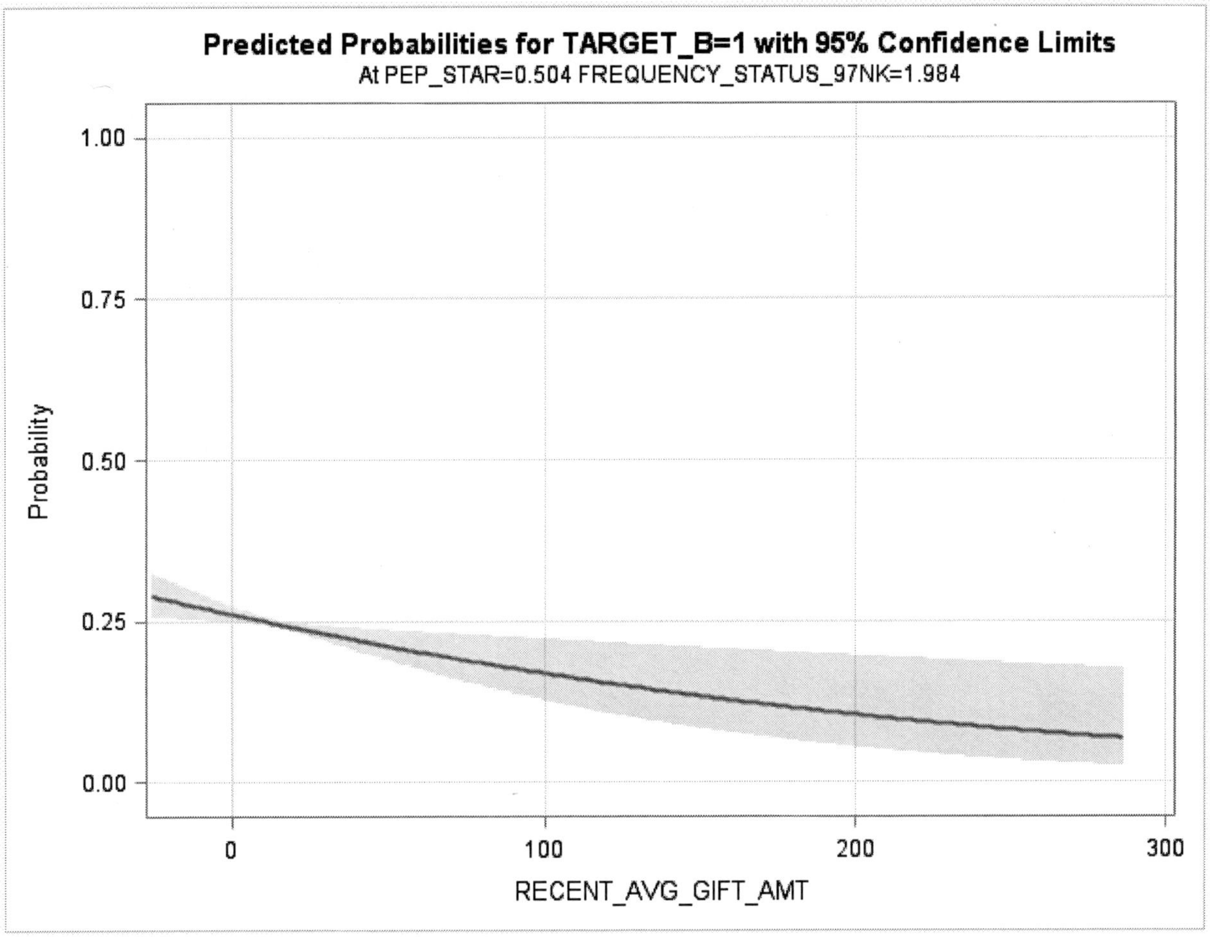

3) The effect plot for **RECENT_AVG_GIFT_AMT** shows a negative relationship between the average donation amount to promotions since June 1994 and the predicted probabilities of responding to the solicitation in June of 1997.

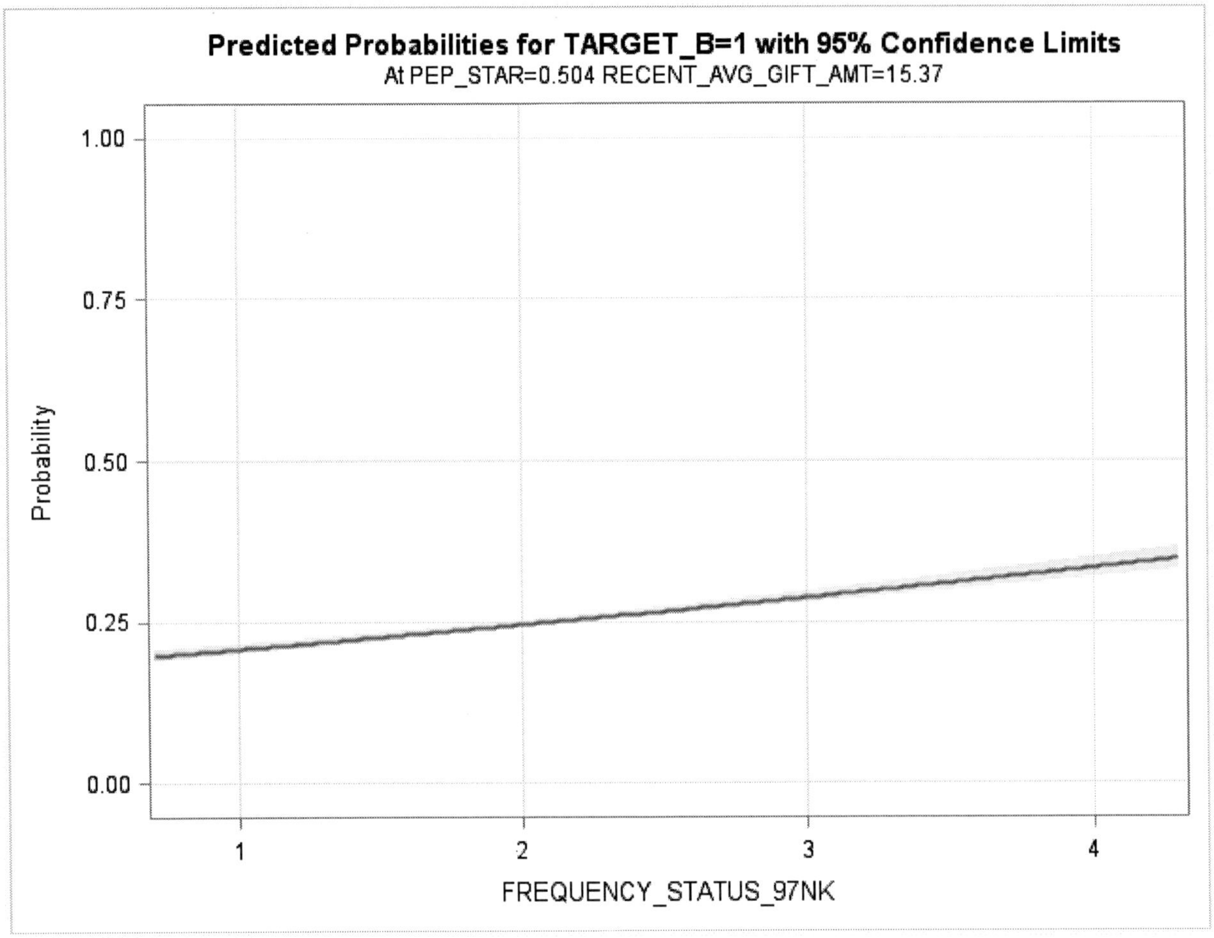
Predicted Probabilities for TARGET_B=1 with 95% Confidence Limits
At PEP_STAR=0.504 RECENT_AVG_GIFT_AMT=15.37
Probability
1.00
0.75
0.50
0.25
0.00
1
2
3
4
FREQUENCY_STATUS_97NK

Solutions to Student Activities (Polls/Quizzes)

2.01 Multiple Choice Poll – Correct Answer

The odds ratio for a $1000-increase in income is 1.074. What does this mean for every $1000-increase in income?

a. The probability of the event increases 7.4%.
b. The logit increases 7.4%.
(c.) The odds of the event increases 7.4%.
d. The log of the odds of the event increases 7.4%.

15

2.02 Multiple Choice Poll – Correct Answer

If the value for the offset is 3.2567, then the model corrected for oversampling will have which of the following?

(a.) An intercept that is 3.2567 lower in value compared to the model fitted to the biased sample
b. Probabilities that are 3.2567% higher than the probabilities from the model fitted to the biased sample
c. Probabilities that are 3.2567% lower than the probabilities from the model fitted to the biased sample
d. Parameter estimates that are 3.2567% lower than the parameter estimates from the model fitted to the biased sample

27

2.03 Multiple Choice Poll – Correct Answer

The c statistic was 0.601. This can be interpreted as the probability of which of the following?

a. A customer donating to the national veterans' organization
b. A customer not donating to the national veterans' organization
c. If one person is randomly selected from the group of donors and another person is randomly selected from the non-donors, 60.1% of the time the donor will have the higher predicted probability of the target event as given by this model

30

Chapter 3 Preparing the Input Variables

3.1 Missing Values

Objectives

- Explain the problem of missing values.
- Discuss the usefulness of missing indicator variables.
- Demonstrate how to impute missing values in the STDIZE procedure.

3

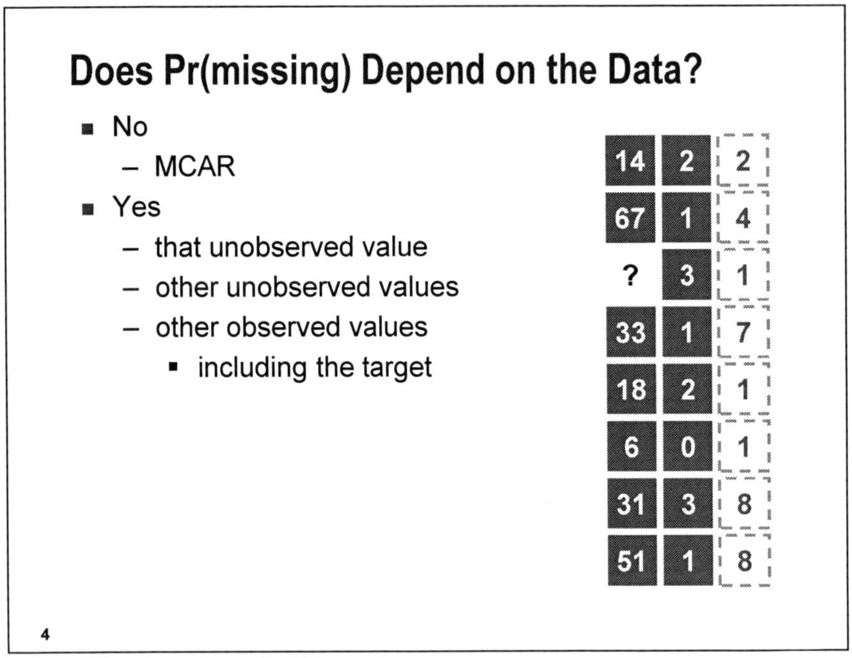

Missing values of the input variables can arise from several different mechanisms (Little 1992). A value is *missing completely at random* (MCAR) if the probability that it is missing is independent of the data. MCAR is a particularly easy mechanism to manage but is unrealistic in most predictive modeling applications.

The probability that a value is missing might depend on the unobserved value. Credit applicants with fewer years at their current job might be less inclined to provide this information.

The probability that a value is missing might depend on observed values of other input variables. Customers with longer tenures might be less likely to have certain historic transactional data. Missingness might depend on a combination of values of correlated inputs.

An even more problematic missing-value mechanism occurs when the probability that a value is missing depends on values of unobserved (lurking) predictors. Transient customers might have missing values on a number of variables.

A fundamental concern for predictive modeling is that the missingness is related to the target. The more transient customers might be the best prospects for a new offer.

Complete Case Analysis

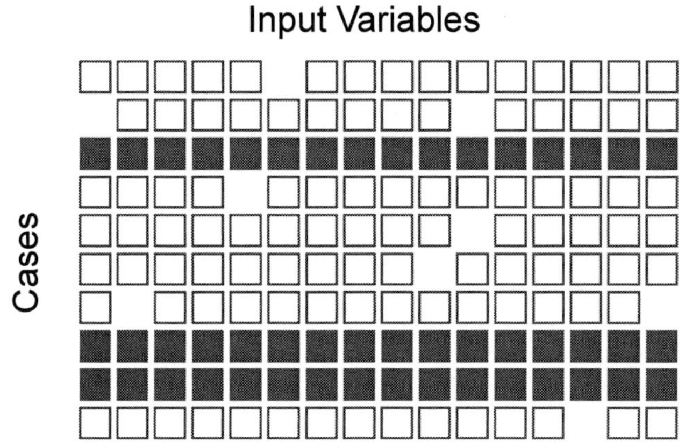

6

The default method for treating missing values in most SAS modeling procedures (including the LOGISTIC procedure) is complete-case analysis. In *complete-case analysis*, only those cases without any missing values are used in the analysis.

Complete-case analysis has some moderately attractive theoretical properties even when the missingness depends on observed values of other inputs (Donner 1982, Jones 1996). However, complete-case analysis has serious practical shortcomings with regard to predictive modeling. Even a smattering of missing values can cause an enormous loss of data in high dimensions. For example, suppose each of the k input variables can be MCAR with probability α; in this situation, the expected proportion of complete cases is $(1-\alpha)^k$.

Therefore, a 1% probability of missing (α=.01) for 100 inputs would leave only 37% of the data for analysis, 200 would leave 13%, and 400 would leave 2%. If the missingness was increased to 5% (α=.05), then <1% of the data would be available with 100 inputs.

New Missing Values

Fitted Model:

$$\text{logit}(\hat{p}) = -2.1 + .072x_1 - .89x_2 - 1.4x_3$$

New Case: $(x_1,\ x_2,\ x_3) = (2,\ ?,\ -.5)$

Predicted Value:

$$\text{logit}(\hat{p}) = -2.1 + .144 - .89(\ \ ) + .7$$

7

Another practical consideration of any treatment of missing values is *scorability* (the practicality of method when it is deployed). The purpose of predictive modeling is scoring new cases. How would a model built on the complete cases score a new case if it had a missing value? To decline to score new incomplete cases would only be practical if there were a very small number of missing values.

Missing Value Imputation

6	03	2.6	0	8.3	42	66	C03
12	04	1.8	0	0.5	86	65	C14
6.5	01	2.3	.33	4.8	37	66	C00
8	01	2.1	1	4.8	37	64	C08
6	01	2.8	1	9.6	22	66	C99
3	01	2.7	0	1.1	28	64	C00
2	02	2.1	1	5.9	21	63	C03
10	03	2.0	0	0.8	0	63	C99
7	01	2.5	0	5.5	62	67	C12
6.5	01	2.4	0	0.9	29	63	C05

8

Because of the aforementioned drawbacks of complete-case analysis, some type of missing value imputation is necessary. Imputation means filling in the missing values with some reasonable value. Many methods have been developed for imputing missing values (Little 1992). The principal consideration for most methods is getting valid statistical inference on the imputed data, not generalization.

Subject matter knowledge is often important for proper handling of missing value imputation. For example, it is fairly common to see missing values incorrectly codes as zeros.

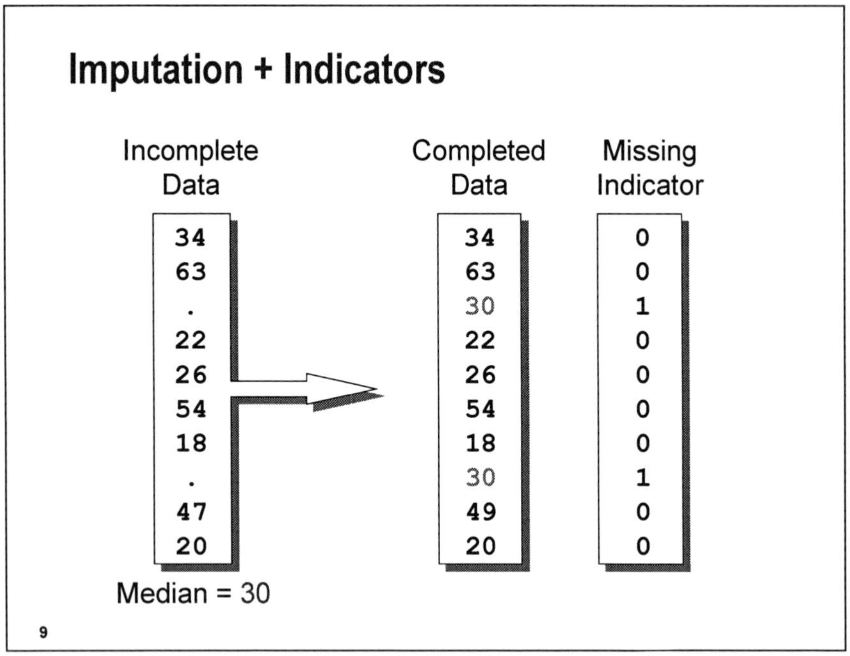

One reasonable strategy for handling missing values in predictive modeling is to do the following steps.

1. Create missing indicators

$$MI_j = \begin{cases} 1 & \text{if } x_j \text{ is missing} \\ 0 & \text{otherwise} \end{cases}$$

   and treat them as new input variables in the analysis.

2. Use median imputation for numeric inputs. Fill the missing value of x_j with the median of the complete cases for that variable.

3. Create a new level representing missing (unknown) for categorical inputs.

If a very large percentage of values is missing (>50%), then the variable might be better handled by omitting it from the analysis or by creating the missing indicator only. If a very small percentage of the values is missing (<1%), then the missing indicator is of little value.

This strategy is somewhat unsophisticated but satisfies two of the most important considerations in predictive modeling: efficient scorability and capturing the relationship of missingness with the target. A new case is easily scored; first replace the missing values with the medians from the development data and then apply the prediction model.

There is a large amount of statistical literature concerning different missing value imputation methods, including discussions of the demerits of mean and median imputation and missing indicators (Donner 1982, Jones 1997). Unfortunately, most of the advice is based on considerations that are peripheral to predictive modeling. There is very little advice when the functional form of the model is not assumed to be perfectly specified, when the goal is to get good predictions that can be practically applied to new cases, when *p*-values and hypothesis tests are of secondary importance, and when the missingness might be highly pathological, in other words, depending on lurking predictors.

3.01 Multiple Choice Poll

Which of the following statements is false regarding missing values in predictive modeling applications?

a. In complete case analysis, there can be an enormous loss of data when the missing values are spread across many variables.
b. Observations with missing values will not be scored in PROC LOGISTIC.
c. Missing indicator variables can be used to capture the relationship between the target variable and missing inputs.
d. The missing completely at random assumption is valid in most predictive modeling applications.

10

Imputing Missing Values

Example: Create missing value indicator variables and replace missing values with the variable median.

```
/*  pmlr03d01.sas */
proc print data=develop(obs=15);
   var ccbal ccpurc income hmown;
run;
```

Obs	CCBal	CCPurc	Income	HMOwn
1	483.65	0	16	1
2	0.00	1	4	1
3	0.00	0	30	1
4	65.76	0	125	1
5	0.00	0	25	1
6	38.62	0	19	0
7	85202.99	0	55	1
8	0.00	0	13	0
9	.	.	20	0
10	0.00	0	54	0
11	0.00	0	.	.
12	0.00	0	25	1
13	.	.	102	1
14	.	.	24	1
15	0.00	0	8	1

Fifteen of the input variables were selected for imputation. Two arrays are created, one called MI, which contains the missing value indicator variables, and one called X, which contains the input variables. It is critical that the order of the variables in the array MI matches the order of the variables in array X. Defining the dimension with an asterisk causes the array elements to be automatically counted. In the DO loop, the DIM function returns the dimension of the array. Thus, the DO loop will execute 15 times in this example. The assignment statement inside the DO loop causes the entries of MI to be 1 if the corresponding entry in X is missing and 0 otherwise.

```
data develop1;
   set develop;
   /* name the missing indicator variables */
   array mi{*} MIAcctAg MIPhone MIPOS MIPOSAmt
               MIInv MIInvBal MICC MICCBal
               MICCPurc MIIncome MIHMOwn MILORes
               MIHMVal MIAge MICRScor;
   /* select variables with missing values */
   array x{*} acctage phone pos posamt
              inv invbal cc ccbal
              ccpurc income hmown lores
              hmval age crscore;
   do i=1 to dim(mi);
      mi{i}=(x{i}=.);
   end;
run;
```

The STDIZE procedure with the REPONLY option can be used to replace only the missing values – a variable value remains unchanged if it was not missing. The METHOD= option enables you to choose several different location measures such as the mean, median, and midrange. The output data set created by the OUT= option contains all the variables in the input data set where the variables listed in the VAR statement are imputed. Only numeric input variables should be used in PROC STDIZE.

```
proc stdize data=develop1
            reponly
            method=median
            out=imputed;
   var &inputs;
run;

proc print data=imputed(obs=12);
   var ccbal miccbal ccpurc miccpurc
       income miincome hmown mihmown;
run;
```

The REPLACE option in PROC STANDARD can be used to replace missing values with the mean of that variable on the nonmissing cases.

Obs	CCBal	MICCBal	CCPurc	MICCPurc	Income	MIIncome	HMOwn	MIHMOwn
1	483.65	0	0	0	16	0	1	0
2	0.00	0	1	0	4	0	1	0
3	0.00	0	0	0	30	0	1	0
4	65.76	0	0	0	125	0	1	0
5	0.00	0	0	0	25	0	1	0
6	38.62	0	0	0	19	0	0	0
7	85202.99	0	0	0	55	0	1	0
8	0.00	0	0	0	13	0	0	0
9	0.00	1	0	1	20	0	0	0
10	0.00	0	0	0	54	0	0	0
11	0.00	0	0	0	35	1	1	1
12	0.00	0	0	0	25	0	1	0

Cluster Imputation

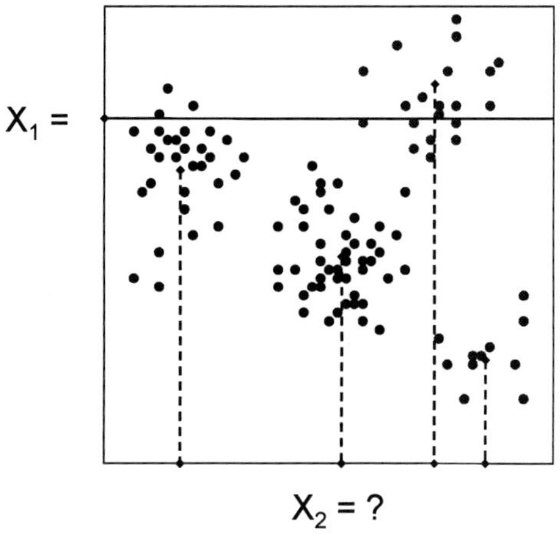

13

Mean imputation uses the unconditional mean of the variable. An attractive extension would be to use the mean conditional on the other inputs. This is referred to as regression imputation. Regression imputation would usually give better estimates of the missing values. Specifically, *k* linear regression models could be built, one for each input variable using the other inputs as predictors. This would presumably give better imputations and be able to accommodate missingness that depends on the values of the other inputs. However, a complication of regression imputation is that the other inputs might themselves have missing values. Consequently, the *k* imputation regressions also need to accommodate missing values.

Cluster-mean imputation is a somewhat more practical alternative:

1. cluster the cases into relatively homogenous subgroups
2. mean-imputation within each group
3. for new cases with multiple missing values, use the cluster mean that is closest in all the nonmissing dimensions.

This method can accommodate missingness that depends on the other input variables. This method is implemented in SAS Enterprise Miner. For large data sets, the FASTCLUS procedure might also be appropriate. (See appendix.)

A simpler but sometimes useful alternative is to define a priori segments (for example, high, middle, low, and unknown income), and then do mean or median imputation within each segment.

Exercises

1. **Missing Value Imputation**

   a. Using the **pva** data set, create missing value indicators for the inputs **DONOR_AGE**, **INCOME_GROUP**, and **WEALTH_RATING**.

   b. Submit the program below to group the variables **RECENT_RESPONSE_PROP** and **RECENT_AVG_GIFT_AMT** into three groups.

```
proc rank data=pva out=pva groups=3;
   var recent_response_prop recent_avg_gift_amt;
   ranks grp_resp grp_amt;
run;
```

   c. Sort **pva** by **GRP_RESP** and **GRP_AMT**.

   d. Use PROC STDIZE with a BY statement to impute missing values for each BY group and output the completed data set. Name the output data set **pva1**.

   e. Use the MEANS procedure to determine the values that the missing values were replaced with.

      1) For the cell **GRP_RESP**=0 and **GRP_AMT**=0, what was the missing value for **DONOR_AGE** replaced with?

> The RANK procedure with the GROUPS= option bins variables into quantiles. The VAR statement lists the variables to be grouped. The RANKS statement names the group indicators in the OUT= data set.

3.02 Multiple Choice Poll

For the cell **GRP_RESP**=0 and **GRP_AMT**=0, what was the missing value for **DONOR_AGE** replaced with?

a. 57
b. 64
c. 58
d. 65

15

3.2 Categorical Inputs

Objectives

- Explain the problem of having numerous levels in a categorical input.
- Illustrate how to cluster levels of a categorical input using the CLUSTER procedure.
- Create a dendrogram using the TREE procedure.

19

Dummy Variables

X
D
B
C
C
A
A
D
C
A
⋮

D_A	D_B	D_C	D_D
0	0	0	1
0	1	0	0
0	0	1	0
0	0	1	0
1	0	0	0
1	0	0	0
0	0	0	1
0	0	1	0
1	0	0	0
⋮	⋮	⋮	⋮

20

With the CLASS statement, you can use categorical input variables in PROC LOGISTIC without having to create dummy variables in a DATA step. You can specify the type of parameterization to use, such as effect coding and reference coding, and the reference level.

Smarter Variables

ZIP
99801
99622
99523
99523
99737
99937
99533
99523
99622
⋮

HomeVal	Urbanicity	Local	...
75	1	1	
100	2	1	
150	1	1	
150	1	0	
150	3	1	
75	3	1	
100	2	1	
150	1	0	
100	3	1	
⋮	⋮	⋮	

21

Expanding categorical inputs into dummy variables can greatly increase the dimension of the input space. A smarter method is to use subject-matter information to create new inputs that represent relevant sources of variation. A categorical input might be best thought of as a link to other data sets. For example, geographic areas are often mapped to several relevant demographic variables.

Quasi-Complete Separation

	0	1	D_A	D_B	D_C	D_D
A	28	7	1	0	0	0
B	16	0	0	1	0	0
C	94	11	0	0	1	0
D	23	21	0	0	0	1

22

Including categorical inputs in the model can cause quasi-complete separation. *Quasi-complete separation* occurs when a level of the categorical input has a target event rate of 0 or 100%. The coefficient of a dummy variable represents the difference in the logits between that level and the reference level. When quasi-complete separation occurs, one of the logits will be infinite. The likelihood will not have a maximum in at least one dimension, so the ML estimate of that coefficient will be infinite. If the zero-cell category is the reference level, then all the coefficients for the dummy variables will be infinite.

Quasi-complete separation complicates model interpretation. It can also affect the convergence of the estimation algorithm. Furthermore, it might lead to incorrect decisions regarding variable selection.

The most common cause of quasi-complete separation in predictive modeling is categorical inputs with rare categories. The best remedy for sparseness is collapsing levels of the categorical variable.

Clustering Levels

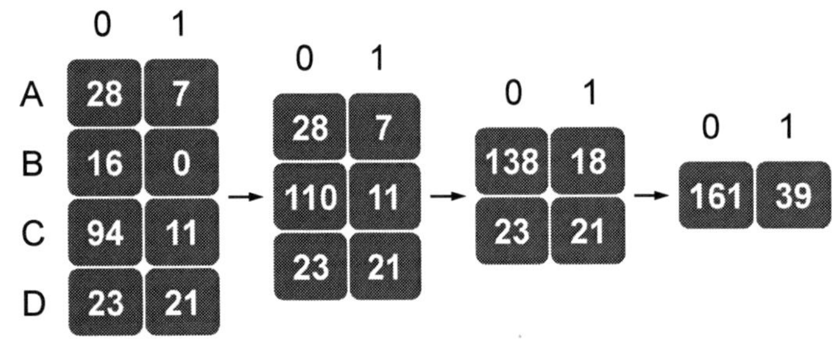

Merged:		B & C	A & BC	ABC & D
χ^2 =	31.7	30.7	28.6	0
	100%	97%	90%	0%

26

Ideally, subject-matter considerations should be used to collapse levels (reduce the dimension) of categorical inputs. This is not always practical in predictive modeling. A simple data-driven method for collapsing levels of contingency tables was developed by Greenacre (1988, 1993). The levels (rows) are hierarchically clustered based on the reduction in the chi-squared test of association between the categorical variable and the target. At each step, the two levels that give the least reduction in the chi-squared statistic are merged. The process is continued until the reduction in chi-squared drops below some threshold (for example, 99%). This method will quickly throw rare categories in with other categories that have similar marginal response rates. While this method is simple and effective, there is a potential loss of information because only univariate associations are considered.

3.03 Multiple Choice Poll

Which of the following statements is false regarding Greenacre's method for collapsing levels of contingency tables?

a. The levels are hierarchically clustered based on the reduction in the chi-squared test of association.
b. Levels with similar marginal response rates are merged.
c. The method accounts for the sample size in each level.
d. The method is appropriate for any categorical input.

27

Clustering Levels of Categorical Inputs

Example: Use PROC MEANS to calculate the response rate and frequency in each of the levels of **branch**. Then use the CLUSTER procedure to cluster the levels of **branch** using Greenacre's method and to create a high resolution dendrogram. Use the DATA step to compute the log of the *p*-value for each collapsed contingency table of the branch levels and find the cluster solution with the lowest *p*-value. Use the TREE procedure to create a SAS data set with the final cluster solution.

The levels of a categorical input can be clustered using Greenacre's method (1988, 1993) in PROC CLUSTER. The procedure was designed for general clustering applications, but with some simple pre-processing of the data, it can be made to cluster levels of categorical variables.

The variable **Branch** has 19 levels. The first step is to create a data set that contains the proportion of the target event (**Ins**) and number of cases in each level. The NWAY option caused the output data set to have 19 observations, one for each of the 19 levels. The output data set also has a variable **prop** for the proportion of target events. It automatically creates the variable **_FREQ_**, which counts the number of cases in each level.

```
/* pmlr03d02.sas */
proc means data=imputed noprint nway;
   class branch;
   var ins;
   output out=level mean=prop;
run;

proc print data=level;
run;
```

Obs	Branch	_TYPE_	_FREQ_	prop
1	B1	1	2819	0.36999
2	B10	1	273	0.40293
3	B11	1	247	0.35628
4	B12	1	549	0.36430
5	B13	1	535	0.37196
6	B14	1	1072	0.19123
7	B15	1	2235	0.24251
8	B16	1	1534	0.27771
9	B17	1	850	0.37059
10	B18	1	541	0.35675
11	B19	1	285	0.38596
12	B2	1	5345	0.32460
13	B3	1	2844	0.38186
14	B4	1	5633	0.37493
15	B5	1	2752	0.38118
16	B6	1	1438	0.37830
17	B7	1	1413	0.34678
18	B8	1	1341	0.38553
19	B9	1	558	0.37814

Using the FREQ statement and METHOD=WARD in PROC CLUSTER gives identical results to Greenacre's method. The OUTTREE= option creates an output data set that can be used by the TREE procedure to create a SAS data set with the final cluster solution. The PLOTS=DENDROGRAM requests a high resolution dendrogram with the VERTICAL option specifying a vertical dendrogram and the HEIGHT=RSQ option specifying that the squared multiple correlation be used as the method to draw the height of the dendrogram. The ID statement specifies a variable that identifies observations in the printed cluster history and in the OUTTREE= data set. The ODS OUTPUT statement will create an output data set called **cluster** from the output object **clusterhistory** that is associated with the results of the clustering algorithm.

```
ods output clusterhistory=cluster;

proc cluster data=level method=ward outtree=fortree
        plots=(dendrogram(vertical height=rsq));
   freq _freq_;
   var prop;
   id branch;
run;
```

Partial Output

Cluster History						
Number of Clusters	Clusters Joined		Freq	Semipartial R-Square	R-Square	Tie
18	B6	B9	1996	0.0000	1.00	
17	B11	B18	788	0.0000	1.00	
16	B19	B8	1626	0.0000	1.00	
15	B1	B17	3669	0.0000	1.00	
14	B3	B5	5596	0.0000	1.00	
13	CL15	B13	4204	0.0000	1.00	
12	CL14	CL18	7592	0.0002	1.00	
11	CL13	B12	4753	0.0002	1.00	
10	CL16	CL12	9218	0.0004	.999	
9	CL17	B7	2201	0.0006	.999	
8	CL11	B4	10386	0.0009	.998	
7	B10	CL10	9491	0.0015	.996	
6	CL8	CL7	19877	0.0058	.990	
5	CL9	B2	7546	0.0130	.977	
4	B15	B16	3769	0.0142	.963	
3	B14	CL4	4841	0.0453	.918	
2	CL6	CL5	27423	0.1399	.778	
1	CL2	CL3	32264	0.7779	.000	

The column labeled **RSquare** in the output is equivalent to the proportion of chi-squared in the 19×2 contingency table remaining after the levels are collapsed. At each step, the levels that give the smallest decrease in chi-squared are merged. The change in chi-squared is listed in the **Semipartial R-Square** column. The rows in the summary represent the results after the listed clusters were merged. The number of clusters is reduced from 18 to 1. When previously collapsed levels are merged, they are denoted using the CL as the prefix and the number of resulting clusters as the suffix. For example, at the sixth step, CL15 represents B1 and B17 that were merged at the fourth step creating 15 clusters.

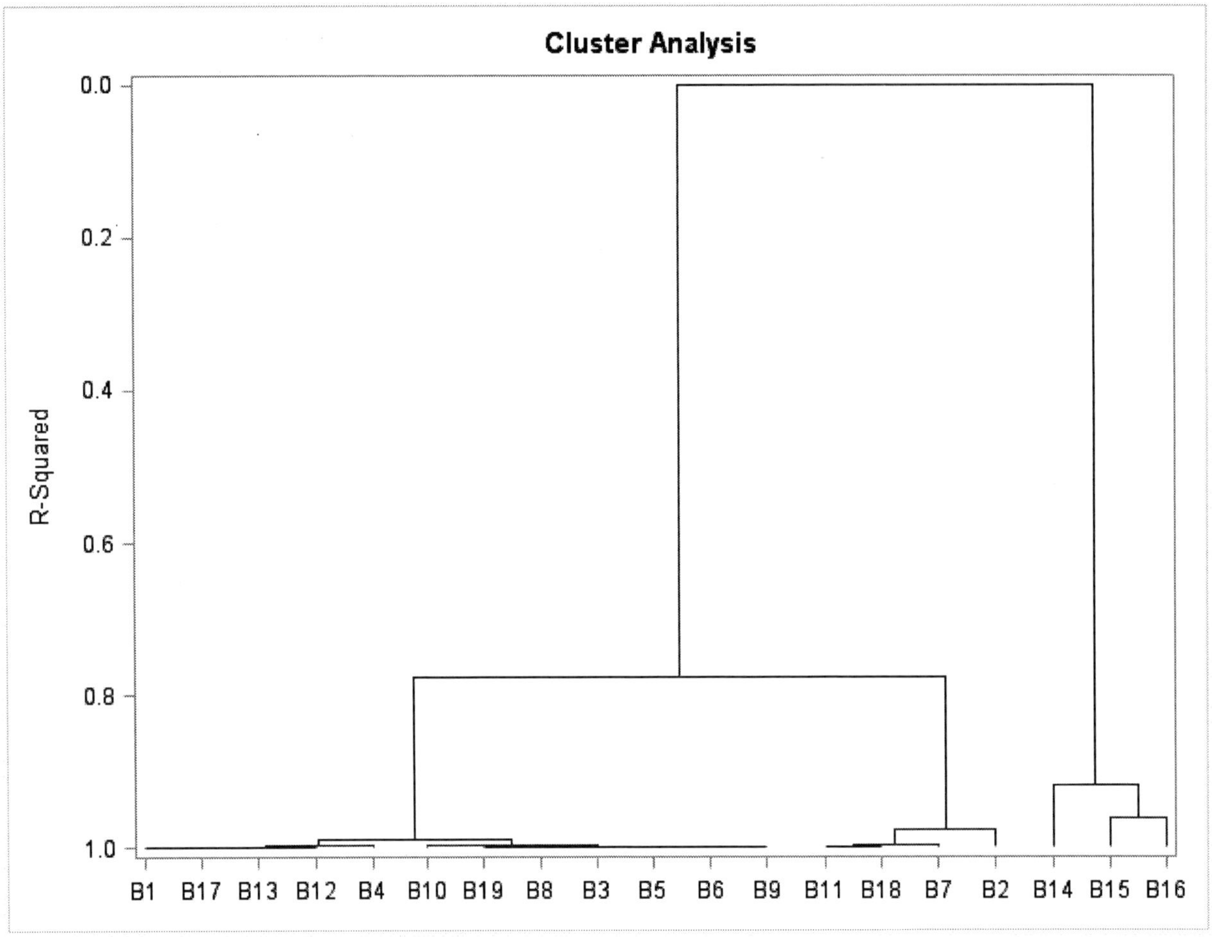

The dendrogram shows that several branches can be combined with a minuscule reduction in chi-squared. The horizontal axis is also roughly ordered by the mean proportion of events in each cluster.

To calculate the optimum number of clusters, the chi-square statistic and the associated *p*-value needs to be computed for each collapsed contingency table. This information can be obtained by multiplying the chi-square statistic from the 19×2 contingency table with the proportion of chi-squared remaining after the levels are collapsed. The FREQ procedure is used to compute the chi-square statistic for the 19×2 contingency table.

```
proc freq data=imputed noprint;
   tables branch*ins / chisq;
   output out=chi(keep=_pchi_) chisq;
run;
```

The DATA step computes the chi-square statistic for each collapsed contingency table. The **_n_** variable is used to put the overall chi-square value in each observation for the data set **cutoff**. The LOGSDF function computes the log of the probability that an observation from a specified distribution is greater than or equal to a specified value. The arguments for the function are the specified distribution in quotation marks, the numeric random variable, and the degrees of freedom. The log of the *p*-value is calculated in order to produce a more visually appealing graph.

```
data cutoff;
   if _n_=1 then set chi;
   set cluster;
   chisquare=_pchi_*rsquared;
   degfree=numberofclusters-1;
   logpvalue=logsdf('CHISQ',chisquare,degfree);
run;
```

To plot the log of the *p*-value by the number of clusters, the SGPLOT procedure will be used.

```
proc sgplot data=cutoff;
   scatter y=logpvalue x=numberofclusters
           / markerattrs=(color=blue symbol=circlefilled);
   xaxis label="Number of Clusters";
   yaxis label="Log of P-Value" min=-170 max=-130;
   title "Plot of the Log of the P-Value by Number of Clusters";
run;
```

Selected SGPLOT procedure statements:

SCATTER	creates a scatter plot where the y= argument specifies the variable for the y-axis and the x= argument specifies the variable for the x-axis.
XAXIS	specifies options for the x-axis.
YAXIS	specifies options for the y-axis.

Selected SCATTER statement option:

MARKERATTRS=	specifies the appearance of the markers in the plot. You can specify the appearance by using a style element or by using suboptions. If you specify a style element, you can also specify suboptions to override specific appearance attributes.

Selected MARKETATTRS= suboptions:

COLOR=	specifies the color of the markers.
SYMBOL=	specifies the symbol for the markers.

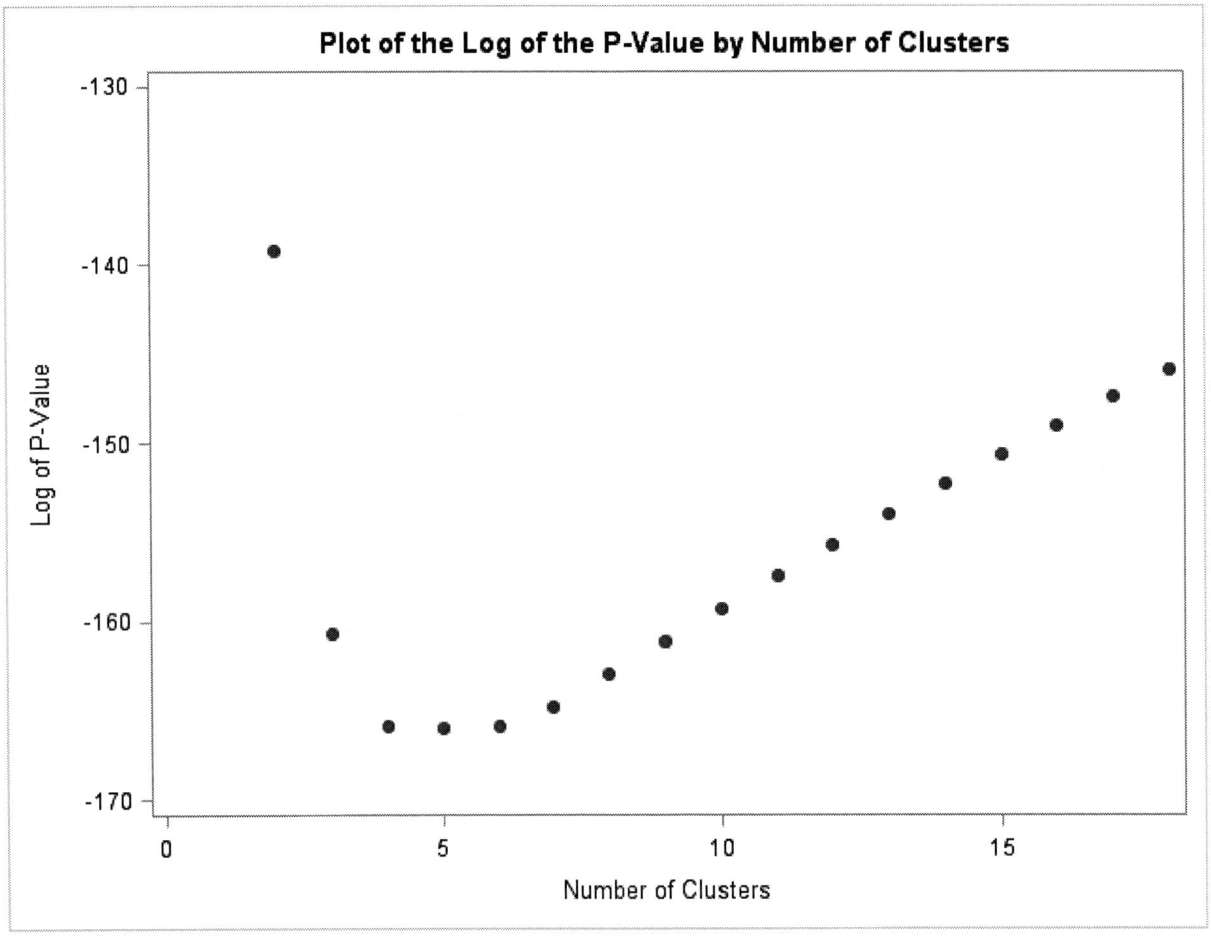

The graph shows that the 4-, 5-, and 6-cluster solutions had the lowest *p*-values.

To find the cluster solution with the lowest *p*-value, and assign that value to the macro variable **NCL**, use the SQL procedure.

```
proc sql;
   select NumberOfClusters into :ncl
   from cutoff
   having logpvalue=min(logpvalue);
quit;
```

Number of Clusters
5

The 5-cluster solution has the smallest log *p*-value.

The TREE procedure produces a SAS data set with the 5 cluster solution. The input data set is the OUTTREE= data set produced in PROC CLUSTER. The **clus** data set from the OUT= option in PROC TREE shows which levels of **branch** are associated with each cluster (if the NCLUSTERS= option is correctly specified).

```
ods html close;
proc tree data=fortree nclusters=&ncl out=clus;
   id branch;
run;
ods html;

proc sort data=clus;
   by clusname;
run;

proc print data=clus;
   by clusname;
   id clusname;
run;
```

CLUSNAME	Branch	CLUSTER
B14	B14	5

CLUSNAME	Branch	CLUSTER
B15	B15	3

CLUSNAME	Branch	CLUSTER
B16	B16	4

CLUSNAME	Branch	CLUSTER
CL5	B11	2
	B18	2
	B7	2
	B2	2

CLUSNAME	Branch	CLUSTER
CL6	B6	1
	B9	1
	B19	1
	B8	1
	B1	1
	B17	1
	B3	1
	B5	1
	B13	1
	B12	1
	B4	1
	B10	1

A DATA step is used to assign the branches to dummy variables. Four dummy variables are created with the second cluster designated as the reference level. Note that the dummy variables are numbered sequentially.

Choosing a cluster near the center of the tree (for example, B11, B18, B7, and B2) as a reference group might lead to better models if the variable selection method that you choose incrementally adds variables to the model (Cohen 1991).

```
data imputed;
   set imputed;
   brclus1=(branch in ('B6','B9','B19','B8','B1','B17',
           'B3','B5','B13','B12','B4','B10'));
   brclus2=(branch='B15');
   brclus3=(branch='B16');
   brclus4=(branch='B14');
run;
```

Exercises

2. Clustering Categorical Input Levels

a. Use Greenacre's correspondence analysis to cluster levels of **CLUSTER_CODE**. First use PROC MEANS to generate a data set with information about the average response rate and sample size for each level of **CLUSTER_CODE**.

b. Use PROC CLUSTER to group those levels together and create a horizontal dendrogram. Use the log of the *p*-value of the appropriate χ^2 test to determine which level of clustering is appropriate.

c. Use PROC SGPLOT to plot the log of the *p*-value by the number of clusters (the range of the y-axis should be -50 to -10) and use PROC TREE to create a SAS data set of the final results.

d. Create indicators to flag membership in those clusters.

1) What is the optimum number of clusters for the **CLUSTER_CODE** variable?

3.04 Multiple Choice Poll

What is the optimum number of clusters for the cluster_code variable?

a. 3
b. 4
c. 5
d. 6

31

3.3 Variable Clustering

Objectives

- Discuss the problem of redundant variables.
- Explain the concept of principal component analysis.
- Demonstrate variable clustering using the VARCLUS procedure.

35

Redundancy

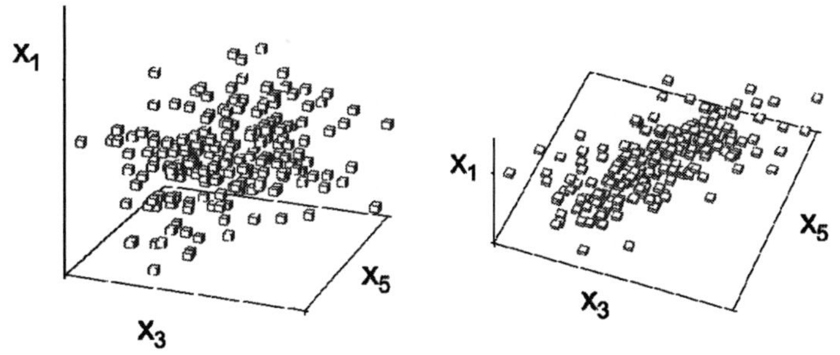

36

Including redundant inputs can degrade the analysis by

- destabilizing the parameter estimates
- increasing the risk of overfitting
- confounding interpretation
- increasing computation time
- increasing scoring effort
- increasing the cost of data collection and augmentation.

Redundancy is an *unsupervised* concept. It does not involve the target variable. On the other hand, the *relevancy* of a variable takes into account the relationship between an input variable and the target variable. In high-dimensional data sets, identifying irrelevant inputs is more difficult than identifying redundant inputs. A good strategy is to first reduce redundancy and then tackle irrelevancy in a lower dimension space.

Variable Clustering

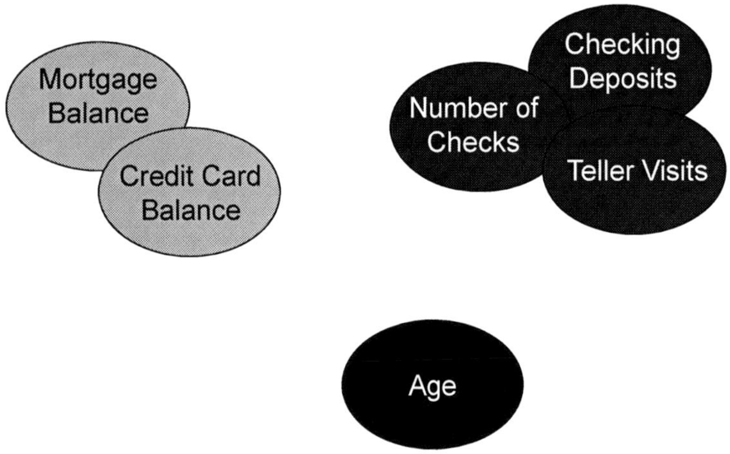

37

One approach to variable reduction is variable clustering. *Variable clustering* finds groups of variables that are as correlated as possible among themselves and as uncorrelated as possible with variables in other clusters. A common strategy is to pick one variable from each cluster based on subject-matter knowledge.

Variable Clustering Example

	X_1	X_2	X_3	X_4	X_5
X_1	1	–.11	–.03	–.69	–.04
X_2	–.11	1	–.14	.07	.04
X_3	–.03	–.14	1	.04	–.73
X_4	–.69	.07	.04	1	.02
X_5	–.04	.04	–.73	.02	1

Correlation Matrix

38

In the example above, it seems that X_1 is correlated with X_4 and X_3 is correlated with X_5. The variable X_2 is correlated with no other variable. Therefore, there should be three variable clusters.

Principal Components

$$PC_{(1)} = W_{(1)1}X_1 + W_{(1)2}X_2 + \ldots + W_{(1)p}X_p$$
$$PC_{(2)} = W_{(2)1}X_1 + W_{(2)2}X_2 + \ldots + W_{(2)p}X_p$$
$$\vdots$$
$$PC_{(p)} = W_{(p)1}X_1 + W_{(p)2}X_2 + \ldots + W_{(p)p}X_p$$

where the weights have been chosen to maximize the quantity

$$\frac{\text{Variance of PC}}{\text{Total Variance}}$$

and the correlation $\text{corr}(PC_{(i)},PC_{(j)})=0$ for each i not equal to j.

39

Variable clustering is based on principal components. *Principal components* are weighted linear combinations of the predictor variables where the weights are chosen to account for the largest amount of variation in the data; total variation in this case is the sum of the sample variances of the predictor variables. The principal components are numbered according to how much variation in the data is accounted for (first principal component accounts for the largest, second principal component accounts for the second largest, and so on) and each principal component accounts for a unique portion of the variation in the data. In other words, they are not correlated.

To obtain a unique solution for the principal components, a constraint is imposed where the sum of the squared weights must equal 1 for each principal component.

Principal Components

	X_1	X_2	X_3	X_4	X_5	PC_1	PC_2	PC_3	PC_4	PC_5	
X_1	1	−.11	−.03	−.69	−.04	1.8	0	0	0	0	PC_1
X_2	−.11	1	−.14	.07	.04	0	1.7	0	0	0	PC_2
X_3	−.03	−.14	1	.04	−.73	0	0	1.0	0	0	PC_3
X_4	−.69	.07	.04	1	.02	0	0	0	0.3	0	PC_4
X_5	−.04	.04	−.73	.02	1	0	0	0	0	0.2	PC_5

Correlation Matrix

Covariance Matrix

40

The correlation matrix is the covariance matrix of the standardized variables. Because each standardized variable has a variance equal to one, the total variability among the standardized variables is just the number of variables. The principal components are produced by an eigen-decomposition of the correlation matrix. The *eigenvalues* are the variances of the PCs; they sum to the number of variables. The first PC corresponds to the first eigenvalue and explains the largest proportion of the variability. Each PC explains a decreasing amount of the total variability. In the above example, the first three PCs explain 90% of the total variability.

Principal components analysis can also be used for reducing redundant dimensions. A set of *k* variables can be transformed into a set of *k* principal components. In practice, dimension reduction is achieved by retaining only the first few PCs provided they explain a sufficient proportion of the total variation. The reduced set of PCs might then be used in place of the original variables in the analysis.

Principal Component Coefficients

	PC_1	PC_2	PC_3	PC_4	PC_5
x_1	–.25	–.65	.09	.69	.15
x_2	.21	.10	.97	.02	.11
x_3	–.65	.28	.04	–.11	.70
x_4	.23	.66	–.14	.70	.07
x_5	.65	–.23	–.19	–.10	.69

41

The chief advantage of variable clustering over principal components is the coefficients. The coefficients of the PCs (*eigenvectors*) are usually nonzero for all the original variables. Thus, even if only a few PCs were used, all the inputs would still have to be retained in the analysis.

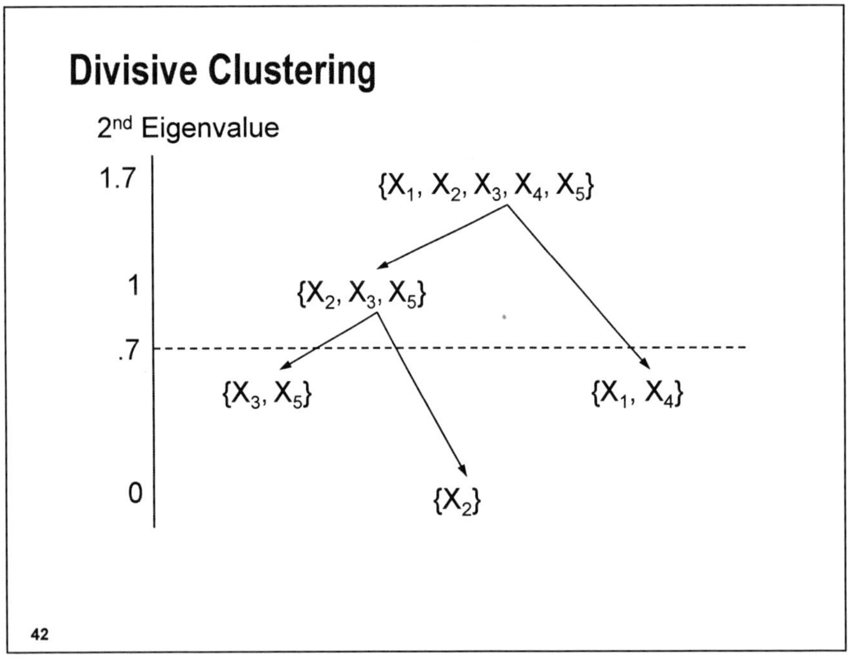

Variable clustering finds groups of variables that are as correlated as possible among themselves and as uncorrelated as possible with variables in other clusters. The basic algorithm is binary and divisive. All variables start in one cluster. A principal components analysis is done on the variables in the cluster. If the second eigenvalue is greater than a specified threshold (in other words, there is more than one dominant dimension), then the cluster is split. The PC scores are then rotated obliquely so that the variables can be split into two groups. This process is repeated for the two child clusters until the second eigenvalue drops below the threshold. (By default, PROC VARCLUS does a nonhierarchical version of this algorithm where variables can also be reassigned to other clusters.)

Larger thresholds for the second eigenvalue give fewer clusters and less of the variation is explained. Smaller thresholds give more clusters and more of the variation is explained. The value 1 is a common choice for the threshold because it represents the average size of the eigenvalues. To account for sampling variability, smaller values such as .7 have been suggested (Jackson 1991).

The VARCLUS Procedure

General form of the VARCLUS procedure:

```
PROC VARCLUS DATA=SAS-data-set <options>;
     VAR variables;
RUN;
```

43

Selected PROC VARCLUS statement options:

MAXEIGEN=*n*	specifies the largest permissible value of the second eigenvalue in each cluster. The default is 1 (using the correlation matrix).
SHORT	suppresses printing of the cluster structure, scoring coefficient, and intercluster correlation matrices.

Selected VARCLUS procedure statement:

VAR	specifies the variables to be clustered. If you do not specify the VAR statement, all numeric variables not listed in other statements are processed.

Cluster Representatives

$$1 - R^2 \text{ ratio} = \frac{1 - R^2_{\text{own cluster}}}{1 - R^2_{\text{next closest}}}$$

Smaller is Better:

$$\frac{1-\uparrow}{1-\downarrow} \Rightarrow \frac{\downarrow}{\uparrow} \Rightarrow \downarrow$$

44

As with principal components analysis, dimension reduction could be achieved by replacing the original variables with the cluster scores (components). A simple alternative is to select a representative variable from each cluster. An ideal representative would have high correlation with its own cluster and have a low correlation with the other clusters. Consequently, variables with the lowest $1-R^2$ ratio (defined above) in each cluster would be good representatives. Of course, subject-matter considerations might dictate the selection of other representatives.

3.05 Multiple Choice Poll

What criteria would you use to pick one variable from each cluster?

a. The importance of the variable based on subject-matter knowledge
b. The cost of collecting data for the variable
c. Whether your audience feels that the variable should be controlled for in the model
d. The strength of the relationship between the variable and the response variable
e. All of the above
f. None of the above

45

Variable Clustering

Example: Cluster the numeric variables in the **imputed** data set. These include the original numeric inputs, the missing indicators, and the dummy variables for the collapsed **branch** (64 total). Use the HI option so that clusters at different levels maintain a hierarchical structure that prevents variables from transferring from one cluster to another after the split is made and the SHORT option to suppress some of the output. Also create a dendrogram of the variable clustering using the PLOTS= option.

```
/* pmlr03d03.sas */
proc varclus data=imputed maxeigen=.7 hi short plots=dendrogram;
   var &inputs brclus1-brclus4 miacctag
       miphone mipos miposamt miinv
       miinvbal micc miccbal miccpurc
       miincome mihmown milores mihmval
       miage micrscor;
   title "Variable Clustering of Imputed Data Set";
run;
```

The output from PROC VARCLUS shows the results for each step in the divisive clustering algorithm. Even with the SHORT option, the amount of printed output is voluminous.

Partial Output

Variable Clustering of Imputed Data Set

Oblique Principal Component Cluster Analysis

Observations	32264	**Proportion**	0
Variables	64	**Maxeigen**	0.7

Clustering algorithm converged.

Cluster Summary for 1 Cluster					
Cluster	**Members**	**Cluster Variation**	**Variation Explained**	**Proportion Explained**	**Second Eigenvalue**
1	64	64	9.228833	0.1442	5.0980

Total variation explained = 9.228833 Proportion = 0.1442

Cluster 1 will be split because it has the largest second eigenvalue, 5.097981, which is greater than the MAXEIGEN=0.7 value.

Clustering algorithm converged.

Cluster Summary for 2 Clusters					
Cluster	Members	Cluster Variation	Variation Explained	Proportion Explained	Second Eigenvalue
1	48	48	9.197492	0.1916	3.4316
2	16	16	5.047174	0.3154	2.0471

Total variation explained = 14.24467 Proportion = 0.2226

The tables with the R-squared statistics contain the results of each iteration of the algorithm except the first one (the cluster with all the variables). The results show which variable is assigned to a specific cluster along with the R-squared statistic for its own cluster and the next closest cluster. The 1-R-squared ratio is also reported.

2 Clusters		R-squared with			
Cluster	Variable	Own Cluster	Next Closest	1-R**2 Ratio	Variable Label
Cluster 1	AcctAge	0.0004	0.0002	0.9998	Age of Oldest Account
	Dep	0.0010	0.0001	0.9991	Checking Deposits
	DepAmt	0.0007	0.0000	0.9993	Amount Deposited
	CashBk	0.0003	0.0000	0.9997	Number Cash Back
	Checks	0.0037	0.0001	0.9963	Number of Checks
	DirDep	0.0001	0.0001	0.9999	Direct Deposit
	NSF	0.0002	0.0001	0.9999	Number Insufficient Fund
	NSFAmt	0.0000	0.0000	1.0000	Amount NSF
	Phone	0.0179	0.0001	0.9821	Number Telephone Banking
	Teller	0.0012	0.0001	0.9989	Teller Visits
	Sav	0.0006	0.0000	0.9994	Saving Account
	SavBal	0.0000	0.0000	1.0000	Saving Balance
	ATM	0.0003	0.0000	0.9997	ATM
	ATMAmt	0.0013	0.0000	0.9987	ATM Withdrawal Amount
	POS	0.0257	0.0000	0.9743	Number Point of Sale
	POSAmt	0.0242	0.0001	0.9759	Amount Point of Sale

	CD	0.0002	0.0000	0.9998	Certificate of Deposit
	CDBal	0.0002	0.0000	0.9998	CD Balance
	LOC	0.0066	0.0000	0.9934	Line of Credit
	LOCBal	0.0014	0.0001	0.9987	Line of Credit Balance
	Inv	0.0052	0.0001	0.9949	Investment
	InvBal	0.0002	0.0000	0.9999	Investment Balance
	ILS	0.0026	0.0000	0.9974	Installment Loan
	ILSBal	0.0024	0.0000	0.9977	Loan Balance
	MM	0.0000	0.0000	1.0000	Money Market
	MMBal	0.0001	0.0000	1.0000	Money Market Balance
	MTG	0.0032	0.0003	0.9970	Mortgage
	MTGBal	0.0006	0.0000	0.9995	Mortgage Balance
	CC	0.1279	0.0007	0.8727	Credit Card
	CCBal	0.0019	0.0000	0.9981	Credit Card Balance
	CCPurc	0.0211	0.0000	0.9789	Credit Card Purchases
	SDB	0.0006	0.0000	0.9995	Safety Deposit Box
	CRScore	0.0001	0.0000	0.9999	Credit Score
	Moved	0.0000	0.0000	1.0000	Recent Address Change
	InArea	0.0003	0.0000	0.9997	Local Address
	brclus1	0.2239	0.0535	0.8200	
	brclus2	0.5331	0.0022	0.4679	
	brclus3	0.0061	0.0019	0.9958	
	brclus4	0.2426	0.0010	0.7582	
	MIAcctAg	0.0000	0.0000	1.0000	
	MIPhone	0.9925	0.0044	0.0076	
	MIPOS	0.9925	0.0044	0.0076	
	MIPOSAmt	0.9925	0.0044	0.0076	

	MIInv	0.9925	0.0044	0.0076	
	MIInvBal	0.9925	0.0044	0.0076	
	MICC	0.9925	0.0044	0.0076	
	MICCBal	0.9925	0.0044	0.0076	
	MICCPurc	0.9925	0.0044	0.0076	
Cluster 2	**DDA**	0.0002	0.0001	0.9999	Checking Account
	DDABal	0.0004	0.0001	0.9997	Checking Balance
	IRA	0.0000	0.0000	1.0000	Retirement Account
	IRABal	0.0001	0.0000	0.9999	IRA Balance
	MMCred	0.0000	0.0000	1.0000	Money Market Credits
	Income	0.0113	0.0000	0.9887	Income
	HMOwn	0.1850	0.0000	0.8150	Owns Home
	LORes	0.0005	0.0001	0.9996	Length of Residence
	HMVal	0.0137	0.0000	0.9863	Home Value
	Age	0.0009	0.0000	0.9991	Age
	MIIncome	0.9857	0.0028	0.0143	
	MIHMOwn	0.9541	0.0030	0.0461	
	MILORes	0.9857	0.0028	0.0143	
	MIHMVal	0.9857	0.0028	0.0143	
	MIAge	0.9194	0.0027	0.0808	
	MICRScor	0.0044	0.0000	0.9956	

Cluster 1 will be split because it has the largest second eigenvalue, 3.431637, which is greater than the MAXEIGEN=0.7 value.

The last iteration of PROC VARCLUS contains the most useful information. It shows the final assignment of the variables to the specific clusters.

41 Clusters		**R-squared with**			
Cluster	**Variable**	**Own Cluster**	**Next Closest**	**1-R**2 Ratio**	**Variable Label**
Cluster 1	**brclus2**	0.5684	0.1194	0.4901	
	MIPhone	0.9962	0.2339	0.0050	
	MIPOS	0.9962	0.2339	0.0050	
	MIPOSAmt	0.9962	0.2339	0.0050	

	MIInv	0.9962	0.2339	0.0050	
	MIInvBal	0.9962	0.2339	0.0050	
	MICC	0.9962	0.2339	0.0050	
	MICCBal	0.9962	0.2339	0.0050	
	MICCPurc	0.9962	0.2339	0.0050	
Cluster 2	**MIIncome**	0.9936	0.1336	0.0074	
	MIHMOwn	0.9624	0.1266	0.0431	
	MILORes	0.9936	0.1336	0.0074	
	MIHMVal	0.9936	0.1336	0.0074	
	MIAge	0.9255	0.1047	0.0832	
Cluster 3	**Dep**	0.7236	0.3474	0.4235	Checking Deposits
	Checks	0.7139	0.1543	0.3383	Number of Checks
	Teller	0.4865	0.0808	0.5586	Teller Visits
Cluster 4	**MTGBal**	0.9687	0.1976	0.0390	Mortgage Balance
	CCBal	0.9687	0.1333	0.0361	Credit Card Balance
Cluster 5	**MM**	0.9746	0.2963	0.0360	Money Market
	MMBal	0.9746	0.2705	0.0348	Money Market Balance
Cluster 6	**Income**	0.8419	0.0268	0.1625	Income
	HMVal	0.8419	0.3218	0.2332	Home Value
Cluster 7	**ILS**	0.9958	0.0315	0.0044	Installment Loan
	ILSBal	0.9958	0.0314	0.0044	Loan Balance
Cluster 8	**POS**	0.9189	0.0711	0.0873	Number Point of Sale
	POSAmt	0.9189	0.0622	0.0864	Amount Point of Sale
Cluster 9	**NSF**	0.7582	0.0484	0.2541	Number Insufficient Fund
	NSFAmt	0.7582	0.0339	0.2503	Amount NSF
Cluster 10	**CD**	0.7252	0.0241	0.2816	Certificate of Deposit
	CDBal	0.7252	0.0263	0.2823	CD Balance
Cluster 11	**IRA**	0.6732	0.0459	0.3426	Retirement Account

	IRABal	0.6732	0.0217	0.3341	IRA Balance
Cluster 12	**Age**	1.0000	0.1985	0.0000	Age
Cluster 13	**LOC**	0.7352	0.0336	0.2740	Line of Credit
	LOCBal	0.7352	0.0632	0.2827	Line of Credit Balance
Cluster 14	**Sav**	1.0000	0.0640	0.0000	Saving Account
Cluster 15	**DDA**	1.0000	0.2874	0.0000	Checking Account
Cluster 16	**Inv**	1.0000	0.0259	0.0000	Investment
Cluster 17	**CRScore**	1.0000	0.1985	0.0000	Credit Score
Cluster 18	**brclus3**	1.0000	0.0801	0.0000	
Cluster 19	**CC**	1.0000	0.1401	0.0000	Credit Card
Cluster 20	**brclus1**	1.0000	0.1882	0.0000	
Cluster 21	**CashBk**	1.0000	0.0050	0.0000	Number Cash Back
Cluster 22	**MIAcctAg**	1.0000	0.0060	0.0000	
Cluster 23	**MICRScor**	1.0000	0.0206	0.0000	
Cluster 24	**Moved**	1.0000	0.0016	0.0000	Recent Address Change
Cluster 25	**AcctAge**	1.0000	0.0219	0.0000	Age of Oldest Account
Cluster 26	**DirDep**	1.0000	0.0948	0.0000	Direct Deposit
Cluster 27	**SavBal**	1.0000	0.0640	0.0000	Saving Balance
Cluster 28	**DDABal**	1.0000	0.1238	0.0000	Checking Balance
Cluster 29	**SDB**	1.0000	0.0130	0.0000	Safety Deposit Box
Cluster 30	**CCPurc**	1.0000	0.1401	0.0000	Credit Card Purchases
Cluster 31	**InArea**	1.0000	0.1159	0.0000	Local Address
Cluster 32	**ATMAmt**	1.0000	0.0490	0.0000	ATM Withdrawal Amount
Cluster 33	**Phone**	1.0000	0.0860	0.0000	Number Telephone Banking
Cluster 34	**MMCred**	1.0000	0.2906	0.0000	Money Market Credits
Cluster 35	**HMOwn**	1.0000	0.3800	0.0000	Owns Home
Cluster 36	**InvBal**	1.0000	0.0259	0.0000	Investment Balance

Cluster 37	**DepAmt**	1.0000	0.1238	0.0000	Amount Deposited
Cluster 38	**brclus4**	1.0000	0.2006	0.0000	
Cluster 39	**ATM**	1.0000	0.1541	0.0000	ATM
Cluster 40	**LORes**	1.0000	0.3800	0.0000	Length of Residence
Cluster 41	**MTG**	1.0000	0.1692	0.0000	Mortgage

No cluster meets the criterion for splitting.

The last table in the output contains the number of clusters for the final iteration. The table also has information about the proportion of variation explained by the clusters and the maximum second eigenvalue in a cluster. This information can be used to decide whether too few or too many clusters have been formed.

Number of Clusters	Total Variation Explained by Clusters	Proportion of Variation Explained by Clusters	Minimum Proportion Explained by a Cluster	Maximum Second Eigenvalue in a Cluster	Minimum R-squared for a Variable	Maximum 1-R**2 Ratio for a Variable
1	9.228833	0.1442	0.1442	5.097981	0.0000	
2	14.244666	0.2226	0.1916	3.431637	0.0000	1.0000
3	17.595965	0.2749	0.1269	2.541211	0.0000	1.4572
4	20.024110	0.3129	0.1269	2.104444	0.0000	1.4572
5	21.979822	0.3434	0.1802	2.047135	0.0000	1.3719
6	23.961430	0.3744	0.1802	2.013311	0.0000	1.3416
7	25.945084	0.4054	0.2023	1.623838	0.0000	1.3428
8	27.446233	0.4288	0.2375	1.449194	0.0000	1.5083
9	28.836743	0.4506	0.2375	1.361978	0.0000	1.5083
10	30.185479	0.4716	0.2504	1.346719	0.0000	1.5083
11	31.531743	0.4927	0.2504	1.293080	0.0003	1.5083
12	32.718882	0.5112	0.2740	1.282023	0.0003	1.4923
13	33.985146	0.5310	0.2915	1.208224	0.0005	1.4923
14	35.066412	0.5479	0.3231	1.161744	0.0005	1.3942
15	36.192826	0.5655	0.3231	1.133198	0.0005	1.1289
16	37.318009	0.5831	0.3231	1.052496	0.0005	1.1289
17	38.322869	0.5988	0.3334	1.051776	0.0022	1.1053
18	39.316470	0.6143	0.3334	1.047393	0.0022	1.1053

19	40.198608	0.6281	0.3334	1.047389	0.0022	1.1053
20	41.003733	0.6407	0.3334	1.008468	0.0022	1.1053
21	42.004913	0.6563	0.3634	1.001662	0.0022	1.1053
22	43.004187	0.6719	0.3634	1.000350	0.0387	1.1053
23	43.994441	0.6874	0.3634	0.993723	0.0387	1.1006
24	44.988164	0.7029	0.3634	0.980590	0.0387	1.1006
25	45.968754	0.7183	0.3634	0.979639	0.0891	1.1006
26	46.820328	0.7316	0.3634	0.975378	0.0891	1.1006
27	47.795707	0.7468	0.3634	0.975309	0.0891	1.1006
28	48.578553	0.7590	0.3634	0.970232	0.0891	1.1006
29	49.547773	0.7742	0.3634	0.955086	0.1885	1.1006
30	50.502860	0.7891	0.3634	0.946039	0.1885	1.1006
31	51.415705	0.8034	0.4554	0.944270	0.1885	1.1006
32	52.303710	0.8172	0.5257	0.874419	0.1885	1.1006
33	53.176667	0.8309	0.5257	0.858297	0.1885	1.1006
34	54.034965	0.8443	0.5257	0.844004	0.1885	1.1006
35	54.878124	0.8575	0.5257	0.839114	0.2933	0.8066
36	55.717238	0.8706	0.5257	0.824195	0.2933	0.8066
37	56.538607	0.8834	0.6174	0.765162	0.4055	0.6283
38	57.303769	0.8954	0.6271	0.745734	0.4055	0.6283
39	58.049504	0.9070	0.6322	0.735552	0.4055	0.6283
40	58.785055	0.9185	0.6414	0.732613	0.4055	0.6283
41	59.513555	0.9299	0.6414	0.687465	0.4865	0.5586

A dendrogram is also produced that shows the variable clustering by the total proportion of variance explained by the clusters at the current level of the tree.

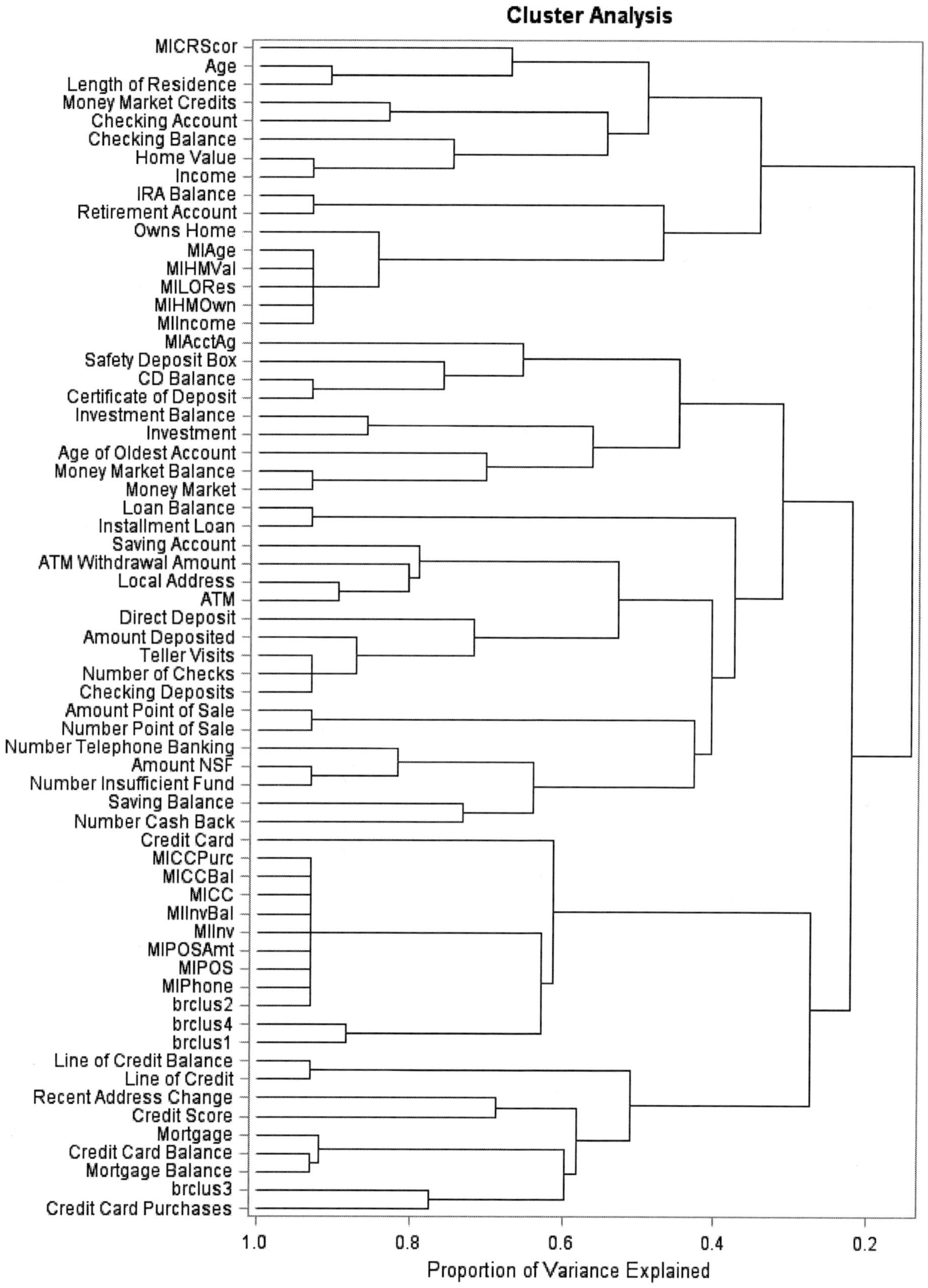
Cluster Analysis
MICRScor
Age
Length of Residence
Money Market Credits
Checking Account
Checking Balance
Home Value
Income
IRA Balance
Retirement Account
Owns Home
MIAge
MIHMVal
MILORes
MIHMOwn
MIIncome
MIAcctAg
Safety Deposit Box
CD Balance
Certificate of Deposit
Investment Balance
Investment
Age of Oldest Account
Money Market Balance
Money Market
Loan Balance
Installment Loan
Saving Account
ATM Withdrawal Amount
Local Address
ATM
Direct Deposit
Amount Deposited
Teller Visits
Number of Checks
Checking Deposits
Amount Point of Sale
Number Point of Sale
Number Telephone Banking
Amount NSF
Number Insufficient Fund
Saving Balance
Number Cash Back
Credit Card
MICCPurc
MICCBal
MICC
MIInvBal
MIInv
MIPOSAmt
MIPOS
MIPhone
brclus2
brclus4
brclus1
Line of Credit Balance
Line of Credit
Recent Address Change
Credit Score
Mortgage
Credit Card Balance
Mortgage Balance
brclus3
Credit Card Purchases
1.0
0.8
0.6
0.4
0.2
Proportion of Variance Explained

Example: Use the Output Delivery System to print out the table of the R-squared statistics from the last iteration of PROC VARCLUS.

The ODS OUTPUT statement creates a SAS data set named **summary** from the output object **clusterquality**, and a SAS data set named **clusters** from each **RSquare** output object. Because there are 40 **RSquare** objects created (one for the 2-cluster solution, one for the 3-cluster solution, and so on, up to the 41-cluster solution), the **clusters** data set concatenates these 40 objects. There is a column called **NumberOfClusters** that indicates to which cluster solution each observation in the **clusters** data set belongs.

The CALL SYMPUT routine creates the macro variable **nvar**, which contains the value of the number of clusters in the last iteration of the clustering algorithm. The COMPRESS function strips blanks from variables. Because the **clusters** data set contains the results of all 41-cluster solutions, the **nvar** macro variable is used to restrict focus to the final result of the VARCLUS algorithm; here, this is the 41-cluster solution. The **nvar** macro variable will be useful later, because if you select one representative from each variable cluster, you will have **nvar** inputs for future modeling consideration.

```
ods html close;
ods output clusterquality=summary
           rsquare=clusters;

proc varclus data=imputed maxeigen=.7 short hi;
   var &inputs brclus1-brclus4 miacctag
       miphone mipos miposamt miinv
       miinvbal micc miccbal miccpurc
       miincome mihmown milores mihmval
       miage micrscor;
run;
ods html;

data _null_;
   set summary;
   call symput('nvar',compress(NumberOfClusters));
run;

proc print data=clusters noobs;
   where NumberOfClusters=&nvar;
   var Cluster Variable RSquareRatio VariableLabel;
run;
```

Cluster	Variable	RSquareRatio	VariableLabel
Cluster 1	brclus2	0.4901	
	MIPhone	0.0050	
	MIPOS	0.0050	
	MIPOSAmt	0.0050	
	MIInv	0.0050	
	MIInvBal	0.0050	

	MICC	0.0050	
	MICCBal	0.0050	
	MICCPurc	0.0050	
Cluster 2	MIIncome	0.0074	
	MIHMOwn	0.0431	
	MILORes	0.0074	
	MIHMVal	0.0074	
	MIAge	0.0832	
Cluster 3	Dep	0.4235	Checking Deposits
	Checks	0.3383	Number of Checks
	Teller	0.5586	Teller Visits
Cluster 4	MTGBal	0.0390	Mortgage Balance
	CCBal	0.0361	Credit Card Balance
Cluster 5	MM	0.0360	Money Market
	MMBal	0.0348	Money Market Balance
Cluster 6	Income	0.1625	Income
	HMVal	0.2332	Home Value
Cluster 7	ILS	0.0044	Installment Loan
	ILSBal	0.0044	Loan Balance
Cluster 8	POS	0.0873	Number Point of Sale
	POSAmt	0.0864	Amount Point of Sale
Cluster 9	NSF	0.2541	Number Insufficient Fund
	NSFAmt	0.2503	Amount NSF
Cluster 10	CD	0.2816	Certificate of Deposit
	CDBal	0.2823	CD Balance
Cluster 11	IRA	0.3426	Retirement Account
	IRABal	0.3341	IRA Balance
Cluster 12	Age	0.0000	Age

Cluster 13	LOC	0.2740	Line of Credit
	LOCBal	0.2827	Line of Credit Balance
Cluster 14	Sav	0.0000	Saving Account
Cluster 15	DDA	0.0000	Checking Account
Cluster 16	InvBal	0.0000	Investment Balance
Cluster 17	CRScore	0.0000	Credit Score
Cluster 18	brclus3	0.0000	
Cluster 19	CC	0.0000	Credit Card
Cluster 20	brclus1	0.0000	
Cluster 21	CashBk	0.0000	Number Cash Back
Cluster 22	MIAcctAg	0.0000	
Cluster 23	MICRScor	0.0000	
Cluster 24	Moved	0.0000	Recent Address Change
Cluster 25	AcctAge	0.0000	Age of Oldest Account
Cluster 26	DirDep	0.0000	Direct Deposit
Cluster 27	SavBal	0.0000	Saving Balance
Cluster 28	DDABal	0.0000	Checking Balance
Cluster 29	SDB	0.0000	Safety Deposit Box
Cluster 30	CCPurc	0.0000	Credit Card Purchases
Cluster 31	InArea	0.0000	Local Address
Cluster 32	ATMAmt	0.0000	ATM Withdrawal Amount
Cluster 33	Phone	0.0000	Number Telephone Banking
Cluster 34	MMCred	0.0000	Money Market Credits
Cluster 35	HMOwn	0.0000	Owns Home
Cluster 36	Inv	0.0000	Investment
Cluster 37	DepAmt	0.0000	Amount Deposited
Cluster 38	brclus4	0.0000	
Cluster 39	ATM	0.0000	ATM
Cluster 40	LORes	0.0000	Length of Residence
Cluster 41	MTG	0.0000	Mortgage

The output shows the cluster number, the names of the variables in each cluster, and the $1–R^2$ ratio (**RSquareRatio**).

To reduce the amount of text that needs to be entered, a new macro variable named **Reduced** is created that contains the names of all the variables selected from PROC VARCLUS. As was mentioned above, subject-matter considerations should play a part in deciding which inputs become the cluster representatives. Consider the first cluster, which consists of the variables **brclus2**, **MIPhone**, **MIPOS**, **MIPOSAmt**, **MIInv**, **MIInvBal**, **MICC**, **MICCBal**, and **MICCPurc**. According to the 1-R-Square ratio, any of the missing indicators would be the best cluster representative. However, closer investigation of the development data set might reveal that the missingness of those eight inputs has more to do with poor data quality than any other source of missing data. If these missing indicators in actuality indicate poor data quality, then their usefulness as predictors with good generalizing power is suspect especially if the pattern of missingness that occurs in the development data is unlikely to exist in the scoring population. With that subject-matter consideration in mind, perhaps **brclus2** is the best cluster representative from cluster 1.

```
%let reduced=
brclus2 miincome checks ccbal
mmbal income ilsbal posamt
nsfamt cd irabal age
loc sav dda invbal
crscore brclus3 cc brclus1
cashbk miacctag micrscor moved
acctage dirdep savbal ddabal
sdb ccpurc inarea atmamt
phone mmcred hmown inv
depamt brclus4 atm lores
mtg;
```

Exercises

3. Variable Clustering

a. Use PROC VARCLUS to cluster all numeric variables in a hierarchical structure (use the macro variable **ex_inputs** along with the missing indicator variables and the cluster group variables). Use MAXEIGEN=.70 as your stopping criterion and create a dendrogram.

1) How many clusters were in your final solution and what proportion of the variation was explained by the clusters?

3.06 Multiple Choice Poll

How many clusters were in the final solution?

a. 25
b. 30
c. 32
d. 35

48

3.4 Variable Screening

Objectives

- Illustrate variable screening using the Spearman and Hoeffding correlation statistics.
- Create empirical logit plots.
- Illustrate a method to accommodate nonlinear relationships between the predictor variables and the target variable.

52

Univariate Screening

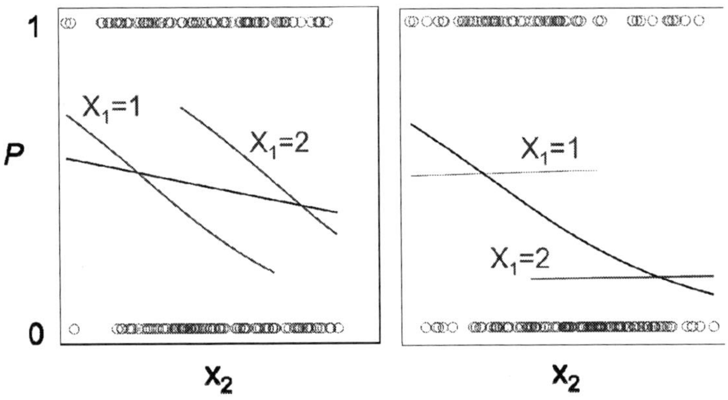

53

It is tempting to use univariate associations to detect irrelevant input variables, where each input variable is screened individually versus the target variable (chi-squared tests, correlation coefficients, two-sample tests, and so on). Only the most important inputs are retained in the analysis. This method does not account for partial associations among the inputs. Inputs could be erroneously omitted or erroneously included. Partial association occurs when the effect of one variable changes in the presence of another variable. Multivariate methods that consider subsets of variables jointly are preferable. The best *k* inputs in a univariate sense would not necessarily be the best *k*-element subset. The presence of interactions can also give misleading univariate associations.

However, even after variable clustering, some further variable reduction might be needed prior to using the variable selection techniques in PROC LOGISTIC. Very liberal univariate screening might be helpful when the number of clusters created in PROC VARCLUS is still relatively large. Because some of the variable selection techniques use the full model, eliminating clearly irrelevant variables (for example, *p*-values greater than .50) will stabilize the full model and might improve the variable selection technique without much risk of eliminating important input variables. Keep in mind that univariate screening can give misleading results when there are partial associations. This problem is minimized because the screening is done after PROC VARCLUS, and is used in eliminating clearly irrelevant variables, rather than searching for the best predictors.

Variable Screening

Example: Use the CORR procedure to examine the associations between the inputs chosen from PROC VARCLUS and the target variable. Use the SPEARMAN option to request the Spearman correlation statistic and the HOEFFDING option to request Hoeffding's D statistic. Also use the RANK option to print the correlation coefficients for each variable in order from highest to lowest. Then create a table that compares the rank order of the Spearman correlation statistic to the rank order of the Hoeffding's D statistic. Finally, create a scatter plot of the ranks of Spearman versus the ranks of Hoeffding's D with PROC SGPLOT. Add reference lines and data labels to the plot.

The Spearman correlation statistic in this example is a correlation of the ranks of the input variables with the binary target. The Spearman correlation statistic was used rather than the Pearson correlation statistic because Spearman is less sensitive to nonlinearities and outliers. However, when variables are not monotonically related to each other, the Spearman correlation statistic can miss important associations. A general and robust similarity measure is Hoeffding's D, which will detect a wide variety of associations between two variables. Hoeffding's D statistic has values between –0.5 to 1, but if there are many ties, smaller values might result.

The output object for the table of Spearman correlation statistics is called SPEARMANCORR, and the output object for the table of Hoeffding's D statistics is called HOEFFDINGCORR.

```
/* pmlr03d04.sas   */
ods html close;
ods output spearmancorr=spearman
           hoeffdingcorr=hoeffding;

proc corr data=imputed spearman hoeffding rank;
   var &reduced;
   with ins;
run;

ods html;
```

The variable names in the SAS data sets **Spearman** and **Hoeffding** are in the variables **best1** through **best41**, the correlation statistics are in the variables **r1** through **r41**, and the *p*-values are in the variables **p1** through **p41**. The macro variable **nvar** was created in the last demonstration. It points to the number of clusters in the final cluster solution from PROC VARCLUS (here it is 41). In order to make a more useful table, a DATA step is used to transpose the variables to observations.

```
data spearman1(keep=variable scorr spvalue ranksp);
   length variable $ 8;
   set spearman;
   array best(*) best1--best&nvar;
   array r(*) r1--r&nvar;
   array p(*) p1--p&nvar;
   do i=1 to dim(best);
      variable=best(i);
      scorr=r(i);
      spvalue=p(i);
      ranksp=i;
      output;
   end;
run;

data hoeffding1(keep=variable hcorr hpvalue rankho);
   length variable $ 8;
   set hoeffding;
   array best(*) best1--best&nvar;
   array r(*) r1--r&nvar;
   array p(*) p1--p&nvar;
   do i=1 to dim(best);
      variable=best(i);
      hcorr=r(i);
      hpvalue=p(i);
      rankho=i;
      output;
   end;
run;
```

The two data sets are then sorted by the variable names and merged by the variable names.

```
proc sort data=spearman1;
   by variable;
run;

proc sort data=hoeffding1;
   by variable;
run;

data correlations;
   merge spearman1 hoeffding1;
   by variable;
run;
```

The final data set is sorted by the rank of the Spearman correlation statistic and then a table is generated showing the rank and associated statistics of the Spearman correlations and Hoeffding's D statistics.

```
proc sort data=correlations;
   by ranksp;
run;

proc print data=correlations label split='*';
   var variable ranksp rankho scorr spvalue hcorr hpvalue;
   label ranksp='Spearman rank*of variables'
         scorr='Spearman Correlation'
         spvalue='Spearman p-value'
         rankho='Hoeffding rank*of variables'
         hcorr='Hoeffding Correlation'
         hpvalue='Hoeffding p-value';
  title "Rank of Spearman Correlations and Hoeffding Correlations";
run;
```

Rank of Spearman Correlations and Hoeffding Correlations

Obs	variable	Spearman rank of variables	Hoeffding rank of variables	Spearman Correlation	Spearman p-value	Hoeffding Correlation	Hoeffding p-value
1	SavBal	1	1	0.25031	0.00000	0.009764437	0.00001
2	CD	2	6	0.20264	0.00000	0.001876987	0.00001
3	DDA	3	5	-0.18493	0.00000	0.002144155	0.00001
4	MMBal	4	11	0.16066	0.00000	0.001117737	0.00001
5	Sav	5	3	0.15164	0.00000	0.002395734	0.00001
6	CC	6	4	0.14683	0.00000	0.002196920	0.00001
7	ATM	7	7	-0.12247	0.00000	0.001480339	0.00001
8	IRABal	8	18	0.10995	0.00000	0.000198562	0.00001
9	Phone	9	14	-0.10400	0.00000	0.000615874	0.00001
10	Inv	10	22	0.09838	0.00000	0.000059608	0.00761
11	MMCred	11	21	0.09509	0.00000	0.000119558	0.00025
12	Checks	12	9	-0.09015	0.00000	0.001239866	0.00001
13	brclus1	13	12	0.08189	0.00000	0.000638991	0.00001
14	CCPurc	14	17	0.08173	0.00000	0.000240566	0.00001
15	POSAmt	15	15	-0.07804	0.00000	0.000445904	0.00001
16	InvBal	16	28	0.07277	0.00000	-.000011379	0.83466
17	SDB	17	19	0.07256	0.00000	0.000175689	0.00001
18	CCBal	18	13	0.07147	0.00000	0.000632818	0.00001
19	DirDep	19	16	-0.07037	0.00000	0.000402104	0.00001
20	ATMAmt	20	8	-0.06809	0.00000	0.001410049	0.00001
21	NSFAmt	21	20	-0.06804	0.00000	0.000119878	0.00025
22	InArea	22	24	-0.06049	0.00000	0.000015869	0.11424
23	brclus4	23	25	-0.06044	0.00000	0.000006379	0.22409
24	brclus2	24	23	-0.05955	0.00000	0.000055090	0.00993
25	DDABal	25	2	0.05611	0.00000	0.003101822	0.00001

26	DepAmt	26	10	-0.04369	0.00000	0.001179781	0.00001
27	CashBk	27	33	-0.04159	0.00000	-.000033143	1.00000
28	brclus3	28	31	-0.03224	0.00000	-.000022896	1.00000
29	Income	29	26	0.01441	0.00966	0.000002916	0.29081
30	ILSBal	30	35	-0.01413	0.01113	-.000037882	1.00000
31	Age	31	27	0.01252	0.02457	-.000000997	0.39375
32	MICRScor	32	40	0.00895	0.10779	-.000043281	1.00000
33	MIAcctAg	33	37	0.00533	0.33881	-.000041551	1.00000
34	Moved	34	41	-0.00466	0.40294	-.000043400	1.00000
35	AcctAge	35	29	-0.00459	0.40928	-.000015364	0.97453
36	LORes	36	32	0.00408	0.46371	-.000026362	1.00000
37	CRScore	37	30	0.00407	0.46454	-.000017633	0.99778
38	LOC	38	38	0.00232	0.67642	-.000042162	1.00000
39	MIIncome	39	36	0.00159	0.77572	-.000038195	1.00000
40	HMOwn	40	34	-0.00060	0.91437	-.000034339	1.00000
41	MTG	41	39	-0.00042	0.93941	-.000042850	1.00000

If the Spearman rank is high but the Hoeffding's D rank is low, then the association is probably not monotonic. Empirical logit plots could be used to investigate this type of relationship.

A graphical representation of this table would aid decision making. PROC SGPLOT is used to create a scatter plot of Spearman ranks against Hoeffding ranks. To label the points with the value of a third variable, the DATALABEL= option is used. Reference lines are added to the appropriate axes using the REFLINE statement.

In order to have reference lines on the plot, the SQL procedure is used to create macro variables that point to the smallest Spearman rank and Hoeffding rank associated with a *p*-value greater than 0.5. This is just for presentation.

```
proc sql noprint;
   select min(ranksp) into :vref
   from (select ranksp
         from correlations
         having spvalue > .5);
   select min(rankho) into :href
   from (select rankho
         from correlations
         having hpvalue > .5);
quit;

proc sgplot data=correlations;
   refline &vref / axis=y;
   refline &href / axis=x;
   scatter y=ranksp x=rankho / datalabel=variable;
   yaxis label="Rank of Spearman";
   xaxis label="Rank of Hoeffding";
   title "Scatter Plot of the Ranks of Spearman vs. Hoeffding";
run;
```

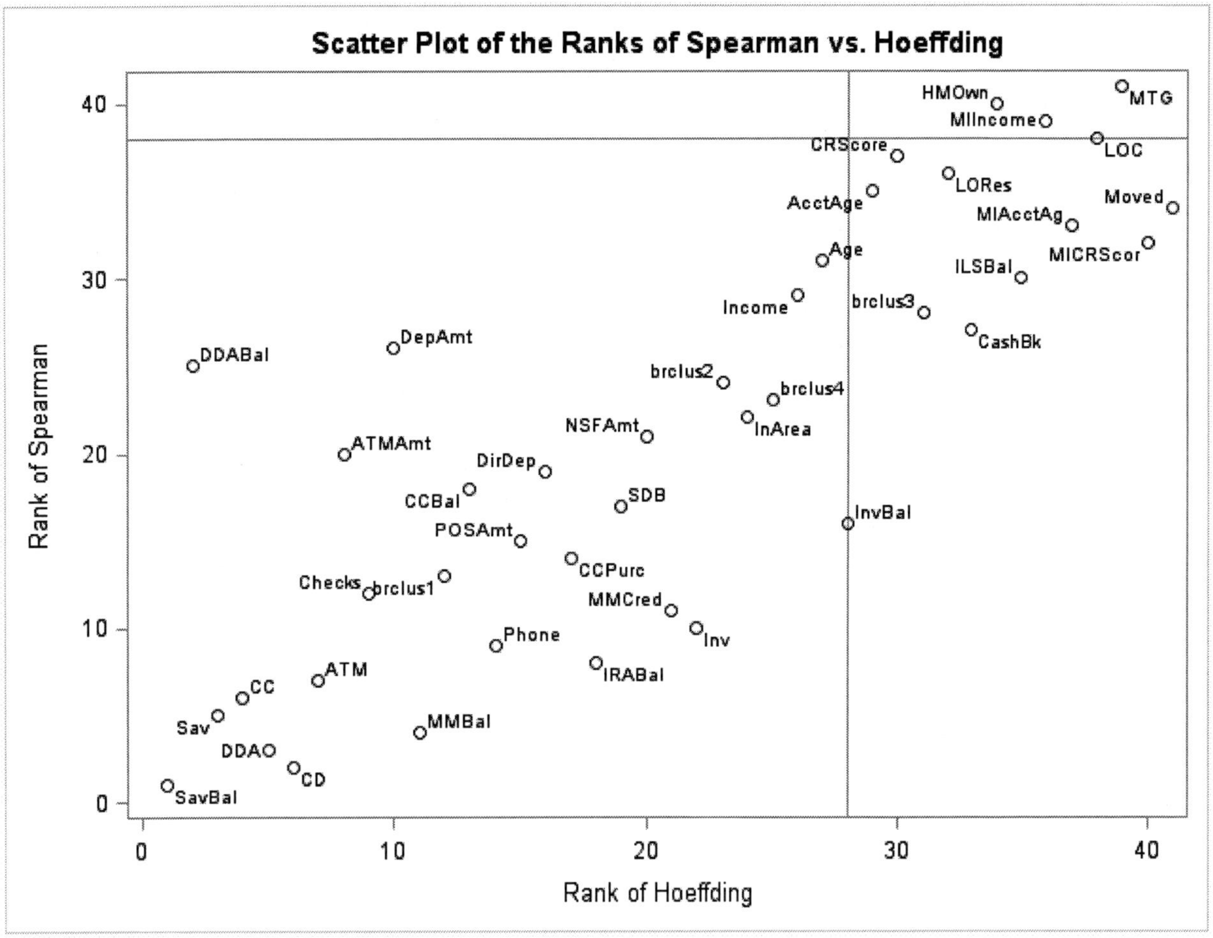

In general, the upper right corner of the plot contains the names of variables that could reasonably be excluded from further analysis, due to their poor rank on both metrics. The criterion to use in eliminating variables is a subjective decision. Thus, four variables are eliminated from the analysis.

In addition to being a useful screening tool, this analysis might point toward further analyses. High ranks for Spearman and low ranks for Hoeffding's D are found for the variables **DDABal**, **DepAmt**, and **ATMAmt**. Even though these variables do not have a monotonic relationship with **Ins**, some other type of relationship is detected by Hoeffding's D statistic. Empirical logit plots should be used to examine these relationships.

The %LET statement creates a macro variable called **screened** that has the names of the variables remaining after the univariate screening method.

```
%let screened =
brclus2 checks ccbal
mmbal income ilsbal posamt
nsfamt cd irabal age
sav dda invbal
crscore brclus3 cc brclus1
cashbk miacctag micrscor moved
acctage dirdep savbal ddabal
sdb ccpurc inarea atmamt
phone mmcred inv
depamt brclus4 atm lores;
```

3.07 Poll

Have you ever constructed logit plots in your work as a predictive modeler?

❍ Yes

❍ No

55

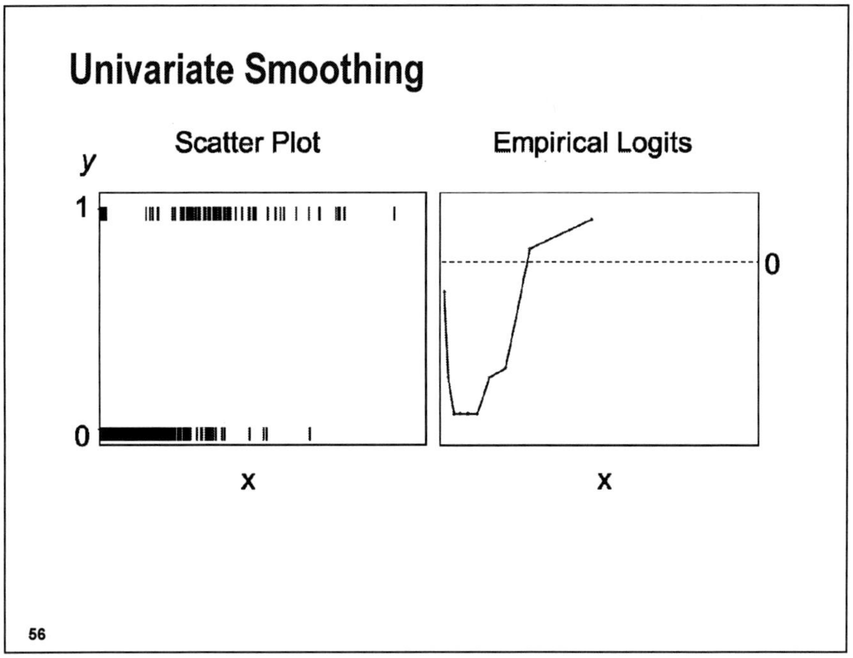

In regression analysis, it is standard practice to examine scatter plots of the target versus each input variable. When the target is binary, these plots are not very enlightening. A useful plot to detect nonlinear relationships is a plot of the empirical logits.

Empirical Logits

$$\ln\left(\frac{m_i + \frac{\sqrt{M_i}}{2}}{M_i - m_i + \frac{\sqrt{M_i}}{2}}\right)$$

where

m_i= number of events

M_i = number of cases

57

Univariate plots of binary data need to be smoothed in order to better reveal the relationship between a continuous input variable and the target. A simple, scalable, and robust smoothing method is to plot empirical logits for quantiles of the input variables. These logits use a minimax estimate of the proportion of events in each bin (Duffy and Santner 1989). This eliminates the problem caused by zero counts and reduces variability.

The number of bins determines the amount of smoothing (for example, the fewer bins, the more smoothing). One large bin would give a constant logit. For very large data sets and intervally scaled inputs, 100 bins often work well. If the standard logistic model were true, then the plots should be linear. Sample variability can cause apparent deviations, particularly when the bin size is too small. However, serious nonlinearities, such as nonmonotonicity, are usually easy to detect.

Empirical Logit Plots

Example: Create an empirical logit plot of checking account balance. Use PROC RANK with the GROUPS= option to bin the input variable. Then use PROC MEANS and a DATA step to generate the values for the logits, and use PROC SGPLOT to create the empirical logit plot.

To create a plot of the empirical logits versus a continuous input variable, the input variable first needs to be binned. In PROC RANK, the bins will be equal size (quantiles) except when the number of tied values exceeds the bin size. In that case, the bin will be enlarged to contain all the tied values. The VAR statement in PROC RANK lists the variable in the DATA= data set to be grouped. The RANKS statement names the variable representing the groups in the OUT= data set. If the RANKS statement is not used, the VAR variable is replaced by the groups.

```
/* pmlr03d05.sas */
%let var=DDABal;

proc rank data=imputed groups=100 out=out;
   var &var;
   ranks bin;
run;

proc print data=out(obs=10);
   var &var bin;
run;
```

Obs	DDABal	bin
1	419.27	44
2	1986.81	76
3	0.00	9
4	1594.84	72
5	2813.45	82
6	1069.78	63
7	1437.57	69
8	1683.28	73
9	190.03	33
10	462.12	46

To compute the empirical logit, the number of target event cases (**Ins**=1) and total cases in each bin needs to be computed. The empirical logits are plotted against the mean of the input variable in each bin. This needs to be computed as well. Both tasks can be done in the MEANS procedure using the CLASS statement. The appropriate statistics (SUM and MEAN) need to be specified in the OUTPUT statement.

```
proc means data=out noprint nway;
   class bin;
   var ins &var;
   output out=bins sum(ins)=ins mean(&var)=&var;
run;

proc print data=bins(obs=10);
run;
```

Obs	bin	_TYPE_	_FREQ_	ins	DDABal
1	0	1	198	21	-31.8287
2	9	1	5987	3179	0.0000
3	19	1	267	26	2.7617
4	20	1	323	26	9.0509
5	21	1	323	38	17.2157
6	22	1	322	51	28.1966
7	23	1	323	38	40.9160
8	24	1	322	47	53.4157
9	25	1	323	45	66.7146
10	26	1	323	64	81.9273

The variable **Ins** contains the number of events while the automatic variable **_FREQ_** contains the bin size.

```
data bins;
   set bins;
   elogit=log((ins+(sqrt(_FREQ_)/2))/
          (_FREQ_-ins+(sqrt(_FREQ_)/2)));
run;
```

PROC SGPLOT allows compatible plots to be laid on top of one another. For example, the SERIES statement connects unmarked points, by default. The REG statement draws a linear regression line through marked data points by default. While this regression line is not necessarily the same line that would result from a logistic regression model on the original (unbinned) data, it might offer a visual cue that suggests whether there is a linear trend in the variable under consideration.

```
proc sgplot data=bins;
   reg y=elogit x=&var /
       curvelabel="Linear Relationship?"
       curvelabelloc=outside
       lineattrs=(color=ligr);
   series y=elogit x=&var;
   title "Empirical Logit against &var";
run;
```

Selected REG statement options:

CURVELABEL	adds a label for the regression curve.
CURVELABELLOC	specifies whether the curve label is placed inside the plot axes (INSIDE) or outside of the plot axes (OUTSIDE).

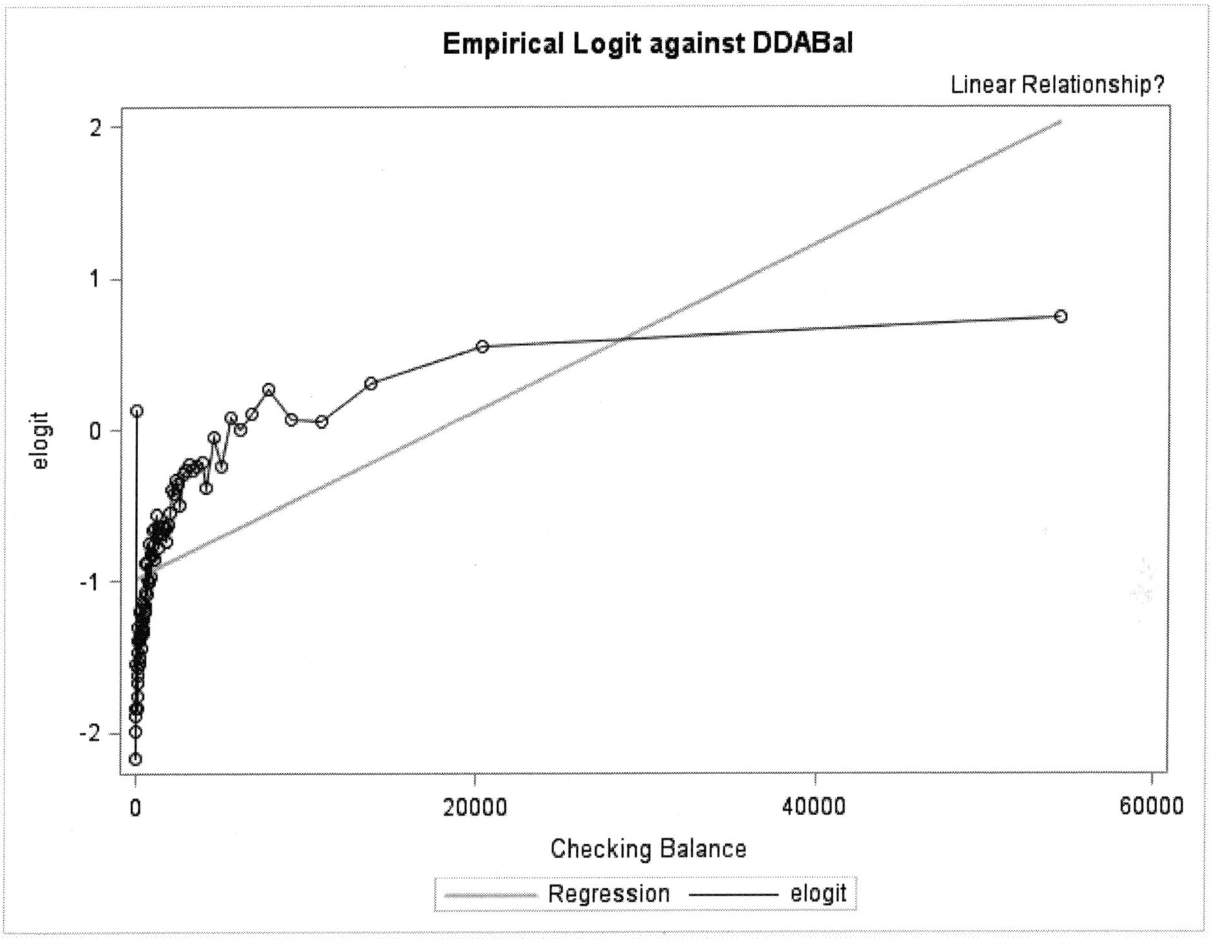

The pattern made by plotting logit against checking account balance has two striking features. There is a spike in the logits at the $0 balance level. Aside from that spike, the trend is monotonic but certainly not linear.

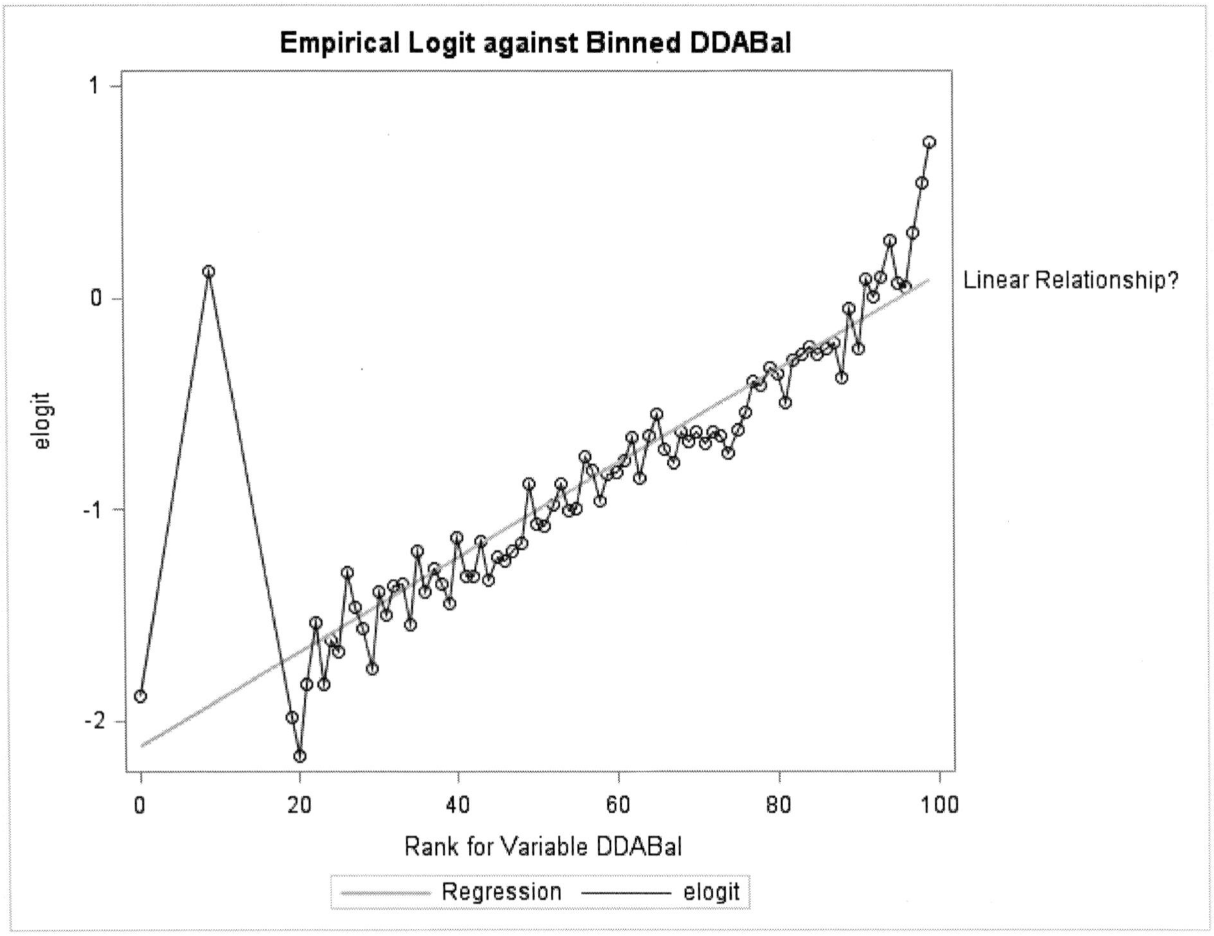

The pattern made by plotting logit against the rank of checking account balance seems to accommodate the nonlinearity of the last plot, but the spike indicates a portion of the population who are not behaving as their balance would lead one to believe. The trend in checking account balance is clear, and this is probably a very good input. How, though, can one account for the nonlinear relationship between response behavior and balance amount?

Exercises

4. Variable Screening and Logit Plots

a. Use the Spearman and Hoeffding correlation coefficients to screen the inputs with the least evidence of a relationship with the target. Use the **ex_reduced** macro variable in PROC CORR and use the LENGTH statement in the DATA step to specify a length of 32 for the character variable called **variable**. Create a table with the Spearman rank of inputs and the Hoeffding rank of inputs and use PROC SGPLOT to create a scatter plot of the ranks of Spearman versus the ranks of Hoeffding.

1) Which input variable shows evidence of a nonlinear relationship with the target?

2) Which input variables can be eliminated due to irrelevancy?

b. Create an empirical logit plot of **LIFETIME_GIFT_RANGE** and the bins of **LIFETIME_GIFT_RANGE**. Use 10 groups in PROC RANK.

1) What transformation would you consider to account for the nonlinear relationship?

3.08 Multiple Choice Poll

What transformation would you consider to account for the nonlinear relationship of **lifetime_gift_range**?

a. None
b. Adding a quadratic term
c. Discretizing the input
d. Adding a cubic term

60

Remedies

1. Hand-Crafted New Input Variables
2. Polynomial Models
3. Flexible Multivariate Function Estimators
4. Do Nothing

61

1. Skilled and patient data analysts can accommodate nonlinearities in a logistic regression model by transforming or discretizing the input variables. This can become impractical with high-dimensional data and increases the risk of overfitting.

2. Polynomial terms might improve model fit but hamper model interpretation and generalization. Quadratic terms and two-factor interactions can be useful additions to a modeler's toolkit but are no panacea. Higher-order polynomials are not reliable smoothers.

3. Methods such as classification trees, generalized additive models, projection pursuit, multivariate adaptive regression splines, radial basis function networks, and multilayer perceptrons are flexible alternatives to logistic regression (Hastie and Tibshirani 1990, Ripley 1996).

4. Standard logistic regression is often robust enough to produce accurate predictions even when there are substantial nonlinear relations between the target and the input variables. Also, more flexible approaches, which might include building in interaction terms, sometimes do not show enough improvement to warrant the extra effort.

3.09 Multiple Choice Poll

How do you accommodate nonlinear effects in your work as a predictive modeler?

a. Hand-crafted new input variables
b. Polynomial models
c. Neural networks
d. Do nothing
e. Other

62

Accommodating Nonlinearities

Example: Re-impute checking account balance when the customer does not have a checking account. Then use PROC SGPLOT to create the empirical logit plots.

In order to use the checking account balance, you might consider taking a logarithmic transformation, a square root transformation, or some other transformation in an attempt to linearize the relationship between the logit and the account balances. This linearization will require two steps. First, that spike at $0 needs to be accounted for. Second, you can transform the balances to some scale that reflects the behavior exhibited in the data.

It seems suspicious that a large portion of the population has exactly $0 in their checking accounts. Investigation (of the data set or of the people who constructed the data set) will show that most of the individuals with exactly $0 balances do not have checking accounts. Their balances have been set to $0 as part of the data pre-processing. This rule seems reasonable from a logical imputation standpoint. How can someone with no checking account have a checking balance? But it is clear from the logit plots that those individuals are behaving like people with much more than $0 in their checking accounts.

PROC MEANS with the CLASS statement yields results for each level of the **DDA** variable; the results of interest are the mean, minimum, and maximum for the **DDABal** and **Ins** variables.

```
/* pmlr03d06.sas */
title;
proc means data=imputed mean min max;
   class dda;
   var ddabal ins;
run;
```

From the output, it is clear that the individuals without checking accounts have had $0 balances imputed for them, and those individuals respond at a higher rate than individuals with checking accounts. If this seems unreasonable, consider that the individuals without checking accounts presumably do their everyday banking with a different bank altogether, and treat this bank as an investment institution.

Checking Account	N Obs	Variable	Label	Mean	Minimum	Maximum
0	5948	DDABal	Checking Balance	0	0	0
		Ins		0.5314391	0	1.0000000
1	26316	DDABal	Checking Balance	2660.49	-774.8300000	278093.83
		Ins		0.3045296	0	1.0000000

There are several possible ways to account for this discrepancy between the **DDABal** value and the empirically observed response behavior. One of the most straightforward is to re-impute. The following code creates a macro variable mean that has the value of the checking account balances of those customers who actually have checking accounts. Then that mean is substituted for the $0 balances[1] of those who do not have checking accounts. The SELECT INTO statement in PROC SQL creates the macro variable, and the following DATA step fills in the $0 balances with the balance of customers who have their accounts at this bank.

```
proc sql;
   select mean(ddabal) into :mean
   from imputed where dda;
quit;

data imputed;
   set imputed;
   if not dda then ddabal=&mean;
run;
```

To evaluate the effectiveness of this re-imputation, take another look at the empirical logit plots.

```
%let var=DDABal;

proc rank data=imputed groups=100 out=out;
   var &var;
   ranks bin;
run;

proc means data=out noprint nway;
   class bin;
   var ins &var;
   output out=bins sum(ins)=ins mean(&var)=&var;
run;

data bins;
   set bins;
   elogit=log((ins+(sqrt(_FREQ_ )/2))/
          ( _FREQ_ -ins+(sqrt(_FREQ_ )/2)));
run;

proc sgplot data=bins;
   reg y=elogit x=&var /
       curvelabel="Linear Relationship?"
       curvelabelloc=outside
       lineattrs=(color=ligr);
   series y=elogit x=&var;
   title "Empirical Logit against &var";
run;
```

[1] Arguably, most, if not all, of these customers have checking accounts somewhere, and therefore do have balances.

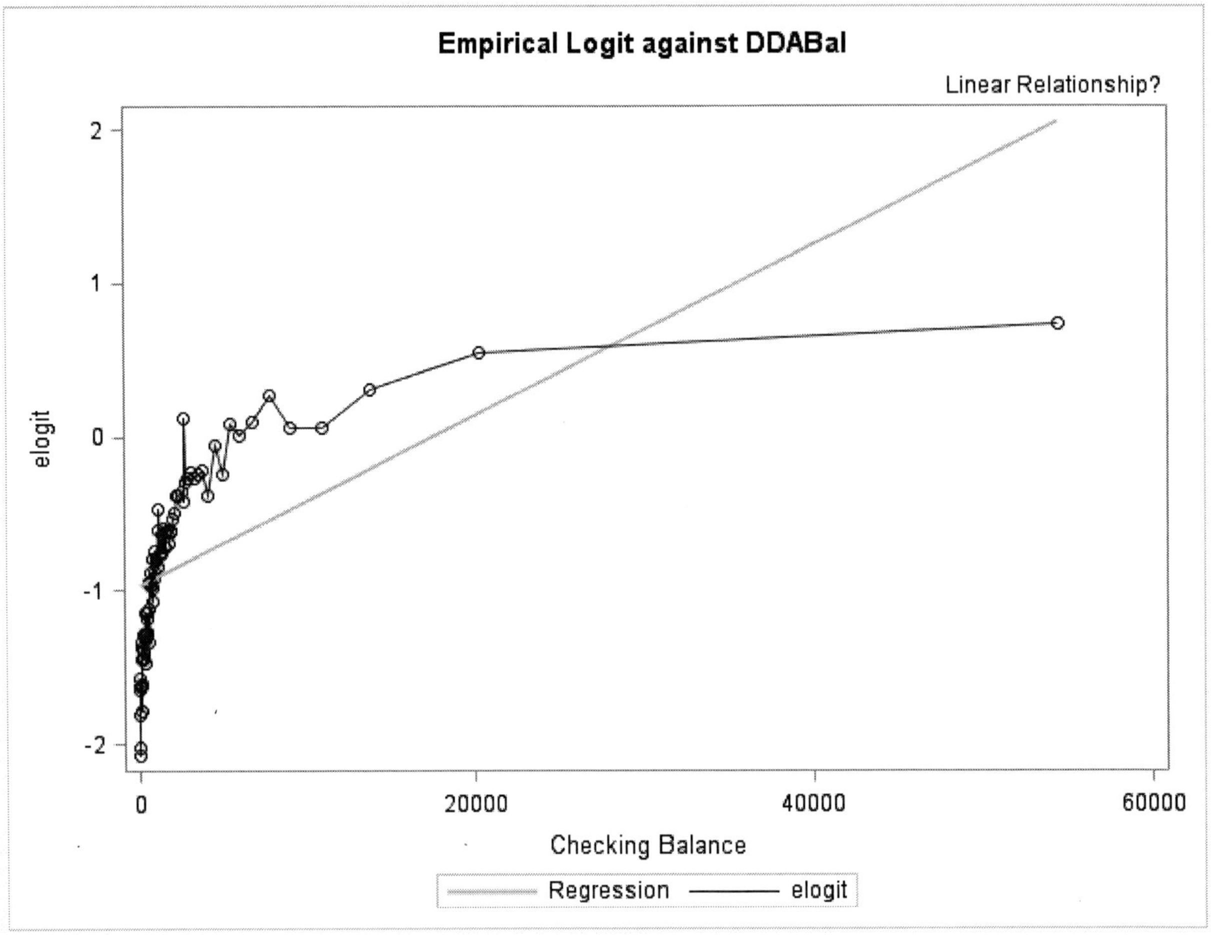

The empirical logit plot of checking account balances still does not show a linear relationship even when the mean is substituted for the $0 balances for the customers who do not have checking accounts.

```
proc sgplot data=bins;
   reg y=elogit x=bin /
       curvelabel="Linear Relationship?"
       curvelabelloc=outside
       lineattrs=(color=ligr);
   series y=elogit x=bin;
   title "Empirical Logit against Binned &var";
run;
```

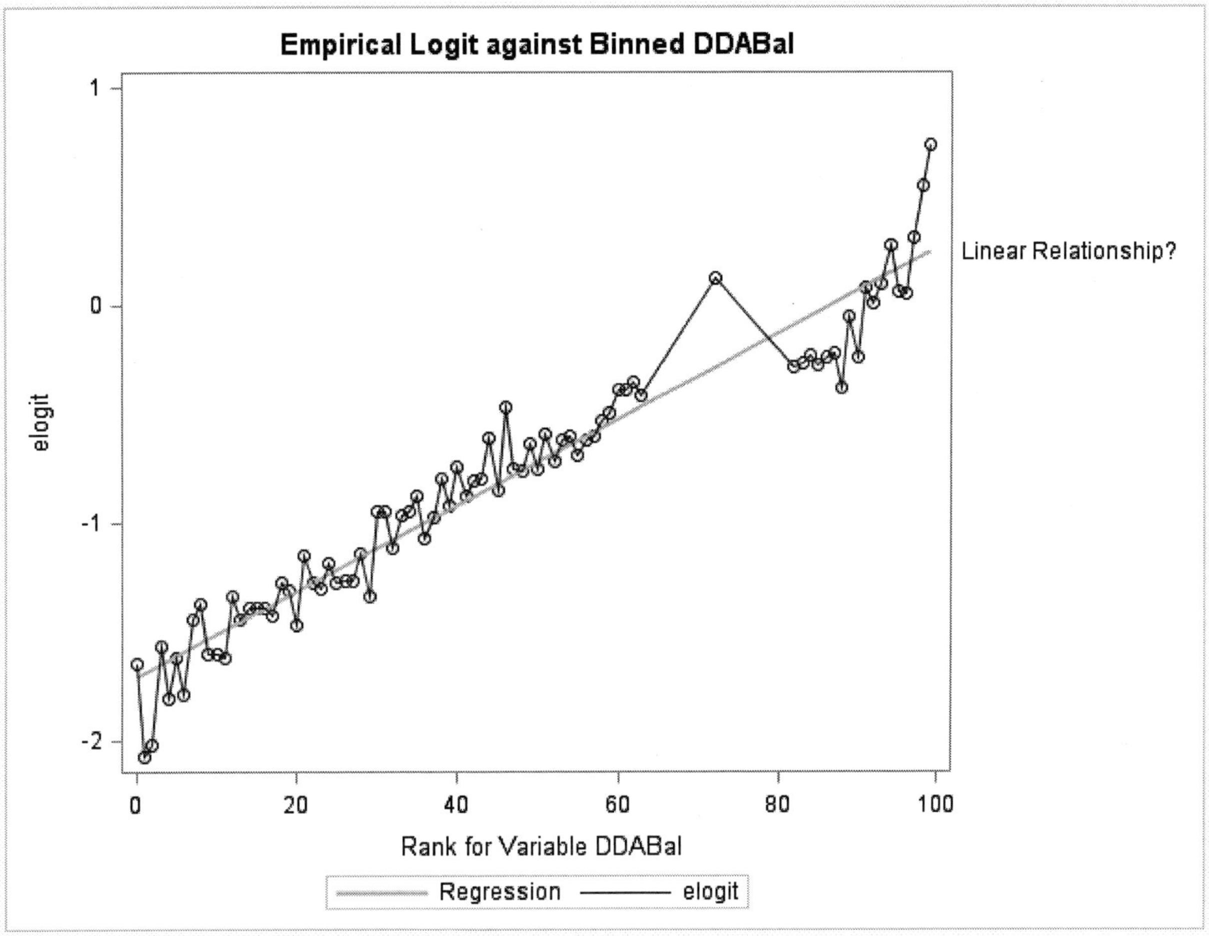

The bins do a very good job of capturing the way that response behavior changes with respect to checking account balances in a fairly linear way.

> ✎ The question of which transformation does the best job of linearizing the relationship is an important one for modelers. You might have several of your favorite transformations; the limitations are usually only the analyst's imagination and the software on the server that houses the database.
>
> Some analysts might reserve the term binning for the practice of creating a categorical predictor from a continuous input. Therefore, it might be more appropriate to label this a *rank-group* or *percentile* transformation.

Regardless of the input's original distribution, the percentiles have a uniform distribution. This uniformly distributed version of **DDABal** has a linear association with the logit. Even better, unlike the log transformation, the percentile transformation affords easy interpretability with odds ratios: a one-unit change in the percentiles results in the corresponding change in the odds of response.

Example: Create a new input, **B_DDABal**, which represents the binned checking account balances. Because you would need the bin assignment rules to create the **B_DDABal** input if it eventually is part of your model, generate DATA step code to perform the binning.

The RANK procedure assigns observations to 100 groups, according to **DDABal**. PROC MEANS creates a data set that contains the maximum **DDABal** value in each bin. This information can be used to assign a new data set its own bins, without running the PROC RANK.

```
proc rank data=imputed groups=100 out=out;
   var ddabal;
   ranks bin;
run;

title;
proc means data=out noprint nway;
   class bin;
   var ddabal;
   output out=endpts max=max;
run;

proc print data=endpts(obs=10);
run;
```

Obs	bin	_TYPE_	_FREQ_	max
1	0	1	323	1.72
2	1	1	322	8.52
3	2	1	322	16.38
4	3	1	323	27.12
5	4	1	323	40.27
6	5	1	322	52.51
7	6	1	323	65.29
8	7	1	323	81.54
9	8	1	322	94.38
10	9	1	323	110.38

Rather than writing out, by hand, a series of rules like IF **DDABal**<=1.72 then bin=0; ELSE IF… for many bins, you can use a DATA step to write the rules. An easy way to do this is to use a FILENAME statement to point to a file and then write the rules to that file using the PUT statement.

The FILENAME statement creates a *fileref*, Rank, which points to the physical file C:\temp\rank.sas. The DATA _NULL_ statement enables you to use the DATA step processing without being required to write out a data set. The FILE statement specifies where you want to put the output of the DATA step (much as the INFILE statement would enable you to specify the input source for a DATA step.) The SET statement brings in the data set **endpts**, which has the maximum balance in each bin. The option END= creates an internal flag that you can use to identify the last record of the data set. You could write IF…THEN…ELSE syntax to do the bin assignment. The following example uses SELECT…WHEN…OTHERWISE to perform the same task. The last record captures everyone with a balance larger than the maximum in the penultimate bin.

```
filename rank "C:\temp\rank.sas";

data _null_;
   file rank;
   set endpts end=last;
   if _n_=1 then put "select;";
   if not last then do;
      put "  when (ddabal <= " max ") B_DDABal=" bin ";";
      end;
   else if last then do;
      put "  otherwise B_DDABal=" bin ";";
      put "end;";
      end;
run;
```

Partial Listing of **rank.sas**

```
select;
   when (ddabal <= 1.72 ) B_DDABal =0 ;
   when (ddabal <= 8.52 ) B_DDABal =1 ;
   when (ddabal <= 16.38 ) B_DDABal =2 ;
   when (ddabal <= 27.12 ) B_DDABal =3 ;
   when (ddabal <= 40.27 ) B_DDABal =4 ;
   when (ddabal <= 52.51 ) B_DDABal =5 ;
   when (ddabal <= 65.29 ) B_DDABal =6 ;
   when (ddabal <= 81.54 ) B_DDABal =7 ;
   when (ddabal <= 94.38 ) B_DDABal =8 ;
   when (ddabal <= 110.38 ) B_DDABal =9 ;
```

To use this code, you can use the %INCLUDE statement embedded in a DATA step. For example, the following code puts **B_DDABal** on the **imputed** data set. The SOURCE option requests that the code be included in the log as well.

```
data imputed;
   set imputed;
   %include rank / source;
run;
```

To see that the recoding worked, evaluate the minimum and maximum checking account balances in each of the bins. PROC MEANS with a CLASS statement will do this.

```
proc means data=imputed min max;
   class B_DDABal;
   var DDABal;
run;
```

Partial Output

Analysis Variable : DDABal Checking Balance			
B_DDABal	N Obs	Minimum	Maximum
0	323	-774.8300000	1.7200000
1	322	1.7300000	8.5200000
2	322	8.5300000	16.3800000
3	323	16.4000000	27.1200000
4	323	27.2400000	40.2700000
5	322	40.4400000	52.5100000
6	323	52.5400000	65.2900000
7	323	65.3700000	81.5400000
8	322	81.5600000	94.3800000
9	323	94.4200000	110.3800000
10	323	110.4000000	125.0000000

Because the binned balance input is a replacement for the **DDABal** column, switch **B_DDABal** for **DDABal** in the **screened** macro variable.

```
%let screened =
brclus2 checks ccbal
mmbal income ilsbal posamt
nsfamt cd irabal age
sav dda invbal
crscore brclus3 cc brclus1
cashbk miacctag micrscor moved
acctage dirdep savbal B_DDABAL
sdb ccpurc inarea atmamt
phone mmcred inv
depamt brclus4 atm lores;
```

Binning is not the only option. Other popular techniques for hand-crafting inputs include the transformations mentioned above as well as splines. Notice that **B_DDABal** is not a categorical input. The point of the linearization exercise is to take advantage of the linear relationship between logits and bins, not add 100 dummy variables to the list of inputs.

If there was any question about data quality, the binning code would have to be much more robust.

3.5 Subset Selection

Objectives

- Discuss the subset selection methods in the LOGISTIC procedure.
- Illustrate the backward selection method.
- Find the subset of variables that minimizes the Schwarz Bayes criterion.

66

All Subsets

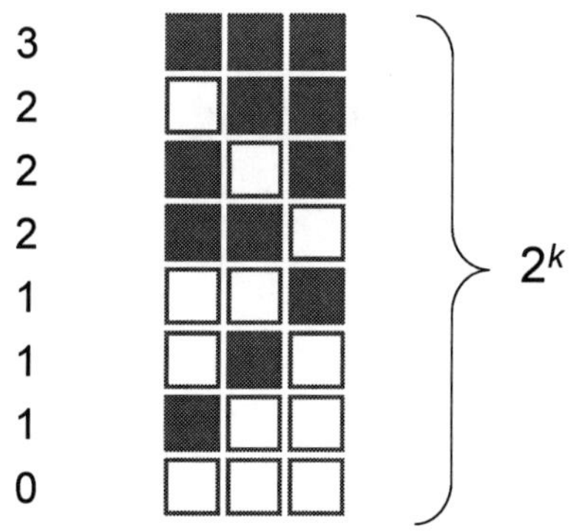

67

Variable selection methods in regression are concerned with finding subsets of the inputs that are jointly important in predicting the target. The most thorough search would consider all possible subsets. This can be prohibitively expensive when the number of inputs, k, is large, as there are 2^k possible subsets to consider.

Stepwise Selection

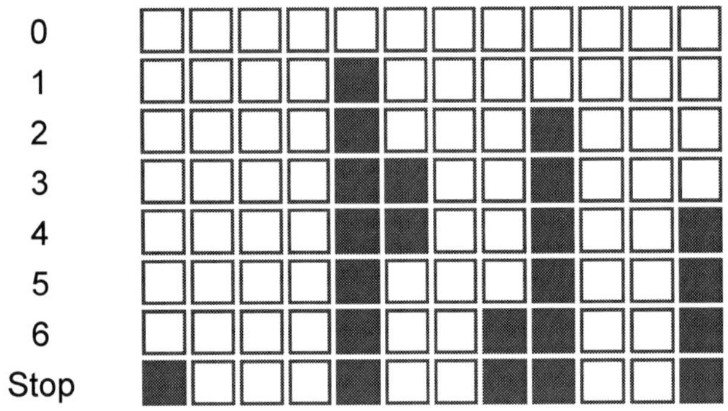

68

Stepwise variable selection is an often criticized and yet heavily used subset selection method. Stepwise selection first searches the 1-input models and selects the best. It then searches the 2-input models that contain the input selected in the first step and selects the best. The model is incrementally built in this fashion until no improvement is made. There is also a backward portion of the algorithm where at each step, the variables in the current model can be removed if they have become unimportant. The usual criterion used for entry and removal from the model is the *p*-value from a significance test that the coefficient is zero, although other criteria can also be used. Note that in subset selection, the *p*-value is merely a tuning parameter that measures the relative strength of the candidate variables.

Stepwise selection was devised to give a computationally efficient alternative to examining all subsets. It is not guaranteed to find the best subset and it can be shown to perform badly in many situations (Harrell 1997).

Backward Elimination

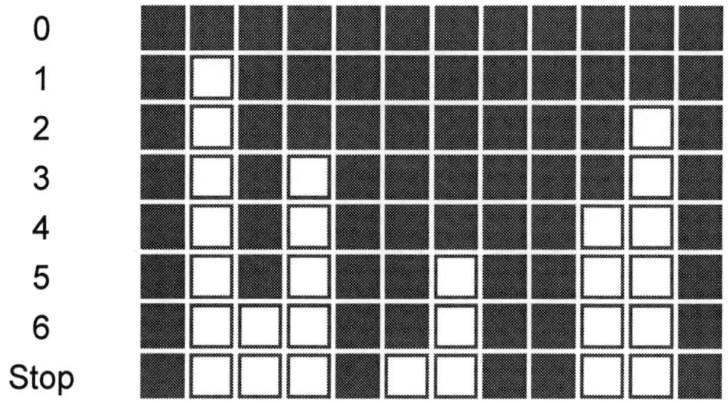

69

Backward variable selection starts with all the candidate variables in the model simultaneously. At each step, the least important input variable is removed (as determined by the *p*-value). Backward elimination is less inclined to exclude important inputs or include spurious inputs than forward (stepwise) methods (Mantel 1970; Harrell 1997). However, it is considered more computationally expensive than stepwise because more steps are usually required and they involve larger models.

Scalability in PROC LOGISTIC

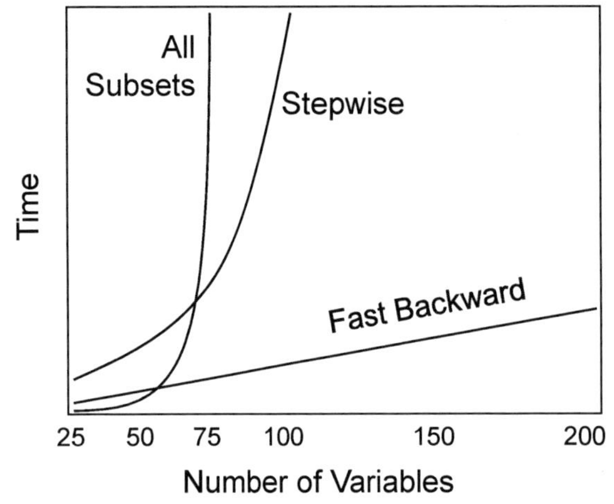

70

Most of the literature on the different subset selection methods has considered linear rather than logistic regression. The conventional wisdom regarding computation time is that **stepwise < backwards < all subsets**.

However, logistic regression (as implemented by PROC LOGISTIC) gives a different story. For up to ≈60 inputs, the results are reversed all subsets < backwards < stepwise.

For any number of inputs, backward elimination (with the FAST option) is more efficient than stepwise. (The above simulation was conducted with 50,000 cases and 200 intercorrelated inputs; 16 of the inputs were important, 6 strongly so.)

Logistic regression requires an iterative optimization algorithm. Each model fit is much more expensive than with linear regression. Each step in the stepwise algorithm requires iterative optimization. To find 16 variables (considering only the forward part of stepwise) would take $16k$–120 separate nonlinear regressions, each of which might require several iterations.

All-subsets selection is executed in PROC LOGISTIC with the SELECTION=SCORE option (SAS Institute Inc. 1997). This method only requires that one model be fit (the full model). The results are then manipulated to calculate a score test for each possible combination of input variables. It also uses a branch and bound method for efficiently searching the many combinations. This method is the fastest until the number of possible combinations becomes unmanageable, at which point the performance acutely deteriorates. If redundant inputs are eliminated first (using variable clustering), then all-subsets selection can be a practical method for predictive modeling.

When combined with the FAST option, backward variable selection requires only a single logistic regression (SAS Institute Inc. 1997). PROC LOGISTIC uses the method of Lawless and Singhal (1978) to manipulate the full model fit to approximate fitting reduced models. The FAST option is extremely efficient because the model is not refitted for every variable removed. Fast backward elimination had the best overall performance, a linear increase in time as the number of inputs increased. Note that ordinary backwards (without the FAST option) would have been slower than stepwise.

The FAST option only provides approximations to the regression coefficients. If you compare models selected by backwards elimination with and without the FAST option, you will see different regression coefficients.

3.10 Multiple Choice Poll

Which of the following statements is true regarding best subsets selection?

a. The models are ranked by the likelihood ratio chi-square.
b. The method uses a forward selection to find the best model.
c. The method is relatively efficient for a small number of variables (for example, less than 50).
d. None of the above.

71

Automatic Subset Selection

Example: Use the backward elimination method in PROC LOGISTIC to find a subset of inputs. Use ODS Graphics to create an odds ratio plot with a horizontal orientation and the statistics displayed. Use all the screened variables and **Res** as the inputs. Specify the FAST option, a significance level of 0.01, and profile likelihood confidence intervals.

```
/* pmlr03d07.sas  */
proc logistic data=imputed plots(only)=oddsratio
        (type=horizontalstat);
   class res (param=ref ref='S');
   model ins(event='1')=&screened res / clodds=pl
         selection=backward fast slstay=.01;
run;
```

Selected MODEL statement options:

SELECTION= specifies the method used to select the variables in the model. BACKWARD requests backward elimination.

FAST uses a computational algorithm to compute a first-order approximation to the remaining slope estimates for each subsequent elimination of a variable from the model. Variables are removed from the model based on these approximate estimates.

SLSTAY= specifies the significance level of the Wald chi-square for an effect to stay in the model in a backward elimination step.

The significance level[2] was chosen arbitrarily for illustrative purposes.

---

[2] The choice of significance level is a multi-faceted question. Analysts with experience may be able to posit a significance level that will secure a model with good generalizing power. If not, the information criterion-based method that follows or the techniques of the following chapters can be used to find a model that generalizes well.

Model Information	
Data Set	WORK.IMPUTED
Response Variable	Ins
Number of Response Levels	2
Model	binary logit
Optimization Technique	Fisher's scoring

Number of Observations Read	32264
Number of Observations Used	32264

Response Profile		
Ordered Value	**Ins**	**Total Frequency**
1	0	21089
2	1	11175

Probability modeled is Ins=1.

Backward Elimination Procedure

Class Level Information			
Class	**Value**	**Design Variables**	
Res	**R**	1	0
	S	0	0
	U	0	1

Step 0. The following effects were entered:

Intercept brclus2 Checks CCBal MMBal Income ILSBal POSAmt NSFAmt CD IRABal Age Sav DDA InvBal CRScore brclus3 CC brclus1 CashBk MIAcctAg MICRScor Moved AcctAge DirDep SavBal B_DDABal SDB CCPurc InArea ATMAmt Phone MMCred Inv DepAmt brclus4 ATM LORes Res

Model Convergence Status
Convergence criterion (GCONV=1E-8) satisfied.

Model Fit Statistics		
Criterion	Intercept Only	Intercept and Covariates
AIC	41633.206	34877.780
SC	41641.587	35213.048
-2 Log L	41631.206	34797.780

Testing Global Null Hypothesis: BETA=0			
Test	Chi-Square	DF	Pr > ChiSq
Likelihood Ratio	6833.4256	39	<.0001
Score	6127.4303	39	<.0001
Wald	4948.1168	39	<.0001

Step 1. Fast Backward Elimination:

Analysis of Effects Removed by Fast Backward Elimination						
Effect Removed	Chi-Square	DF	Pr > ChiSq	Residual Chi-Square	DF	Pr > Residual ChiSq
CCPurc	0.0020	1	0.9646	0.0020	1	0.9646
POSAmt	0.0219	1	0.8824	0.0238	2	0.9882
MMCred	0.0292	1	0.8643	0.0530	3	0.9968
Age	0.0707	1	0.7904	0.1237	4	0.9982
Res	1.1392	2	0.5657	1.2629	6	0.9737
InvBal	0.3452	1	0.5569	1.6081	7	0.9783
CRScore	0.3567	1	0.5504	1.9648	8	0.9821
Moved	0.4602	1	0.4975	2.4250	9	0.9828
Income	0.7832	1	0.3762	3.2081	10	0.9761
LORes	0.6500	1	0.4201	3.8581	11	0.9739
InArea	1.5256	1	0.2168	5.3838	12	0.9439
DDA	1.9730	1	0.1601	7.3568	13	0.8828

DepAmt	3.6400	1	0.0564	10.9968	14	0.6863
CashBk	3.7577	1	0.0526	14.7545	15	0.4692
MICRScor	3.8363	1	0.0502	18.5908	16	0.2905
SDB	4.9697	1	0.0258	23.5605	17	0.1319

Model Convergence Status
Convergence criterion (GCONV=1E-8) satisfied.

Model Fit Statistics		
Criterion	Intercept Only	Intercept and Covariates
AIC	41633.206	34867.832
SC	41641.587	35060.611
-2 Log L	41631.206	34821.832

Testing Global Null Hypothesis: BETA=0			
Test	Chi-Square	DF	Pr > ChiSq
Likelihood Ratio	6809.3739	22	<.0001
Score	6106.8287	22	<.0001
Wald	4940.7225	22	<.0001

Residual Chi-Square Test		
Chi-Square	DF	Pr > ChiSq
23.8360	17	0.1240

The residual chi-square tests the significance of the variables not in the model. The results suggest that you have included all of the useful inputs.

Summary of Backward Elimination

Step	Effect Removed	DF	Number In	Wald Chi-Square	Pr > ChiSq	Variable Label
1	CCPurc	1	37	0.0020	0.9646	Credit Card Purchases
1	POSAmt	1	36	0.0219	0.8824	Amount Point of Sale
1	MMCred	1	35	0.0292	0.8643	Money Market Credits
1	Age	1	34	0.0707	0.7904	Age
1	Res	2	33	1.1392	0.5657	Area Classification
1	InvBal	1	32	0.3452	0.5569	Investment Balance
1	CRScore	1	31	0.3567	0.5504	Credit Score
1	Moved	1	30	0.4602	0.4975	Recent Address Change
1	Income	1	29	0.7832	0.3762	Income
1	LORes	1	28	0.6500	0.4201	Length of Residence
1	InArea	1	27	1.5256	0.2168	Local Address
1	DDA	1	26	1.9730	0.1601	Checking Account
1	DepAmt	1	25	3.6400	0.0564	Amount Deposited
1	CashBk	1	24	3.7577	0.0526	Number Cash Back
1	MICRScor	1	23	3.8363	0.0502	
1	SDB	1	22	4.9697	0.0258	Safety Deposit Box

Type 3 Analysis of Effects

Effect	DF	Wald Chi-Square	Pr > ChiSq
brclus2	1	83.6630	<.0001
Checks	1	78.1056	<.0001
CCBal	1	10.8949	0.0010
MMBal	1	303.5887	<.0001
ILSBal	1	13.9290	0.0002
NSFAmt	1	15.8824	<.0001
CD	1	575.0271	<.0001

IRABal	1	10.0394	0.0015
Sav	1	337.2491	<.0001
brclus3	1	62.2114	<.0001
CC	1	102.9569	<.0001
brclus1	1	10.1704	0.0014
MIAcctAg	1	10.7583	0.0010
AcctAge	1	74.3892	<.0001
DirDep	1	28.0906	<.0001
SavBal	1	387.4137	<.0001
B_DDABal	1	1396.4525	<.0001
ATMAmt	1	62.0174	<.0001
Phone	1	18.6455	<.0001
Inv	1	56.9924	<.0001
brclus4	1	80.1846	<.0001
ATM	1	59.0375	<.0001

The results show that PROC LOGISTIC using the backward elimination method reduced the number of variables down from 38 to 22.

Analysis of Maximum Likelihood Estimates					
Parameter	DF	Estimate	Standard Error	Wald Chi-Square	Pr > ChiSq
Intercept	1	-1.9702	0.0469	1765.5881	<.0001
brclus2	1	-0.5780	0.0632	83.6630	<.0001
Checks	1	-0.0265	0.00300	78.1056	<.0001
CCBal	1	-5.31E-7	1.609E-7	10.8949	0.0010
MMBal	1	0.000043	2.455E-6	303.5887	<.0001
ILSBal	1	-0.00002	5.893E-6	13.9290	0.0002
NSFAmt	1	0.00389	0.000977	15.8824	<.0001
CD	1	0.9093	0.0379	575.0271	<.0001
IRABal	1	6.795E-6	2.145E-6	10.0394	0.0015

Sav	1	0.5521	0.0301	337.2491	<.0001
brclus3	1	-0.5460	0.0692	62.2114	<.0001
CC	1	0.2920	0.0288	102.9569	<.0001
brclus1	1	0.1021	0.0320	10.1704	0.0014
MIAcctAg	1	-0.1775	0.0541	10.7583	0.0010
AcctAge	1	-0.0189	0.00219	74.3892	<.0001
DirDep	1	-0.1675	0.0316	28.0906	<.0001
SavBal	1	0.000044	2.249E-6	387.4137	<.0001
B_DDABal	1	0.0191	0.000511	1396.4525	<.0001
ATMAmt	1	0.000037	4.652E-6	62.0174	<.0001
Phone	1	-0.0646	0.0150	18.6455	<.0001
Inv	1	0.6075	0.0805	56.9924	<.0001
brclus4	1	-0.8114	0.0906	80.1846	<.0001
ATM	1	-0.2380	0.0310	59.0375	<.0001

Association of Predicted Probabilities and Observed Responses			
Percent Concordant	77.4	**Somers' D**	0.550
Percent Discordant	22.4	**Gamma**	0.552
Percent Tied	0.2	**Tau-a**	0.249
Pairs	235669575	**c**	0.775

Odds Ratio Estimates and Profile-Likelihood Confidence Intervals				
Effect	Unit	Estimate	95% Confidence Limits	
brclus2	1.0000	0.561	0.495	0.635
Checks	1.0000	0.974	0.968	0.980
CCBal	1.0000	1.000	1.000	1.000
MMBal	1.0000	1.000	1.000	1.000
ILSBal	1.0000	1.000	1.000	1.000
NSFAmt	1.0000	1.004	1.002	1.006
CD	1.0000	2.483	2.305	2.674
IRABal	1.0000	1.000	1.000	1.000
Sav	1.0000	1.737	1.638	1.842
brclus3	1.0000	0.579	0.505	0.663
CC	1.0000	1.339	1.266	1.417
brclus1	1.0000	1.107	1.040	1.179
MIAcctAg	1.0000	0.837	0.753	0.931
AcctAge	1.0000	0.981	0.977	0.986
DirDep	1.0000	0.846	0.795	0.900
SavBal	1.0000	1.000	1.000	1.000
B_DDABal	1.0000	1.019	1.018	1.020
ATMAmt	1.0000	1.000	1.000	1.000
Phone	1.0000	0.937	0.910	0.965
Inv	1.0000	1.836	1.569	2.151
brclus4	1.0000	0.444	0.371	0.530
ATM	1.0000	0.788	0.742	0.838

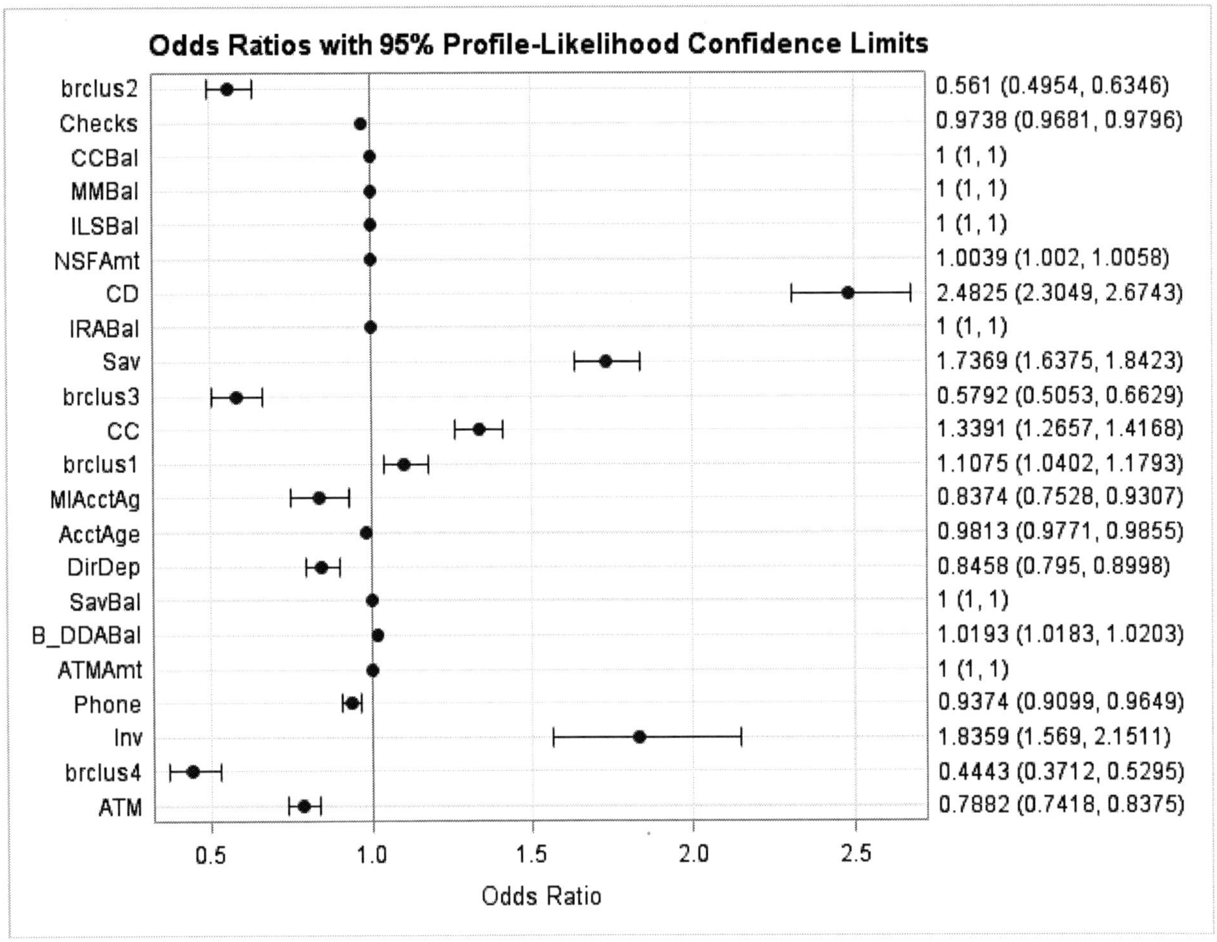

The UNITS statement is helpful in situations where there is a large scale of measurement such that even a very significant coefficient can be a small number close to 0. In these cases, because decimal accuracy is not shown to greater accuracy in the output, the odds ratio will appear as 1.000 and the confidence band shows (1,1) (an example is the variable **CCBal** shown above).

Example: Use the all subsets selection method (SELECTION=SCORE) to find a subset of inputs. Use the BEST= option to limit the amount of output. Because the best subsets method does not support class variables, create dummy variables for **Res** in a DATA step.

```
data imputed;
   set imputed;
   resr=(res='R');
   resu=(res='U');
run;

proc logistic data=imputed;
   model ins(event='1')=&screened resr resu
   / selection=score best=1;
run;
```

Selected MODEL statement option:

BEST=*n* specifies that *n* models with the highest score chi-square statistics are to be displayed for each model size. It is used exclusively with the SCORE model selection method.

Partial Output

Regression Models Selected by Score Criterion		
Number of Variables	Score Chi-Square	Variables Included in Model
1	2781.3404	B_DDABal
2	3711.5967	CD B_DDABal
3	4380.4694	CD SavBal B_DDABal
4	4763.8784	CD Sav SavBal B_DDABal
5	5147.5244	MMBal CD Sav SavBal B_DDABal
6	5376.0884	Checks MMBal CD Sav SavBal B_DDABal
7	5567.6038	Checks MMBal CD Sav CC SavBal B_DDABal
8	5681.4645	Checks MMBal CD Sav CC brclus1 SavBal B_DDABal
9	5749.8760	Checks MMBal CD Sav CC brclus1 SavBal B_DDABal Inv
10	5807.1711	brclus2 Checks MMBal CD Sav brclus3 CC SavBal B_DDABal brclus4
11	5872.1641	brclus2 Checks MMBal CD Sav brclus3 CC SavBal B_DDABal Inv brclus4
12	5924.1821	brclus2 Checks MMBal CD Sav brclus3 CC DirDep SavBal B_DDABal Inv brclus4
13	5961.7085	brclus2 Checks MMBal CD Sav brclus3 CC AcctAge DirDep SavBal B_DDABal Inv brclus4
14	6009.4822	brclus2 Checks MMBal CD Sav brclus3 CC AcctAge SavBal B_DDABal ATMAmt Inv brclus4 ATM
15	6041.6934	brclus2 Checks MMBal CD Sav brclus3 CC AcctAge DirDep SavBal B_DDABal ATMAmt Inv brclus4 ATM
16	6055.6418	brclus2 Checks MMBal ILSBal CD Sav brclus3 CC AcctAge DirDep SavBal B_DDABal ATMAmt Inv brclus4 ATM
17	6066.3278	brclus2 Checks MMBal ILSBal CD Sav brclus3 CC AcctAge DirDep SavBal B_DDABal ATMAmt Phone Inv brclus4 ATM
18	6076.9589	brclus2 Checks MMBal ILSBal NSFAmt CD Sav brclus3 CC AcctAge DirDep SavBal B_DDABal ATMAmt Phone Inv brclus4 ATM
19	6086.9879	brclus2 Checks MMBal ILSBal NSFAmt CD IRABal Sav brclus3 CC AcctAge DirDep SavBal B_DDABal ATMAmt Phone Inv brclus4 ATM
20	6096.2229	brclus2 Checks MMBal ILSBal NSFAmt CD IRABal Sav brclus3 CC brclus1 AcctAge DirDep SavBal B_DDABal ATMAmt Phone Inv brclus4 ATM
21	6102.9309	brclus2 Checks MMBal ILSBal NSFAmt CD IRABal Sav brclus3 CC brclus1 MIAcctAg AcctAge DirDep SavBal B_DDABal ATMAmt Phone Inv brclus4 ATM
22	6108.7723	brclus2 Checks MMBal ILSBal NSFAmt CD IRABal Sav brclus3 CC brclus1 MIAcctAg AcctAge DirDep SavBal B_DDABal SDB ATMAmt Phone Inv brclus4 ATM
23	6112.6250	brclus2 Checks CCBal MMBal ILSBal NSFAmt CD IRABal Sav brclus3 CC brclus1 MIAcctAg AcctAge DirDep SavBal B_DDABal SDB ATMAmt Phone Inv brclus4 ATM
24	6116.5398	brclus2 Checks CCBal MMBal ILSBal NSFAmt CD IRABal Sav brclus3 CC brclus1 MIAcctAg AcctAge DirDep SavBal B_DDABal SDB ATMAmt Phone Inv DepAmt brclus4 ATM
25	6119.1566	brclus2 Checks CCBal MMBal ILSBal NSFAmt CD IRABal Sav brclus3 CC brclus1 CashBk MIAcctAg AcctAge DirDep SavBal B_DDABal SDB ATMAmt Phone Inv DepAmt brclus4 ATM
26	6121.6564	brclus2 Checks CCBal MMBal ILSBal NSFAmt CD IRABal Sav brclus3 CC brclus1 CashBk MIAcctAg MICRScor AcctAge DirDep SavBal B_DDABal SDB ATMAmt Phone Inv DepAmt brclus4 ATM
27	6122.8056	brclus2 Checks CCBal MMBal ILSBal NSFAmt CD IRABal Sav brclus3 CC brclus1 CashBk MIAcctAg MICRScor AcctAge DirDep SavBal B_DDABal SDB InArea ATMAmt Phone Inv DepAmt brclus4 ATM
28	6123.7653	brclus2 Checks CCBal MMBal ILSBal NSFAmt CD IRABal Sav brclus3 CC brclus1 CashBk MIAcctAg MICRScor Moved AcctAge DirDep SavBal B_DDABal SDB InArea ATMAmt Phone Inv DepAmt brclus4 ATM
29	6124.7237	brclus2 Checks CCBal MMBal ILSBal NSFAmt CD IRABal Sav brclus3 CC brclus1 CashBk MIAcctAg MICRScor Moved AcctAge DirDep SavBal B_DDABal SDB InArea ATMAmt Phone Inv DepAmt brclus4 ATM resu
30	6125.6389	brclus2 Checks CCBal MMBal Income ILSBal NSFAmt CD IRABal Sav brclus3 CC brclus1 CashBk MIAcctAg MICRScor Moved AcctAge DirDep SavBal B_DDABal SDB InArea ATMAmt Phone Inv DepAmt brclus4 ATM resu
31	6126.2643	brclus2 Checks CCBal MMBal Income ILSBal NSFAmt CD IRABal Sav brclus3 CC brclus1 CashBk MIAcctAg MICRScor Moved AcctAge DirDep SavBal B_DDABal SDB InArea ATMAmt Phone Inv DepAmt brclus4 ATM LORes resu
32	6126.6521	brclus2 Checks CCBal MMBal Income ILSBal NSFAmt CD IRABal Sav InvBal brclus3 CC brclus1 CashBk MIAcctAg MICRScor Moved AcctAge DirDep SavBal B_DDABal SDB InArea ATMAmt Phone Inv DepAmt brclus4 ATM LORes resu
33	6126.9319	brclus2 Checks CCBal MMBal Income ILSBal NSFAmt CD IRABal Sav InvBal brclus3 CC brclus1 CashBk MIAcctAg MICRScor Moved AcctAge DirDep SavBal B_DDABal SDB InArea ATMAmt Phone MMCred Inv DepAmt brclus4 ATM LORes resu

34	6127.1608	brclus2 Checks CCBal MMBal Income ILSBal NSFAmt CD IRABal Sav InvBal CRScore brclus3 CC brclus1 CashBk MIAcctAg MICRScor Moved AcctAge DirDep SavBal B_DDABal SDB InArea ATMAmt Phone MMCred Inv DepAmt brclus4 ATM LORes resu
35	6127.3019	brclus2 Checks CCBal MMBal Income ILSBal NSFAmt CD IRABal Sav InvBal CRScore brclus3 CC brclus1 CashBk MIAcctAg MICRScor Moved AcctAge DirDep SavBal B_DDABal SDB CCPurc InArea ATMAmt Phone MMCred Inv DepAmt brclus4 ATM LORes resu
36	6127.3788	brclus2 Checks CCBal MMBal Income ILSBal NSFAmt CD IRABal Sav DDA InvBal CRScore brclus3 CC brclus1 CashBk MIAcctAg MICRScor Moved AcctAge DirDep SavBal B_DDABal SDB CCPurc InArea ATMAmt Phone MMCred Inv DepAmt brclus4 ATM LORes resu
37	6127.4088	brclus2 Checks CCBal MMBal Income ILSBal POSAmt NSFAmt CD IRABal Sav DDA InvBal CRScore brclus3 CC brclus1 CashBk MIAcctAg MICRScor Moved AcctAge DirDep SavBal B_DDABal SDB CCPurc InArea ATMAmt Phone MMCred Inv DepAmt brclus4 ATM LORes resu
38	6127.4291	brclus2 Checks CCBal MMBal Income ILSBal POSAmt NSFAmt CD IRABal Sav DDA InvBal CRScore brclus3 CC brclus1 CashBk MIAcctAg MICRScor Moved AcctAge DirDep SavBal B_DDABal SDB CCPurc InArea ATMAmt Phone MMCred Inv DepAmt brclus4 ATM LORes resr resu
39	6127.4303	brclus2 Checks CCBal MMBal Income ILSBal POSAmt NSFAmt CD IRABal Age Sav DDA InvBal CRScore brclus3 CC brclus1 CashBk MIAcctAg MICRScor Moved AcctAge DirDep SavBal B_DDABal SDB CCPurc InArea ATMAmt Phone MMCred Inv DepAmt brclus4 ATM LORes resr resu

The score test statistic increases with model size. The Bayesian Information criterion (BIC) is often used for model selection. The BIC is essentially the –2 log likelihood plus a penalty term that increases as the model gets bigger. The penalty term for BIC is $(k+1)\cdot\ln(n)$, where k is the number of variables in the model and n is the sample size. Smaller values of BIC are preferable. The BIC is the same as the Schwarz criterion (SC) except when the event/trials syntax is used.

When the SELECTION=SCORE option is used, output data sets are not available. However, the Output Delivery System can be used to create an output data set with the variables selected in the all subsets selection. The SCORE statement can then be used with the FITSTAT option to generate model fit statistics for each model selected in the all subsets selection. Since a series of logistic regression models will have to be scored, the scoring process will be in a macro DO Loop.

Example: Generate fit statistics for the models generated in the all subsets selection. First create an output data set with the results of the all subsets selection. Then use a macro DO loop to score each of the models.

```
ods html close;
ods output bestsubsets=score;

proc logistic data=imputed;
   model ins(event='1')=&screened resr resu
   / selection=score best=1;
run;
```

The names and number of variables selected from the all subsets selection are transferred to macro variables using an SQL SELECT INTO function. The automatic macro variable **sqlobs** gives the number of models produced overall.

```
proc sql noprint;
  select variablesinmodel into :inputs1 - :inputs999
  from score;
  select NumberOfVariables into :ic1 - :ic999
  from score;
quit;

%let lastindx = &SQLOBS;
```

The macro **fitstat** consists of a DO Loop that scores each model selected from the all subsets selection and generates model fit statistics using PROC LOGISTIC. The FITSTAT option in the SCORE statement displays the fit statistics for the data that you are scoring. The macro variable **im** is set equal to the variable names in the **model_indx** model. The macro variable **ic** is set equal to the number of variables in the **model_indx** model. Since a data set is created with the predicted information for each model that is scored by PROC LOGISTIC, PROC DATASETS is used to delete these unnecessary data sets. Only the data sets with the fit statistics for each model scored are kept.

```
%macro fitstat( );

%do model_indx=1 %to &lastindx;

%let im=&&inputs&model_indx;
%let ic=&&ic&model_indx;

ods output scorefitstat=stat&ic;
proc logistic data=imputed;
  model ins(event='1')=&im;
  score data=imputed out=scored fitstat
        priorevent=&pi1;
run;

proc datasets
   library=work
   nodetails
   nolist;
   delete scored;
run;
quit;

%end;
%mend fitstat;

%fitstat( );
```

The data sets with the model fit statistics are concatenated and sorted by the Bayesian Information criterion.

```
data modelfit;
   set stat1 - stat&lastindx;
   model = _n_;
run;

proc sort data = modelfit;
   by bic;
run;

ods html;
proc print data=modelfit;
   var model auc aic bic misclass adjrsquare brierscore;
   title "Fit Statistics from Models selected from Best-Subsets";
run;
```

Fit Statistics from Models selected from Best-Subsets

Obs	model	AUC	AIC	BIC	MisClass	AdjRSquare	BrierScore
1	23	0.77528	76707.56	76908.72	0.3413	0.262675	0.309532
2	24	0.775461	76701.07	76910.61	0.3413	0.262808	0.309527
3	22	0.775162	76724.26	76917.04	0.3415	0.262377	0.309628
4	21	0.775114	76732.8	76917.2	0.3414	0.262203	0.309667
5	25	0.7755	76699.68	76917.6	0.3413	0.262945	0.309535
6	26	0.775602	76696.3	76922.61	0.3413	0.263078	0.309532
7	20	0.774951	76750.15	76926.16	0.3416	0.261836	0.309726
8	27	0.775602	76696.91	76931.6	0.3414	0.263105	0.309529
9	19	0.774827	76766.33	76933.96	0.3415	0.261477	0.309775
10	28	0.775612	76697.83	76940.9	0.3414	0.26312	0.309526
11	29	0.775639	76697.84	76949.29	0.3413	0.263154	0.30952
12	18	0.774381	76791.97	76951.23	0.3415	0.261063	0.309831
13	30	0.775654	76698.67	76958.51	0.3413	0.263176	0.309518
14	31	0.775658	76699.18	76967.39	0.3414	0.263204	0.309512
15	16	0.773929	76828.16	76970.64	0.3415	0.260018	0.309872
16	17	0.774113	76819.94	76970.82	0.3416	0.260549	0.309913
17	32	0.775658	76700	76976.6	0.3414	0.263219	0.309507
18	15	0.773762	76850.84	76984.94	0.3415	0.259481	0.309937
19	33	0.775654	76702.15	76987.12	0.3414	0.26322	0.309508
20	34	0.775658	76703.29	76996.65	0.3414	0.263231	0.309505
21	35	0.775659	76705.26	77007	0.3414	0.263231	0.309505
22	36	0.77571	76702.76	77012.88	0.3413	0.263327	0.309486
23	14	0.773171	76893.24	77018.97	0.3415	0.25837	0.309984
24	37	0.775712	76704.86	77023.36	0.3413	0.263328	0.309487
25	38	0.775713	76706.61	77033.5	0.3414	0.263334	0.309486
26	39	0.77572	76708.52	77043.79	0.3414	0.263336	0.309487

27	13	0.772241	77024.15	77141.49	0.3416	0.255786	0.310351
28	12	0.771391	77121.63	77230.6	0.3420	0.25384	0.31062
29	11	0.770202	77212.73	77313.31	0.3418	0.251723	0.31077
30	10	0.768908	77338.15	77430.34	0.3417	0.249626	0.311126
31	9	0.767185	77473.31	77557.13	0.3420	0.24606	0.311331
32	8	0.765747	77605.88	77681.32	0.3419	0.243802	0.311693
33	7	0.763662	77838.11	77905.17	0.3419	0.238982	0.312278
34	6	0.76079	78156.98	78215.65	0.3419	0.231237	0.312798
35	5	0.75644	78506.17	78556.46	0.3415	0.223337	0.313456
36	4	0.743741	79305.55	79347.46	0.3418	0.207368	0.315024
37	3	0.74197	79483.37	79516.89	0.3407	0.199229	0.314439
38	2	0.703312	82362.33	82387.48	0.3464	0.153639	0.324211
39	1	0.677748	84004.13	84020.9	0.3464	0.117493	0.327571

Besides the BIC, other displayed statistics include the area under the ROC curve (AUC), Akaike's information criterion (AIC), the misclassification rate, the maximum-rescaled R-square statistic (AdjRSquare), and the Brier score. The Brier score measures the average squared deviation between predicted probabilities for a set of events and their outcomes, so a lower score represents higher accuracy. The AdjRSquare statistics, which can achieve a maximum value of 1, are most useful for comparing competing models that are not necessarily nested—larger values indicate better models.

The results reveal that the 23-input model has the smallest value of **bic**. The following SQL code creates a macro variable **selected** that contains the names of the inputs in that model.

```
proc sql;
   select VariablesInModel into :selected
   from score
   where numberofvariables=23;
quit;
```

Variables Included in Model
brclus2 Checks CCBal MMBal ILSBal NSFAmt CD IRABal Sav brclus3 CC brclus1 MIAcctAg AcctAge DirDep SavBal B_DDABal SDB ATMAmt Phone Inv brclus4 ATM

These automatic selection routines raise several questions. For techniques like stepwise selection and backward elimination, what are good stopping rules? For best subsets, what number of inputs yields the best model?

The answers to these questions lie in the purposes of the models. The goal of most predictive modeling is generalization. Hence, the best model is the model that generalizes to new cases the best. How does one measure generalizing ability of a model? What are some statistics that summarize a model's performance? The next chapter offers several suggestions for comparing and selecting models.

Exercises

5. Compare Variable Selection Methods

a. Fit a logistic regression model to the **pva1** data set with **TARGET_B** as the target variable and the macro variable **ex_screened** as the predictor variable. Model the probability that the target variable equals 1 and use the SCORE method with the BEST=1 option.

1) What is the best 1 variable model?

2) What is the best 2 variable model?

b. Use the **fitstat** macro to determine which model is the best according to the BIC criterion. Create a macro variable for the variable names in the final model.

1) Which variables made it to the final model?

c. Fit the final model in PROC LOGISTIC. Use the macro variable created for the variable names and use the NAMELEN=32 option in the PROC LOGISTIC statement.

1) What is the c statistic for the final model?

3.11 Multiple Choice Poll

What is the c statistic for the final model?

a. .610
b. .612
c. .613
d. .615

75

3.6 Chapter Summary

Preparing the data for predictive modeling can be laborious. First, missing values need to be replaced with reasonable values. Missing indicator variables are also needed if missingness is related to the target. If there are nominal input variables with numerous levels, the levels should be collapsed to reduce the likelihood of quasi-complete separation and to reduce the redundancy among the levels. Furthermore, if there are numerous input variables, variable clustering should be performed to reduce the redundancy among the variables. In addition, there are several selection methods in the LOGISTIC procedure to select a subset of variables.

To assist in identifying nonlinear associations, the Hoeffding's D statistic can be used. A variable with a low rank in the Spearman correlation statistic but with a high rank in the Hoeffding's D statistic might indicate that the association with the target is nonlinear.

General form of the STDIZE procedure:

PROC STDIZE DATA=*SAS-data-set* <*options*>;
    VAR *variables*;
RUN;

General form of the CLUSTER procedure:

PROC CLUSTER DATA=*SAS-data-set* <*options*>;
    FREQ *variable*;
    VAR *variable*;
    ID *variable*;
RUN;

General form of the VARCLUS procedure:

PROC VARCLUS DATA=*SAS-data-set* <*options*>;
    VAR *variables*;
RUN;

3.7 Solutions

Solutions to Exercises

1. **Missing Value Imputation**

   a. Using the **pva** data set, create missing value indicators for the inputs **DONOR_AGE**, **INCOME_GROUP**, and **WEALTH_RATING**.

   b. Submit the program below to group the variables **RECENT_RESPONSE_PROP** and **RECENT_AVG_GIFT_AMT** into three groups.

   c. Sort **pva** by **GRP_RESP** and **GRP_AMT**.

   d. Use PROC STDIZE with a BY statement to impute missing values for each BY group and output the completed data set. Name the output data set **pva1**.

   e. Use the MEANS procedure to determine the values that the missing values were replaced with.

An electronic copy of the solution program is in **pmlr03s01.sas**.

```
data pva(drop=i);
   set pva;
   /* name the missing indicator variables */
   array mi{*} mi_DONOR_AGE mi_INCOME_GROUP
               mi_WEALTH_RATING;
   /* select variables with missing values */
   array x{*} DONOR_AGE INCOME_GROUP WEALTH_RATING;
   do i=1 to dim(mi);
      mi{i}=(x{i}=.);
   end;
run;

proc rank data=pva out=pva groups=3;
   var recent_response_prop recent_avg_gift_amt;
   ranks grp_resp grp_amt;
run;

proc sort data=pva out=pva;
   by grp_resp grp_amt;
run;

proc stdize data=pva method=median reponly out=pva1;
   by grp_resp grp_amt;
   var DONOR_AGE INCOME_GROUP WEALTH_RATING;
run;

proc means data=pva1 median;
   class grp_resp grp_amt;
   var DONOR_AGE INCOME_GROUP WEALTH_RATING;
run;
```

Rank for Variable RECENT_RESPONSE_PROP	Rank for Variable RECENT_AVG_GIFT_AMT	N Obs	Variable	Median
0	0	969	DONOR_AGE	64.0000000
			INCOME_GROUP	4.0000000
			WEALTH_RATING	5.0000000
	1	2325	DONOR_AGE	59.0000000
			INCOME_GROUP	4.0000000
			WEALTH_RATING	5.0000000
	2	3216	DONOR_AGE	57.0000000
			INCOME_GROUP	4.0000000
			WEALTH_RATING	6.0000000
1	0	1396	DONOR_AGE	65.0000000
			INCOME_GROUP	4.0000000
			WEALTH_RATING	5.0000000
	1	2557	DONOR_AGE	58.0000000
			INCOME_GROUP	4.0000000
			WEALTH_RATING	5.0000000
	2	2394	DONOR_AGE	57.0000000
			INCOME_GROUP	4.0000000
			WEALTH_RATING	6.0000000
2	0	4244	DONOR_AGE	63.0000000
			INCOME_GROUP	4.0000000
			WEALTH_RATING	5.0000000
	1	1430	DONOR_AGE	61.0000000
			INCOME_GROUP	4.0000000
			WEALTH_RATING	5.0000000
	2	841	DONOR_AGE	59.0000000
			INCOME_GROUP	4.0000000
			WEALTH_RATING	6.0000000

1) For the cell **GRP_RESP**=0 and **GRP_AMT**=0, the missing value for **DONOR_AGE** was replaced with a value of 64.

2. Clustering Categorical Input Levels

a. Use Greenacre's correspondence analysis to cluster levels of **CLUSTER_CODE**. First use PROC MEANS to generate a data set with information about the average response rate and sample size for each level of **CLUSTER_CODE**.

b. Use PROC CLUSTER to group those levels together and to generate a horizontal dendrogram. Use the log of the *p*-value of the appropriate χ^2 test to determine which level of clustering is appropriate.

c. Use PROC SGPLOT to plot the log of the *p*-value by the number of clusters (the range of the y-axis should be -50 to -10) and use PROC TREE to create a data set of the final results.

d. Create indicators to flag membership in those clusters.

An electronic copy of the solution program is in **pmlr03s02.sas**.

```
proc means data=pva1 noprint nway;
   class CLUSTER_CODE;
   var target_b;
   output out=level mean=prop;
run;

ods output clusterhistory=cluster;
proc cluster data=level method=ward outtree=fortree
      plots=(dendrogram(horizontal height=rsq));
   freq _freq_;
   var prop;
   id CLUSTER_CODE;
run;
```

Partial Output

Cluster History

Number of Clusters	Clusters Joined		Freq	Semipartial R-Square	R-Square	Tie
53	16	38	624	0.0000	1.00	T
52	09	43	621	0.0000	1.00	
51	23	39	805	0.0000	1.00	
50	03	40	1130	0.0000	1.00	
49	07	34	468	0.0000	1.00	
48	27	31	915	0.0000	1.00	
47	49	51	1135	0.0000	1.00	
46	18	24	1414	0.0000	1.00	
45	06	10	510	0.0000	1.00	
44	21	30	872	0.0000	1.00	

43	CL49	33	577	0.0000	1.00	
42	01	14	693	0.0000	1.00	
41	22	36	967	0.0000	1.00	
40	05	29	369	0.0000	1.00	
39	45	52	542	0.0000	1.00	
38	CL45	32	662	0.0000	1.00	
37	04	48	293	0.0000	1.00	
36	08	37	582	0.0000	1.00	
35	12	26	833	0.0000	1.00	
34	15	25	496	0.0000	1.00	
33	CL53	CL46	2038	0.0000	1.00	
32	19	42	382	0.0000	1.00	
31	CL50	46	1499	0.0000	1.00	
30	CL52	50	777	0.0000	1.00	
29	41	44	814	0.0000	1.00	
28	02	11	864	0.0000	1.00	
27	CL36	CL44	1454	0.0000	1.00	
26	CL40	CL34	865	0.0000	1.00	
25	13	20	896	0.0000	1.00	
24	CL39	CL47	1677	0.0000	1.00	
23	CL32	CL41	1349	0.0001	1.00	
22	CL42	35	1420	0.0001	1.00	
21	17	CL48	1264	0.0001	.999	
20	CL43	CL51	1382	0.0002	.999	
19	CL25	53	1199	0.0002	.999	
18	CL38	47	847	0.0002	.999	
17	CL28	CL37	1157	0.0002	.999	
16	CL30	CL24	2454	0.0004	.998	

15	CL35	CL23	2182	0.0005	.998	
14	CL22	CL31	2919	0.0006	.997	
13	.	28	797	0.0008	.996	
12	CL26	CL20	2247	0.0010	.995	
11	CL17	CL15	3339	0.0015	.994	
10	CL12	CL21	3511	0.0038	.990	
9	CL27	CL16	3908	0.0040	.986	
8	CL18	CL29	1661	0.0042	.982	
7	CL14	CL33	4957	0.0052	.977	
6	CL13	CL19	1996	0.0081	.969	
5	CL11	CL10	6850	0.0218	.947	
4	CL6	CL7	6953	0.0394	.907	
3	CL8	CL9	5569	0.0494	.858	
2	CL4	CL5	13803	0.1881	.670	
1	CL2	CL3	19372	0.6698	.000	

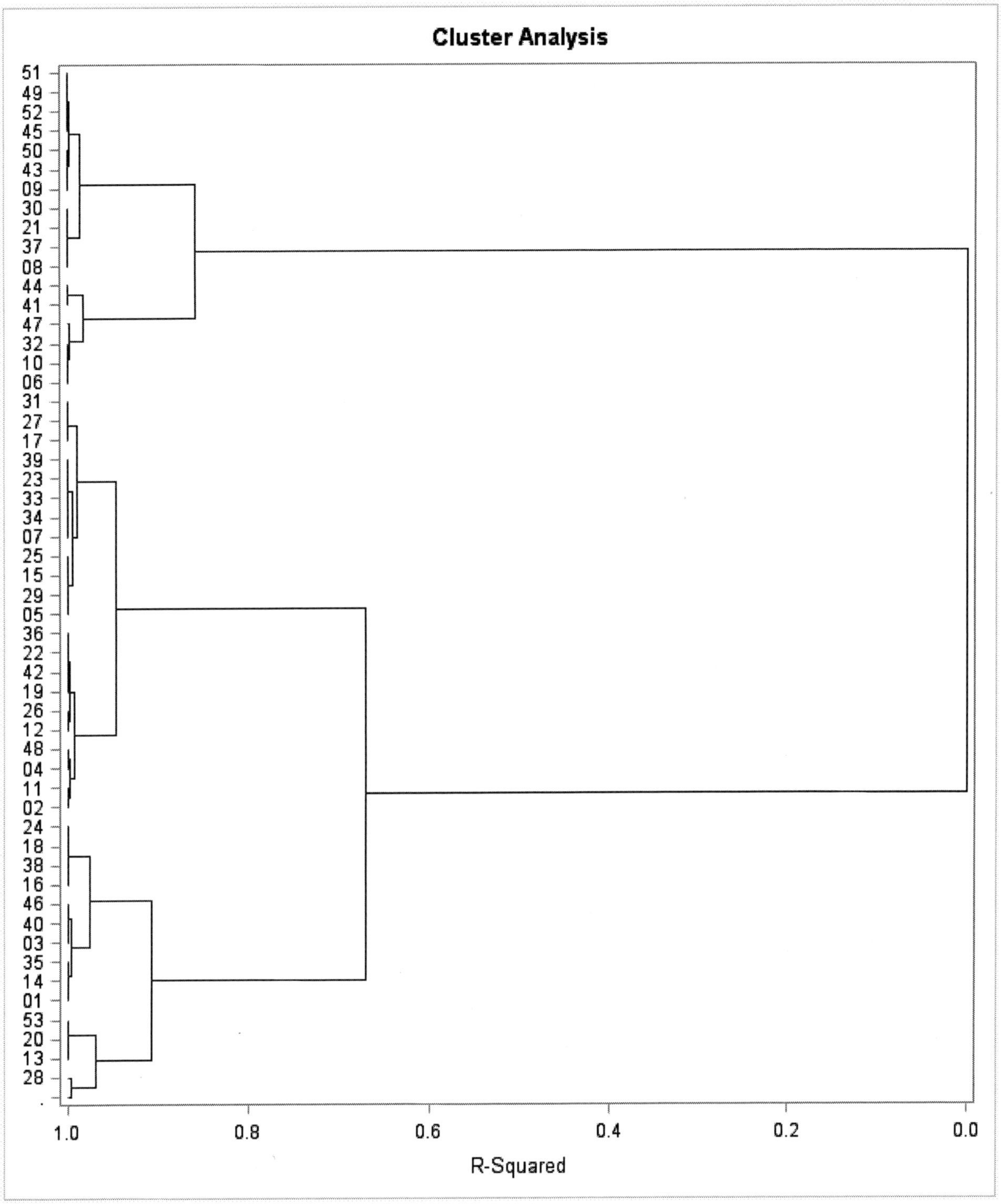


```
proc freq data=pva1 noprint;
   tables CLUSTER_CODE*TARGET_B / chisq;
   output out=chi(keep=_pchi_) chisq;
run;
```

```
data cutoff;
   if _n_ = 1 then set chi;
   set cluster;
   chisquare=_pchi_*rsquared;
   degfree=numberofclusters-1;
   logpvalue=logsdf('CHISQ',chisquare,degfree);
run;

proc sgplot data=cutoff;
   scatter y=logpvalue x=numberofclusters
         / markerattrs=(color=blue symbol=circlefilled);
   xaxis label="Number of Clusters";
   yaxis label="Log of P-Value" min=-50 max=-10;
   title "Plot of the Log of the P-Value by Number of Clusters";
run;
```

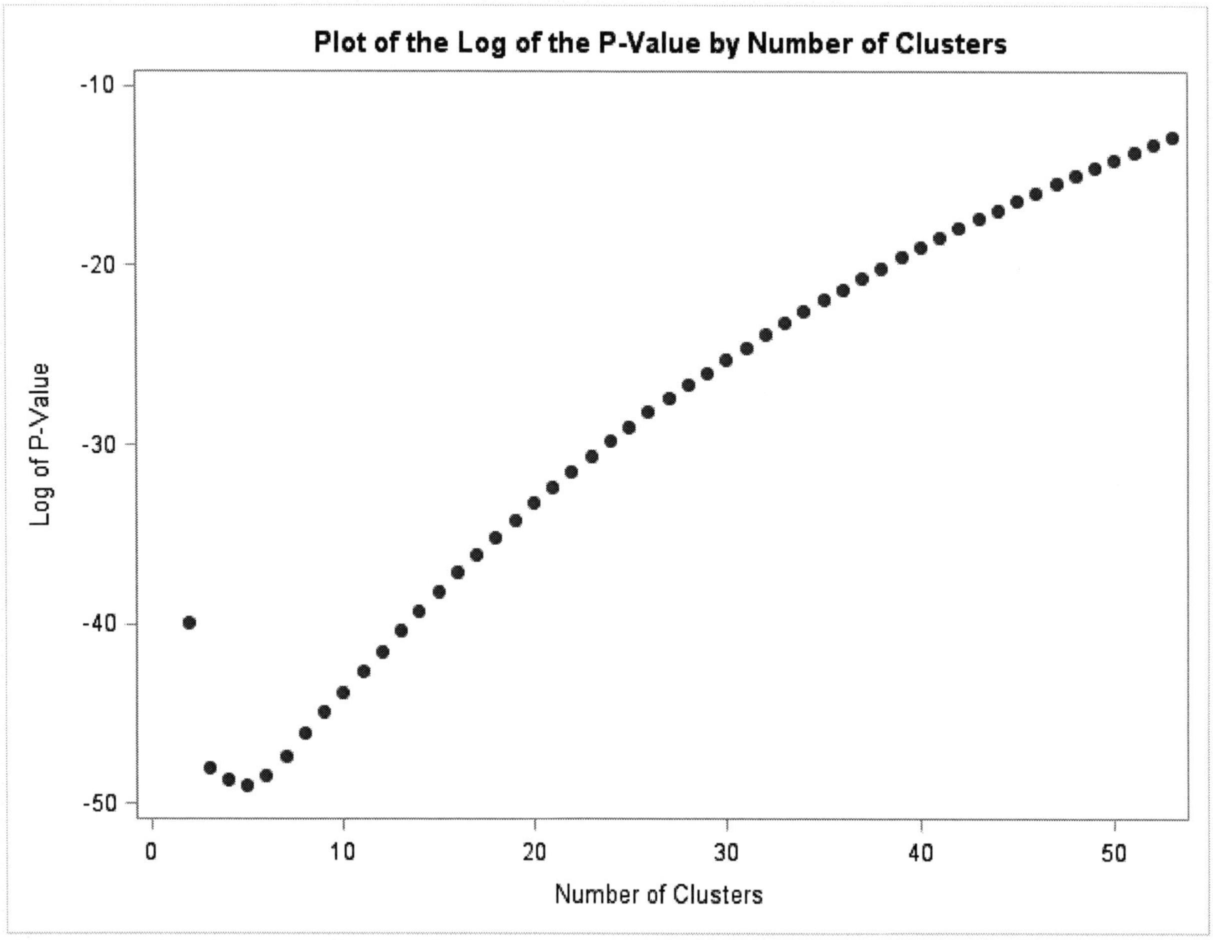


```
proc sql;
   select NumberOfClusters into :ncl
   from cutoff
   having logpvalue=min(logpvalue);
quit;
```

Number of Clusters
5

```
ods html close;
proc tree data=fortree nclusters=&ncl out=clus;
   id cluster_code;
run;
ods html;

proc sort data=clus;
   by clusname;
run;

proc print data=clus;
   by clusname;
   id clusname;
   title "Cluster Assignments";
run;
```

Cluster Assignments

CLUSNAME	CLUSTER_CODE	CLUSTER
CL5	23	3
	39	3
	07	3
	34	3
	27	3
	31	3
	33	3
	22	3
	36	3
	05	3
	29	3
	04	3
	48	3
	12	3
	26	3

	15	3
	25	3
	19	3
	42	3
	02	3
	11	3
	17	3

CLUSNAME	CLUSTER_CODE	CLUSTER
CL6	13	5
	20	5
	53	5
	.	5
	28	5

CLUSNAME	CLUSTER_CODE	CLUSTER
CL7	16	1
	38	1
	03	1
	40	1
	18	1
	24	1
	01	1
	14	1
	46	1
	35	1

CLUSNAME	CLUSTER_CODE	CLUSTER
CL8	06	4
	10	4
	32	4
	41	4
	44	4
	47	4

CLUSNAME	CLUSTER_CODE	CLUSTER
CL9	09	2
	43	2
	49	2
	51	2
	21	2
	30	2
	45	2
	52	2
	08	2
	37	2
	50	2

```
data pval;
   set pval;
   ClusCdGrp1 = CLUSTER_CODE in("13", "20", "53", ".", "28");
   ClusCdGrp2 = CLUSTER_CODE in("16", "38", "03", "40", "18",
                                "24", "01", "14", "46", "35");
   ClusCdGrp3 = CLUSTER_CODE in("06", "10", "32", "41", "44", "47");
   ClusCdGrp4 = CLUSTER_CODE in("09", "43", "49", "51",
                                "21", "30", "45", "52",
                                "08", "37", "50");
run;
```

1) The optimum number of clusters for the **CLUSTER_CODE** variable is 5.

3. Variable Clustering

a. Use PROC VARCLUS to cluster all numeric variables in a hierarchical structure (use the macro variable **ex_inputs** along with the missing indicator variables and the cluster group variables). Use MAXEIGEN=.70 as your stopping criterion and create a dendrogram.

An electronic copy of the solution program is in **pmlr03s03.sas**.

```
proc varclus data=pva1 short hi maxeigen=0.70 plots=dendrogram;
   var &ex_inputs mi_DONOR_AGE mi_INCOME_GROUP
       mi_WEALTH_RATING ClusCdGrp1 ClusCdGrp2
       ClusCdGrp3 ClusCdGrp4;
   title "Variable Clustering of PVA data set";
run;
```

Partial Output

32 Clusters		R-squared with		
Cluster	Variable	Own Cluster	Next Closest	1-R**2 Ratio
Cluster 1	MONTHS_SINCE_ORIGIN	0.8709	0.2470	0.1715
	LIFETIME_CARD_PROM	0.9315	0.2918	0.0967
	LIFETIME_PROM	0.9182	0.2645	0.1112
	LIFETIME_GIFT_AMOUNT	0.4984	0.2765	0.6933
	LIFETIME_GIFT_COUNT	0.7123	0.4296	0.5043
	MONTHS_SINCE_FIRST_GIFT	0.8847	0.2532	0.1543
	mi_WEALTH_RATING	0.5449	0.1182	0.5161
Cluster 2	LIFETIME_AVG_GIFT_AMT	0.9023	0.6735	0.2991
	LIFETIME_MIN_GIFT_AMT	0.9023	0.2578	0.1316
Cluster 3	MEDIAN_HOME_VALUE	0.7325	0.0952	0.2957
	MEDIAN_HOUSEHOLD_INCOME	0.8109	0.1980	0.2358
	PER_CAPITA_INCOME	0.8345	0.1492	0.1945
	nses1	0.5581	0.1778	0.5374
Cluster 4	FREQUENCY_STATUS_97NK	0.6765	0.2014	0.4051
	RECENT_RESPONSE_PROP	0.8340	0.1529	0.1960
	RECENT_CARD_RESPONSE_PROP	0.6596	0.0656	0.3643
	RECENT_RESPONSE_COUNT	0.8270	0.2874	0.2427
	RECENT_CARD_RESPONSE_COUNT	0.8301	0.2236	0.2189
Cluster 5	CARD_PROM_12	0.8222	0.1011	0.1978
	NUMBER_PROM_12	0.8222	0.3309	0.2658

Cluster 6	nses_	1.0000	0.1396	0.0000
	nurb_	1.0000	0.1396	0.0000
Cluster 7	mi_DONOR_AGE	0.7237	0.1571	0.3278
	mi_INCOME_GROUP	0.7237	0.3547	0.4283
Cluster 8	nses4	0.7331	0.1404	0.3105
	ClusCdGrp3	0.7331	0.0382	0.2775
Cluster 9	PCT_VIETNAM_VETERANS	0.7146	0.0772	0.3092
	PCT_WWII_VETERANS	0.7146	0.1771	0.3468
Cluster 10	LIFETIME_GIFT_RANGE	0.9359	0.2758	0.0885
	LIFETIME_MAX_GIFT_AMT	0.9359	0.5536	0.1436
Cluster 11	nses3	1.0000	0.1139	0.0000
Cluster 12	PCT_OWNER_OCCUPIED	1.0000	0.0736	0.0000
Cluster 13	INCOME_GROUP	1.0000	0.1417	0.0000
Cluster 14	PEP_STAR	0.7500	0.3532	0.3865
	STATUS_ES	0.7500	0.2171	0.3193
Cluster 15	nurbu	1.0000	0.0997	0.0000
Cluster 16	nurbt	1.0000	0.0772	0.0000
Cluster 17	PCT_MALE_MILITARY	1.0000	0.0226	0.0000
Cluster 18	DONOR_AGE	1.0000	0.0402	0.0000
Cluster 19	STATUS_FL	1.0000	0.1462	0.0000
Cluster 20	MOR_HIT_RATE	1.0000	0.0459	0.0000
Cluster 21	ClusCdGrp1	1.0000	0.0592	0.0000
Cluster 22	nurbr	0.7371	0.0974	0.2912
	ClusCdGrp4	0.7371	0.2310	0.3419
Cluster 23	nurbs	1.0000	0.1061	0.0000
Cluster 24	RECENT_STAR_STATUS	1.0000	0.1210	0.0000
Cluster 25	PUBLISHED_PHONE	1.0000	0.0997	0.0000
Cluster 26	MONTHS_SINCE_LAST_GIFT	1.0000	0.2099	0.0000

Cluster 27	IN_HOUSE	1.0000	0.1862	0.0000
Cluster 28	WEALTH_RATING	1.0000	0.2021	0.0000
Cluster 29	RECENT_AVG_GIFT_AMT	0.8785	0.4455	0.2191
	RECENT_AVG_CARD_GIFT_AMT	0.6297	0.1994	0.4626
	LAST_GIFT_AMT	0.7806	0.4931	0.4328
Cluster 30	home01	1.0000	0.3399	0.0000
Cluster 31	ClusCdGrp2	1.0000	0.0802	0.0000
Cluster 32	PCT_MALE_VETERANS	1.0000	0.1396	0.0000

No cluster meets the criterion for splitting.

Number of Clusters	Total Variation Explained by Clusters	Proportion of Variation Explained by Clusters	Minimum Proportion Explained by a Cluster	Maximum Second Eigenvalue in a Cluster	Minimum R-squared for a Variable	Maximum 1-R**2 Ratio for a Variable
1	7.864678	0.1404	0.1404	5.568126	0.0000	
2	12.420243	0.2218	0.1897	4.212711	0.0004	0.9997
3	16.595971	0.2964	0.2588	3.013748	0.0007	1.0075
4	19.482981	0.3479	0.2588	2.424482	0.0007	1.0275
5	21.651264	0.3866	0.2634	1.961928	0.0007	1.0575
6	23.599426	0.4214	0.2634	1.800516	0.0007	1.1874
7	25.368423	0.4530	0.2634	1.763991	0.0007	1.3573
8	26.879837	0.4800	0.3360	1.428525	0.0007	1.3612
9	28.133241	0.5024	0.3360	1.350485	0.0007	1.3612
10	29.069488	0.5191	0.3360	1.285995	0.0010	1.3612
11	30.291685	0.5409	0.3360	1.146334	0.0010	1.3598
12	31.434587	0.5613	0.3589	1.107165	0.0010	1.3598
13	32.450036	0.5795	0.3589	1.077754	0.0010	1.0968
14	33.353621	0.5956	0.3589	1.006684	0.0010	1.0968
15	34.348075	0.6134	0.4473	0.999840	0.0010	1.0761
16	35.347376	0.6312	0.4473	0.998937	0.0022	1.0209
17	36.345581	0.6490	0.4473	0.951359	0.1296	0.9068

18	37.295435	0.6660	0.4473	0.927057	0.1646	0.8765
19	38.126866	0.6808	0.4473	0.924090	0.1705	0.8703
20	39.005175	0.6965	0.4522	0.919871	0.1705	0.8703
21	39.919862	0.7129	0.4832	0.918306	0.1705	0.8703
22	40.728030	0.7273	0.5558	0.880605	0.1705	0.8703
23	41.571456	0.7423	0.5558	0.857141	0.1705	0.8703
24	42.427463	0.7576	0.5558	0.820652	0.3502	0.7327
25	43.207298	0.7716	0.5805	0.795547	0.3502	0.7327
26	43.858458	0.7832	0.6258	0.794179	0.3502	0.7327
27	44.529691	0.7952	0.6258	0.785040	0.3502	0.7327
28	45.259930	0.8082	0.6258	0.766411	0.4778	0.6933
29	45.840511	0.8186	0.6258	0.748457	0.4984	0.6933
30	46.588968	0.8319	0.6334	0.733165	0.4984	0.6933
31	47.322133	0.8450	0.6356	0.728718	0.4984	0.6933
32	48.050850	0.8581	0.7146	0.678626	0.4984	0.6933

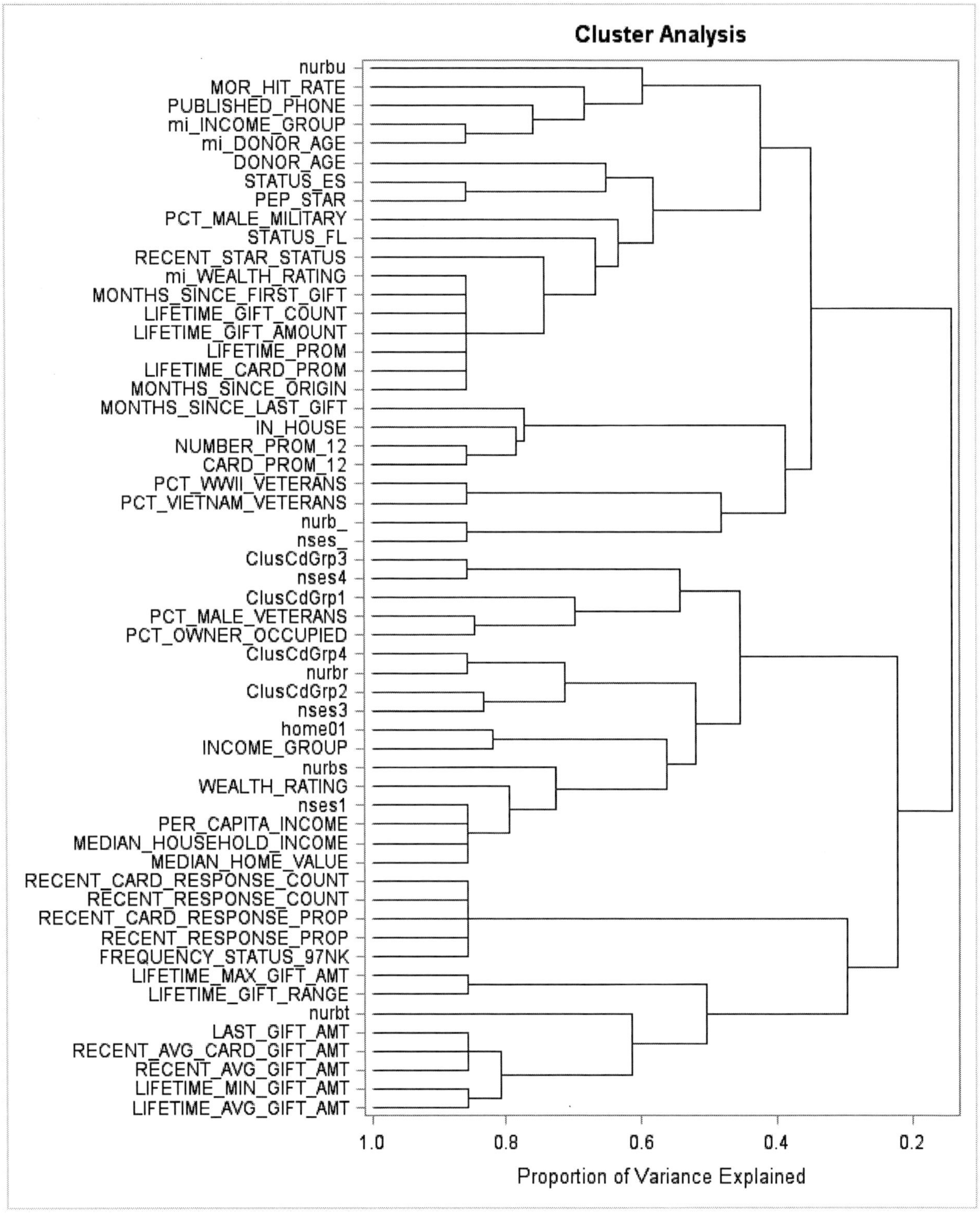

1) The number of clusters in the final solution is 32 and the proportion of the variation that was explained by the clusters is 0.8581.

4. Variable Screening and Logit Plots

a. Use the Spearman and Hoeffding correlation coefficients to screen the inputs with the least evidence of a relationship with the target. Use the **ex_reduced** macro variable in PROC CORR and use the LENGTH statement in the DATA step to specify a length of 32 for the character variable called **variable**. Create a table with the Spearman rank of inputs and the Hoeffding rank of inputs and use PROC SGPLOT to create a scatter plot of the ranks of Spearman versus the ranks of Hoeffding.

An electronic copy of the solution program is in **pmlr03s04.sas**.

```
ods html close;
ods output spearmancorr=spearman
           hoeffdingcorr=hoeffding;

proc corr data=pval spearman hoeffding rank;
   var &ex_reduced;
   with target_b;
run;

ods html;

data spearman1(keep=variable scorr spvalue ranksp);
   length variable $ 32;
   set spearman;
   array best(*) best1--best&nvar;
   array r(*) r1--r&nvar;
   array p(*) p1--p&nvar;
   do i=1 to dim(best);
      variable=best(i);
      scorr=r(i);
      spvalue=p(i);
      ranksp=i;
      output;
   end;
run;

data hoeffding1(keep=variable hcorr hpvalue rankho);
   length variable $ 32;
   set hoeffding;
   array best(*) best1--best&nvar;
   array r(*) r1--r&nvar;
   array p(*) p1--p&nvar;
   do i=1 to dim(best);
      variable=best(i);
      hcorr=r(i);
      hpvalue=p(i);
      rankho=i;
      output;
   end;
run;
```

```
proc sort data=spearman1;
   by variable;
run;

proc sort data=hoeffding1;
   by variable;
run;

data correlations;
   merge spearman1 hoeffding1;
   by variable;
run;

proc sort data=correlations;
   by ranksp;
run;

proc print data=correlations label split='*';
   var variable ranksp rankho;
   label ranksp='Spearman rank*of variables'
         rankho='Hoeffding rank*of variables';
   title "Ranks of Variables Based on Spearman and Hoeffding";
run;
```

Ranks of Variables Based on Spearman and Hoeffding

Obs	variable	Spearman rank of variables	Hoeffding rank of variables
1	RECENT_RESPONSE_PROP	1	1
2	RECENT_AVG_GIFT_AMT	2	2
3	STATUS_ES	3	5
4	LIFETIME_MIN_GIFT_AMT	4	3
5	MONTHS_SINCE_LAST_GIFT	5	4
6	RECENT_STAR_STATUS	6	7
7	LIFETIME_CARD_PROM	7	6
8	STATUS_FL	8	14
9	PER_CAPITA_INCOME	9	8
10	ClusCdGrp3	10	16
11	IN_HOUSE	11	21
12	DONOR_AGE	12	9

13	ClusCdGrp2	13	13
14	INCOME_GROUP	14	12
15	ClusCdGrp1	15	26
16	CARD_PROM_12	16	11
17	nses3	17	18
18	LIFETIME_GIFT_RANGE	18	10
19	MOR_HIT_RATE	19	15
20	nurbr	20	23
21	nses_	21	32
22	nurbs	22	25
23	PCT_MALE_VETERANS	23	17
24	home01	24	24
25	nurbu	25	29
26	PCT_OWNER_OCCUPIED	26	19
27	PCT_VIETNAM_VETERANS	27	22
28	mi_DONOR_AGE	28	27
29	nurbt	29	30
30	WEALTH_RATING	30	20
31	PUBLISHED_PHONE	31	28
32	PCT_MALE_MILITARY	32	31

```
proc sql noprint;
   select min(ranksp) into :vref
   from (select ranksp
         from correlations
         having spvalue > .5);
   select min(rankho) into :href
   from (select rankho
         from correlations
         having hpvalue > .5);
run;
quit;
```

```
proc sgplot data=correlations;
   refline &vref / axis=y;
   refline &href / axis=x;
   scatter y=ranksp x=rankho / datalabel=variable;
   yaxis label="Rank of Spearman";
   xaxis label="Rank of Hoeffding";
   title "Scatter Plot of the Ranks of Spearman vs. Hoeffding";
run;
```

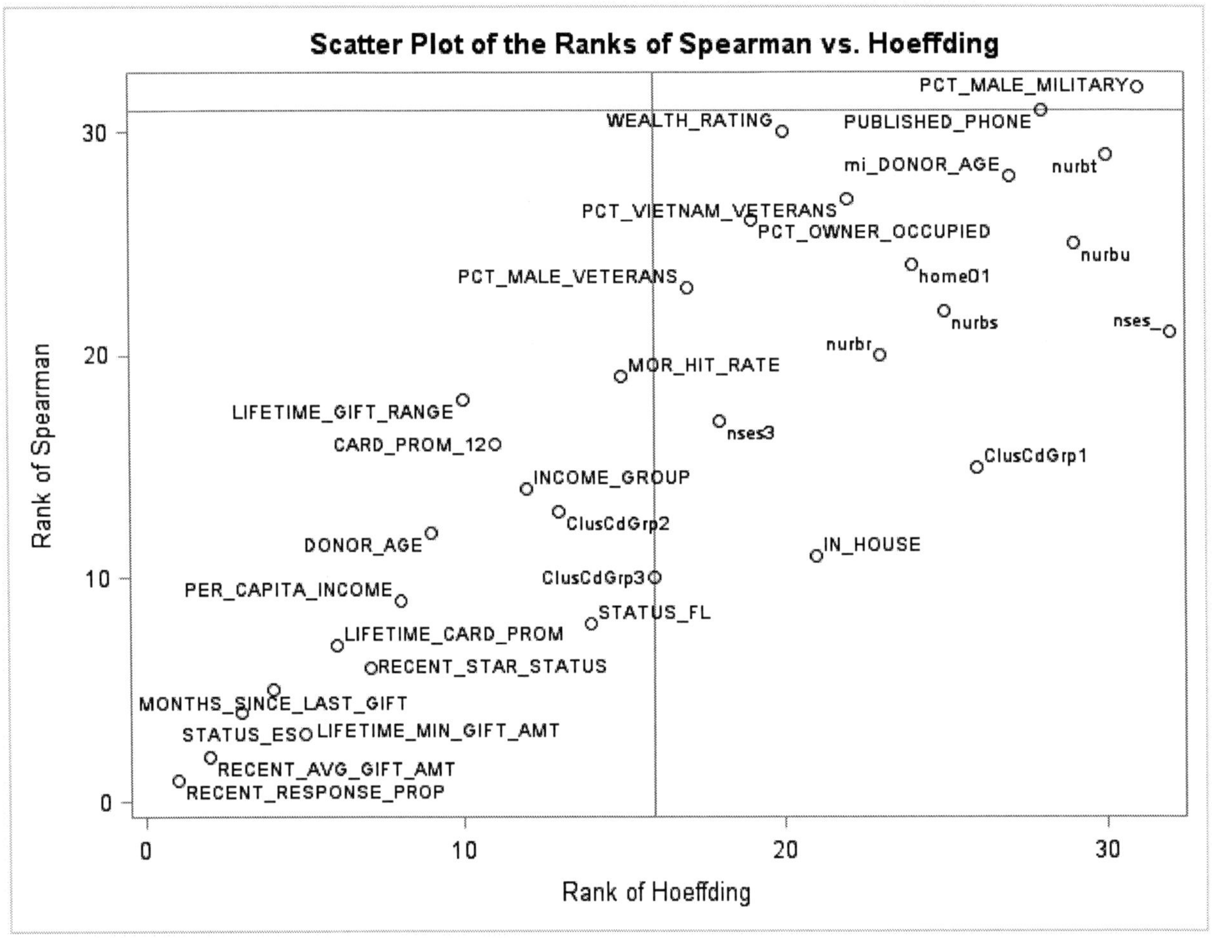

1) The input variable **LIFETIME_GIFT_RANGE** shows evidence of a nonlinear relationship with the target.

2) The input variables **PCT_MALE_MILITARY** and **PUBLISHED_PHONE** can be eliminated due to irrelevancy.

b. Create an empirical logit plot of **LIFETIME_GIFT_RANGE** and the bins of **LIFETIME_GIFT_RANGE**. Use 10 groups in PROC RANK.

```
%let var = LIFETIME_GIFT_RANGE;
proc rank data=pva1 groups=10 out=out;
   var &var;
   ranks bin;
run;
```

```
proc means data=out noprint nway;
   class bin;
   var target_b &var;
   output out=bins sum(target_b)=target_b
          mean(&var)=&var;
run;

data bins;
   set bins;
   elogit=log((target_b+(sqrt(_FREQ_ )/2))/
          ( _FREQ_ -target_b+(sqrt(_FREQ_ )/2)));
run;

proc sgplot data = bins;
   reg y=elogit x=&var /
       curvelabel="Linear Relationship?"
       curvelabelloc=outside
       lineattrs=(color=ligr);
   series y=elogit x=&var;
   title "Empirical Logit against &var";
run;
```

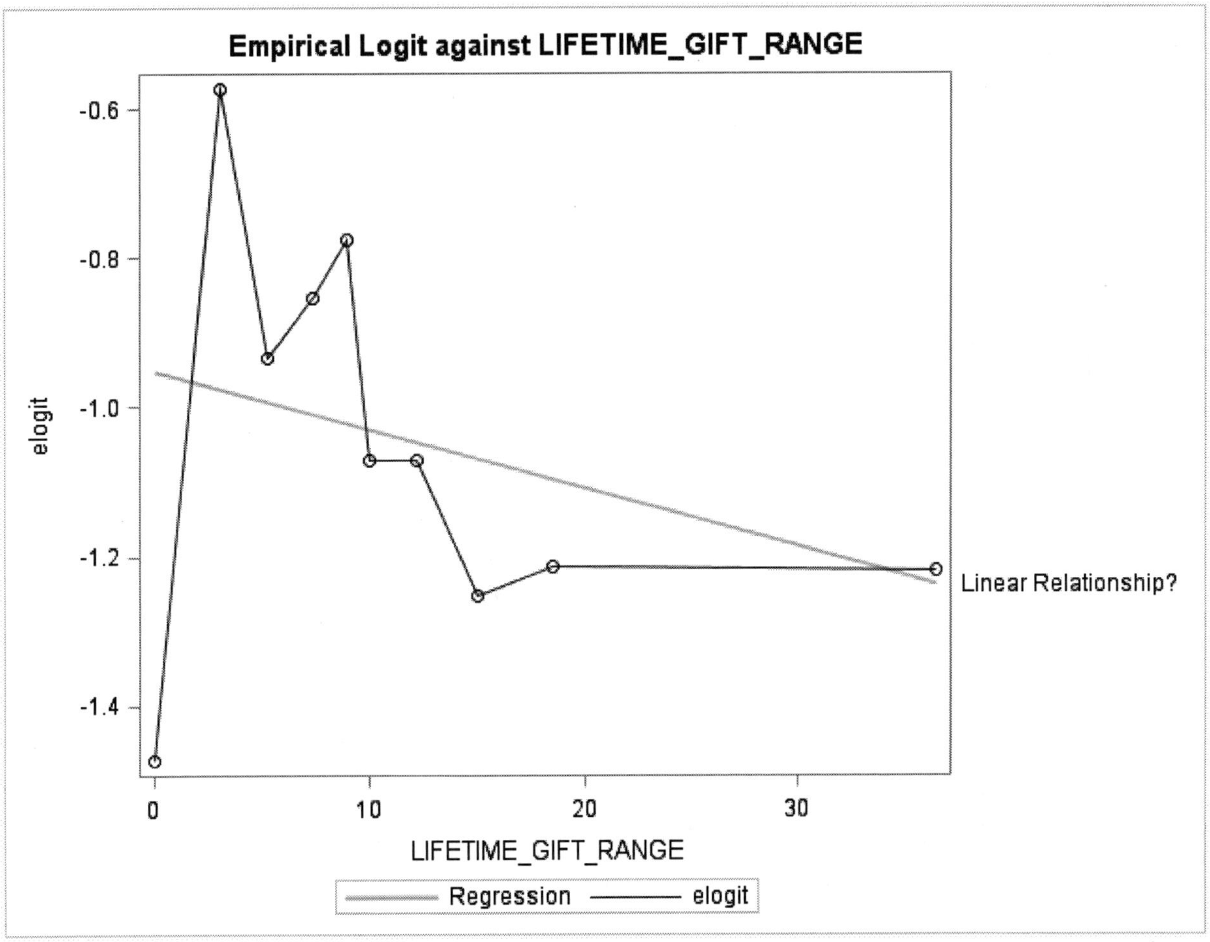

```
proc sgplot data=bins;
   reg y=elogit x=bin /
       curvelabel="Linear Relationship?"
       curvelabelloc=outside
       lineattrs=(color=ligr);
   series y=elogit x=bin;
   title "Empirical Logit against Binned &var";
run;
```

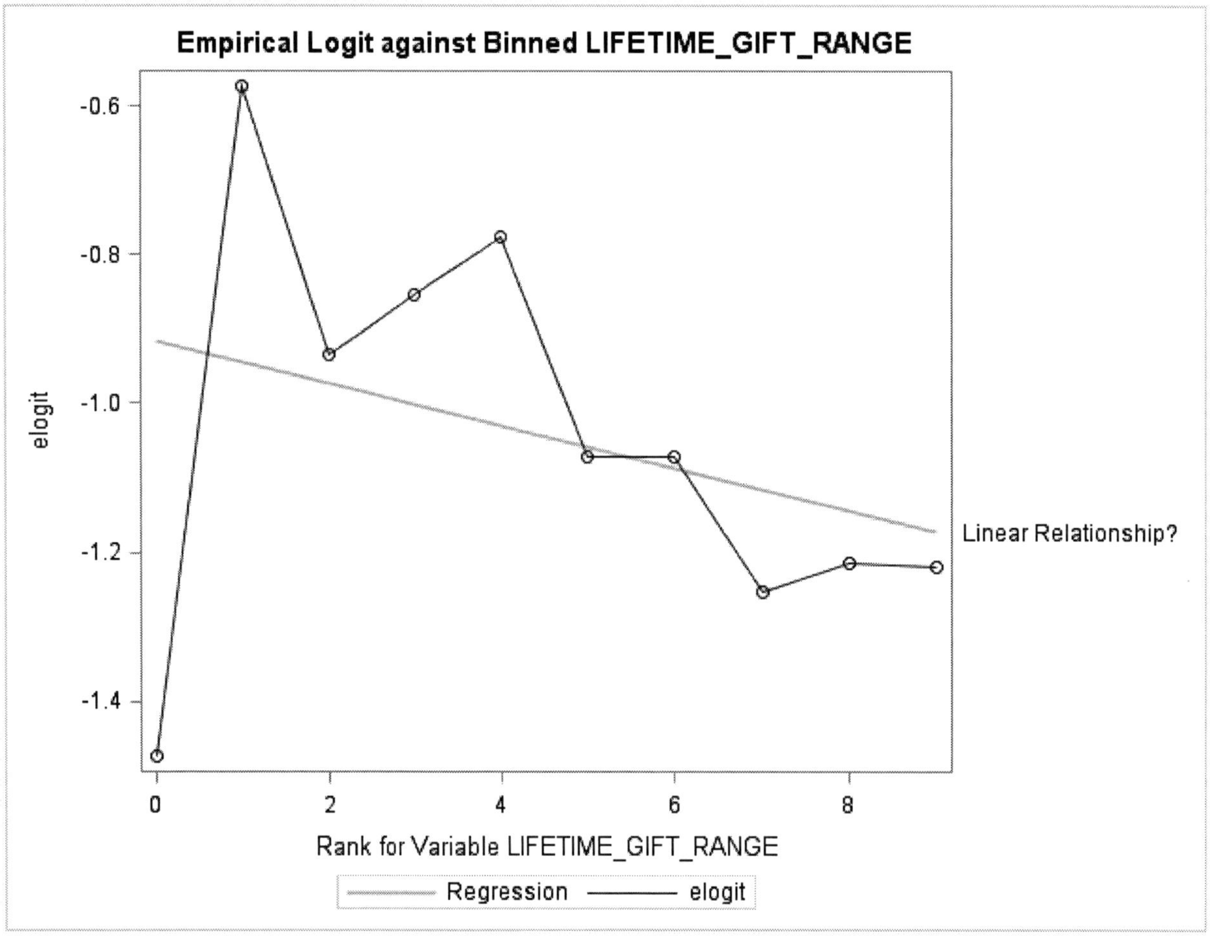

1) The relationship looks quadratic. Therefore, adding a quadratic term might be useful.

5. Compare Variable Selection Methods

a. Fit a logistic regression model to the **pva1** data set with **TARGET_B** as the target variable and the macro variable **ex_screened** as the predictor variable. Model the probability that the target variable equals 1 and use the SCORE method with the BEST=1 option.

An electronic copy of the solution program is in **pmlr03s05.sas**.

```
proc logistic data=pva1;
   model target_b(event='1')= &ex_screened / selection=score best=1;
   title "Models Selected by All Subsets Selection";
run;
```

Partial Output

Regression Models Selected by Score Criterion		
Number of Variables	Score Chi-Square	Variables Included in Model
1	271.3053	RECENT_RESPONSE_PROP
2	373.8733	LIFETIME_CARD_PROM RECENT_RESPONSE_PROP
3	425.2582	LIFETIME_CARD_PROM RECENT_RESPONSE_PROP MONTHS_SINCE_LAST_GIFT
4	471.9683	LIFETIME_CARD_PROM RECENT_RESPONSE_PROP INCOME_GROUP MONTHS_SINCE_LAST_GIFT
5	502.0768	LIFETIME_CARD_PROM PER_CAPITA_INCOME RECENT_RESPONSE_PROP MONTHS_SINCE_LAST_GIFT RECENT_AVG_GIFT_AMT
6	532.0701	LIFETIME_CARD_PROM RECENT_RESPONSE_PROP ClusCdGrp3 INCOME_GROUP MONTHS_SINCE_LAST_GIFT RECENT_AVG_GIFT_AMT
7	551.9727	LIFETIME_CARD_PROM PER_CAPITA_INCOME RECENT_RESPONSE_PROP ClusCdGrp3 INCOME_GROUP MONTHS_SINCE_LAST_GIFT RECENT_AVG_GIFT_AMT
8	568.4713	LIFETIME_CARD_PROM RECENT_RESPONSE_PROP ClusCdGrp3 INCOME_GROUP ClusCdGrp1 MONTHS_SINCE_LAST_GIFT RECENT_AVG_GIFT_AMT ClusCdGrp2
9	584.3013	LIFETIME_CARD_PROM RECENT_RESPONSE_PROP ClusCdGrp3 INCOME_GROUP STATUS_FL ClusCdGrp1 MONTHS_SINCE_LAST_GIFT RECENT_AVG_GIFT_AMT ClusCdGrp2
10	596.3164	LIFETIME_CARD_PROM RECENT_RESPONSE_PROP ClusCdGrp3 INCOME_GROUP STATUS_ES STATUS_FL ClusCdGrp1 MONTHS_SINCE_LAST_GIFT RECENT_AVG_GIFT_AMT ClusCdGrp2
11	605.5415	LIFETIME_CARD_PROM PER_CAPITA_INCOME RECENT_RESPONSE_PROP ClusCdGrp3 INCOME_GROUP STATUS_ES STATUS_FL ClusCdGrp1 MONTHS_SINCE_LAST_GIFT RECENT_AVG_GIFT_AMT ClusCdGrp2
12	613.2143	LIFETIME_CARD_PROM PER_CAPITA_INCOME RECENT_RESPONSE_PROP ClusCdGrp3 INCOME_GROUP STATUS_ES DONOR_AGE STATUS_FL ClusCdGrp1 MONTHS_SINCE_LAST_GIFT RECENT_AVG_GIFT_AMT ClusCdGrp2
13	618.0685	LIFETIME_CARD_PROM PER_CAPITA_INCOME RECENT_RESPONSE_PROP nses_ ClusCdGrp3 INCOME_GROUP STATUS_ES DONOR_AGE STATUS_FL ClusCdGrp1 MONTHS_SINCE_LAST_GIFT RECENT_AVG_GIFT_AMT ClusCdGrp2
14	621.5581	LIFETIME_CARD_PROM PER_CAPITA_INCOME RECENT_RESPONSE_PROP CARD_PROM_12 nses_ ClusCdGrp3 INCOME_GROUP STATUS_ES DONOR_AGE STATUS_FL ClusCdGrp1 MONTHS_SINCE_LAST_GIFT RECENT_AVG_GIFT_AMT ClusCdGrp2
15	624.6587	LIFETIME_CARD_PROM PER_CAPITA_INCOME RECENT_RESPONSE_PROP CARD_PROM_12 nses_ ClusCdGrp3 INCOME_GROUP STATUS_ES DONOR_AGE STATUS_FL ClusCdGrp1 MONTHS_SINCE_LAST_GIFT RECENT_AVG_GIFT_AMT ClusCdGrp2 LIFETIME_GIFT_RANGE2
16	626.7553	LIFETIME_CARD_PROM LIFETIME_MIN_GIFT_AMT PER_CAPITA_INCOME RECENT_RESPONSE_PROP CARD_PROM_12 nses_ ClusCdGrp3 INCOME_GROUP STATUS_ES DONOR_AGE STATUS_FL ClusCdGrp1 MONTHS_SINCE_LAST_GIFT RECENT_AVG_GIFT_AMT ClusCdGrp2 LIFETIME_GIFT_RANGE2
17	628.6737	LIFETIME_CARD_PROM LIFETIME_MIN_GIFT_AMT PER_CAPITA_INCOME RECENT_RESPONSE_PROP CARD_PROM_12 nses_ mi_DONOR_AGE ClusCdGrp3 INCOME_GROUP STATUS_ES DONOR_AGE STATUS_FL ClusCdGrp1 MONTHS_SINCE_LAST_GIFT RECENT_AVG_GIFT_AMT ClusCdGrp2 LIFETIME_GIFT_RANGE2
18	630.3633	LIFETIME_CARD_PROM LIFETIME_MIN_GIFT_AMT PER_CAPITA_INCOME RECENT_RESPONSE_PROP CARD_PROM_12 nses_ mi_DONOR_AGE ClusCdGrp3 INCOME_GROUP STATUS_ES DONOR_AGE STATUS_FL ClusCdGrp1 MONTHS_SINCE_LAST_GIFT IN_HOUSE RECENT_AVG_GIFT_AMT ClusCdGrp2 LIFETIME_GIFT_RANGE2
19	631.7936	LIFETIME_CARD_PROM LIFETIME_MIN_GIFT_AMT PER_CAPITA_INCOME RECENT_RESPONSE_PROP CARD_PROM_12 nses_ mi_DONOR_AGE ClusCdGrp3 nses3 INCOME_GROUP STATUS_ES DONOR_AGE STATUS_FL ClusCdGrp1 MONTHS_SINCE_LAST_GIFT IN_HOUSE RECENT_AVG_GIFT_AMT ClusCdGrp2 LIFETIME_GIFT_RANGE2
20	633.1877	LIFETIME_CARD_PROM LIFETIME_MIN_GIFT_AMT PER_CAPITA_INCOME RECENT_RESPONSE_PROP CARD_PROM_12 nses_ mi_DONOR_AGE ClusCdGrp3 nses3 INCOME_GROUP STATUS_ES DONOR_AGE STATUS_FL ClusCdGrp1 RECENT_STAR_STATUS MONTHS_SINCE_LAST_GIFT IN_HOUSE RECENT_AVG_GIFT_AMT ClusCdGrp2 LIFETIME_GIFT_RANGE2
21	633.9693	LIFETIME_CARD_PROM LIFETIME_MIN_GIFT_AMT PER_CAPITA_INCOME RECENT_RESPONSE_PROP CARD_PROM_12 nses_ mi_DONOR_AGE ClusCdGrp3 nses3 INCOME_GROUP STATUS_ES DONOR_AGE STATUS_FL ClusCdGrp1 RECENT_STAR_STATUS MONTHS_SINCE_LAST_GIFT IN_HOUSE RECENT_AVG_GIFT_AMT ClusCdGrp2 PCT_OWNER_OCCUPIED LIFETIME_GIFT_RANGE2
22	634.8284	LIFETIME_CARD_PROM LIFETIME_MIN_GIFT_AMT PER_CAPITA_INCOME RECENT_RESPONSE_PROP CARD_PROM_12 nses_ mi_DONOR_AGE ClusCdGrp3 nses3 INCOME_GROUP STATUS_ES nurbt DONOR_AGE STATUS_FL ClusCdGrp1 RECENT_STAR_STATUS MONTHS_SINCE_LAST_GIFT IN_HOUSE RECENT_AVG_GIFT_AMT ClusCdGrp2 PCT_OWNER_OCCUPIED LIFETIME_GIFT_RANGE2
23	635.3926	LIFETIME_CARD_PROM LIFETIME_MIN_GIFT_AMT PER_CAPITA_INCOME RECENT_RESPONSE_PROP CARD_PROM_12 nses_ mi_DONOR_AGE ClusCdGrp3 PCT_VIETNAM_VETERANS nses3 INCOME_GROUP STATUS_ES nurbt DONOR_AGE STATUS_FL ClusCdGrp1 RECENT_STAR_STATUS MONTHS_SINCE_LAST_GIFT IN_HOUSE RECENT_AVG_GIFT_AMT ClusCdGrp2 PCT_OWNER_OCCUPIED LIFETIME_GIFT_RANGE2

24	635.8319	LIFETIME_CARD_PROM LIFETIME_MIN_GIFT_AMT PER_CAPITA_INCOME RECENT_RESPONSE_PROP CARD_PROM_12 nses_mi_DONOR_AGE ClusCdGrp3 PCT_VIETNAM_VETERANS nses3 INCOME_GROUP STATUS_ES nurbt DONOR_AGE STATUS_FL ClusCdGrp1 RECENT_STAR_STATUS MONTHS_SINCE_LAST_GIFT IN_HOUSE RECENT_AVG_GIFT_AMT home01 ClusCdGrp2 PCT_OWNER_OCCUPIED LIFETIME_GIFT_RANGE2
25	636.1834	LIFETIME_CARD_PROM LIFETIME_MIN_GIFT_AMT PER_CAPITA_INCOME RECENT_RESPONSE_PROP CARD_PROM_12 nses_mi_DONOR_AGE ClusCdGrp3 PCT_VIETNAM_VETERANS LIFETIME_GIFT_RANGE nses3 INCOME_GROUP STATUS_ES nurbt DONOR_AGE STATUS_FL ClusCdGrp1 RECENT_STAR_STATUS MONTHS_SINCE_LAST_GIFT IN_HOUSE RECENT_AVG_GIFT_AMT home01 ClusCdGrp2 PCT_OWNER_OCCUPIED LIFETIME_GIFT_RANGE2
26	636.2983	LIFETIME_CARD_PROM LIFETIME_MIN_GIFT_AMT PER_CAPITA_INCOME RECENT_RESPONSE_PROP CARD_PROM_12 nses_mi_DONOR_AGE ClusCdGrp3 PCT_VIETNAM_VETERANS LIFETIME_GIFT_RANGE nses3 INCOME_GROUP STATUS_ES nurbt DONOR_AGE STATUS_FL MOR_HIT_RATE ClusCdGrp1 RECENT_STAR_STATUS MONTHS_SINCE_LAST_GIFT IN_HOUSE RECENT_AVG_GIFT_AMT home01 ClusCdGrp2 PCT_OWNER_OCCUPIED LIFETIME_GIFT_RANGE2
27	636.3980	LIFETIME_CARD_PROM LIFETIME_MIN_GIFT_AMT PER_CAPITA_INCOME RECENT_RESPONSE_PROP CARD_PROM_12 nses_mi_DONOR_AGE ClusCdGrp3 PCT_VIETNAM_VETERANS LIFETIME_GIFT_RANGE nses3 INCOME_GROUP STATUS_ES nurbt DONOR_AGE STATUS_FL MOR_HIT_RATE ClusCdGrp1 nurbs RECENT_STAR_STATUS MONTHS_SINCE_LAST_GIFT IN_HOUSE RECENT_AVG_GIFT_AMT home01 ClusCdGrp2 PCT_OWNER_OCCUPIED LIFETIME_GIFT_RANGE2
28	636.4237	LIFETIME_CARD_PROM LIFETIME_MIN_GIFT_AMT PER_CAPITA_INCOME RECENT_RESPONSE_PROP CARD_PROM_12 nses_mi_DONOR_AGE ClusCdGrp3 PCT_VIETNAM_VETERANS LIFETIME_GIFT_RANGE nses3 INCOME_GROUP STATUS_ES nurbt DONOR_AGE STATUS_FL MOR_HIT_RATE ClusCdGrp1 nurbr nurbs RECENT_STAR_STATUS MONTHS_SINCE_LAST_GIFT IN_HOUSE RECENT_AVG_GIFT_AMT home01 ClusCdGrp2 PCT_OWNER_OCCUPIED LIFETIME_GIFT_RANGE2
29	636.4243	LIFETIME_CARD_PROM LIFETIME_MIN_GIFT_AMT PER_CAPITA_INCOME RECENT_RESPONSE_PROP CARD_PROM_12 nses_mi_DONOR_AGE ClusCdGrp3 PCT_VIETNAM_VETERANS LIFETIME_GIFT_RANGE nses3 PCT_MALE_VETERANS INCOME_GROUP STATUS_ES nurbt DONOR_AGE STATUS_FL MOR_HIT_RATE ClusCdGrp1 nurbr nurbs RECENT_STAR_STATUS MONTHS_SINCE_LAST_GIFT IN_HOUSE RECENT_AVG_GIFT_AMT home01 ClusCdGrp2 PCT_OWNER_OCCUPIED LIFETIME_GIFT_RANGE2
30	636.4247	LIFETIME_CARD_PROM LIFETIME_MIN_GIFT_AMT PER_CAPITA_INCOME RECENT_RESPONSE_PROP CARD_PROM_12 nses_mi_DONOR_AGE ClusCdGrp3 PCT_VIETNAM_VETERANS LIFETIME_GIFT_RANGE nses3 PCT_MALE_VETERANS INCOME_GROUP STATUS_ES nurbu nurbt DONOR_AGE STATUS_FL MOR_HIT_RATE ClusCdGrp1 nurbr nurbs RECENT_STAR_STATUS MONTHS_SINCE_LAST_GIFT IN_HOUSE RECENT_AVG_GIFT_AMT home01 ClusCdGrp2 PCT_OWNER_OCCUPIED LIFETIME_GIFT_RANGE2
31	636.4248	LIFETIME_CARD_PROM LIFETIME_MIN_GIFT_AMT PER_CAPITA_INCOME RECENT_RESPONSE_PROP CARD_PROM_12 nses_mi_DONOR_AGE ClusCdGrp3 PCT_VIETNAM_VETERANS LIFETIME_GIFT_RANGE nses3 PCT_MALE_VETERANS INCOME_GROUP STATUS_ES nurbu nurbt DONOR_AGE STATUS_FL MOR_HIT_RATE ClusCdGrp1 nurbr nurbs RECENT_STAR_STATUS MONTHS_SINCE_LAST_GIFT IN_HOUSE WEALTH_RATING RECENT_AVG_GIFT_AMT home01 ClusCdGrp2 PCT_OWNER_OCCUPIED LIFETIME_GIFT_RANGE2

1) The best 1 variable model is **RECENT_RESPONSE_PROP**.

2) The best 2 variable model is **LIFETIME_CARD_PROM** and **RECENT_RESPONSE_PROP**.

b. Use the **fitstat** macro to determine which model is the best according to the BIC criterion. Create a macro variable for the variable names in the final model.

```
ods html close;
ods output bestsubsets=score;
proc logistic data=pva1;
   model target_b(event='1')= &ex_screened
         / selection=score best=1;
run;

proc sql noprint;
  select variablesinmodel into :exinputs1 - :exinputs999
  from score;
  select NumberOfVariables into :exic1 - :exic999
  from score;
quit;

%let lastindx = &SQLOBS;

%macro fitstat( );
```

```
%do model_indx=1 %to &lastindx;

%let ex_im=&&exinputs&model_indx;
%let ex_ic=&&exic&model_indx;

ods output scorefitstat=ex_stat&ex_ic;
proc logistic data=pva1;
  model target_b(event='1')=&ex_im;
  score data=pva1 out=scored fitstat
        priorevent=&ex_pi1;
run;

proc datasets
   library=work
   nodetails
   nolist;
   delete scored;
run;
quit;

%end;
%mend fitstat;

%fitstat( );

data exmodelfit;
   set ex_stat1 - ex_stat&lastindx;
   model = _n_;
run;

proc sort data = exmodelfit;
   by bic;
run;

ods html;
proc print data=exmodelfit;
   var model auc aic bic misclass adjrsquare brierscore;
   title "Fit Statistics from Models selected from Best-Subsets";
run;
```

Fit Statistics from Models selected from Best-Subsets

Obs	model	AUC	AIC	BIC	MisClass	AdjRSquare	BrierScore
1	11	0.613459	29787.39	29881.85	0.2500	0.045528	0.223913
2	12	0.614129	29779.63	29881.96	0.2500	0.046117	0.223865
3	10	0.612642	29796.96	29883.55	0.2500	0.044842	0.223965
4	13	0.614278	29776.01	29886.21	0.2500	0.046439	0.223829
5	9	0.611889	29808.51	29887.23	0.2500	0.044019	0.22403

6	14	0.614741	29774.14	29892.21	0.2500	0.04666	0.223818
7	15	0.614917	29771.41	29897.36	0.2499	0.046893	0.223777
8	8	0.610759	29827.41	29898.26	0.2500	0.042674	0.224103
9	16	0.614846	29771.26	29905.07	0.2499	0.047001	0.223758
10	7	0.609289	29845.66	29908.63	0.2500	0.041448	0.224225
11	17	0.615009	29770.77	29912.46	0.2499	0.047154	0.223749
12	18	0.615081	29771.29	29920.85	0.2499	0.047229	0.223741
13	6	0.607519	29868.57	29923.67	0.2500	0.039959	0.224337
14	19	0.615211	29771.33	29928.76	0.2499	0.047351	0.223733
15	20	0.615421	29771.54	29936.84	0.2499	0.047459	0.223721
16	21	0.615489	29772.57	29945.74	0.2499	0.047516	0.223717
17	5	0.603405	29907.15	29954.38	0.2500	0.037422	0.224509
18	22	0.61555	29773.52	29954.57	0.2499	0.047577	0.22371
19	23	0.615649	29774.78	29963.7	0.2499	0.047622	0.223707
20	24	0.615739	29776.2	29972.99	0.2499	0.04766	0.223705
21	25	0.61581	29777.42	29982.08	0.2499	0.047702	0.2237
22	4	0.599826	29946.22	29985.58	0.2500	0.034807	0.224695
23	26	0.615827	29779.29	29991.82	0.2499	0.04771	0.2237
24	27	0.615862	29781.13	30001.53	0.2499	0.047721	0.223699
25	28	0.615867	29783.1	30011.38	0.2499	0.047722	0.223699
26	29	0.615868	29785.1	30021.25	0.2499	0.047722	0.223699
27	30	0.615872	29787.1	30031.12	0.2499	0.047722	0.223699
28	3	0.592942	30002.67	30034.15	0.2500	0.031283	0.224959
29	31	0.615856	29789.09	30040.98	0.2499	0.047724	0.2237
30	2	0.590185	30065.55	30089.16	0.2500	0.027213	0.225339
31	1	0.575721	30188.17	30203.91	0.2500	0.01968	0.225954

```
proc sql;
   select VariablesInModel into :ex_selected
   from score
   where numberofvariables=11;
quit;
```

Variables Included in Model
LIFETIME_CARD_PROM PER_CAPITA_INCOME RECENT_RESPONSE_PROP ClusCdGrp3 INCOME_GROUP STATUS_ES STATUS_FL ClusCdGrp1 MONTHS_SINCE_LAST_GIFT RECENT_AVG_GIFT_AMT ClusCdGrp2

1) The variables in the final model are **LIFETIME_CARD_PROM**, **PER_CAPITA_INCOME**, **RECENT_RESPONSE_PROP**, **ClusCdGrp3**, **INCOME_GROUP**, **STATUS_ES**, **STATUS_FL**, **ClusCdGrp1**, **MONTHS_SINCE_LAST_GIFT**, **RECENT_AVG_GIFT_AMT**, and **ClusCdGrp2**.

c. Fit the final model in PROC LOGISTIC. Use the macro variable created for the variable names and use the NAMELEN=32 option in the PROC LOGISTIC statement.

```
proc logistic data=pva1 namelen=32;
   model target_b(event='1') = &ex_selected;
run;
```

Model Information	
Data Set	WORK.PVA1
Response Variable	TARGET_B
Number of Response Levels	2
Model	binary logit
Optimization Technique	Fisher's scoring

Number of Observations Read	19372
Number of Observations Used	19372

Response Profile

Ordered Value	TARGET_B	Total Frequency
1	0	14529
2	1	4843

Probability modeled is TARGET_B=1.

Model Convergence Status
Convergence criterion (GCONV=1E-8) satisfied.

Model Fit Statistics

Criterion	Intercept Only	Intercept and Covariates
AIC	21789.113	21206.225
SC	21796.984	21300.684
-2 Log L	21787.113	21182.225

Testing Global Null Hypothesis: BETA=0			
Test	Chi-Square	DF	Pr > ChiSq
Likelihood Ratio	604.8879	11	<.0001
Score	605.5415	11	<.0001
Wald	581.9543	11	<.0001

Analysis of Maximum Likelihood Estimates					
Parameter	DF	Estimate	Standard Error	Wald Chi-Square	Pr > ChiSq
Intercept	1	-1.2019	0.1256	91.5915	<.0001
LIFETIME_CARD_PROM	1	0.0112	0.00233	23.1304	<.0001
PER_CAPITA_INCOME	1	6.279E-6	2.045E-6	9.4322	0.0021
RECENT_RESPONSE_PROP	1	1.5552	0.1700	83.7123	<.0001
ClusCdGrp3	1	-0.2733	0.0680	16.1506	<.0001
INCOME_GROUP	1	0.0531	0.0110	23.4985	<.0001
STATUS_ES	1	0.1519	0.0454	11.2127	0.0008
STATUS_FL	1	-0.3088	0.0753	16.8339	<.0001
ClusCdGrp1	1	0.2617	0.0624	17.5941	<.0001
MONTHS_SINCE_LAST_GIFT	1	-0.0347	0.00433	64.1513	<.0001
RECENT_AVG_GIFT_AMT	1	-0.0109	0.00209	27.4563	<.0001
ClusCdGrp2	1	0.1596	0.0403	15.6942	<.0001

Odds Ratio Estimates			
Effect	Point Estimate	95% Wald Confidence Limits	
LIFETIME_CARD_PROM	1.011	1.007	1.016
PER_CAPITA_INCOME	1.000	1.000	1.000
RECENT_RESPONSE_PROP	4.736	3.394	6.608
ClusCdGrp3	0.761	0.666	0.869
INCOME_GROUP	1.055	1.032	1.077
STATUS_ES	1.164	1.065	1.272
STATUS_FL	0.734	0.634	0.851
ClusCdGrp1	1.299	1.150	1.468
MONTHS_SINCE_LAST_GIFT	0.966	0.958	0.974
RECENT_AVG_GIFT_AMT	0.989	0.985	0.993
ClusCdGrp2	1.173	1.084	1.269

Association of Predicted Probabilities and Observed Responses			
Percent Concordant	61.0	Somers' D	0.227
Percent Discordant	38.3	Gamma	0.229
Percent Tied	0.7	Tau-a	0.085
Pairs	70363947	c	0.613

1) The c statistic for the final model is 0.613.

Solutions to Student Activities (Polls/Quizzes)

3.01 Multiple Choice Poll – Correct Answer

Which of the following statements is false regarding missing values in predictive modeling applications?

a. In complete case analysis, there can be an enormous loss of data when the missing values are spread across many variables.

b. Observations with missing values will not be scored in PROC LOGISTIC.

c. Missing indicator variables can be used to capture the relationship between the target variable and missing inputs.

(d.) The missing completely at random assumption is valid in most predictive modeling applications.

11

3.02 Multiple Choice Poll – Correct Answer

For the cell **GRP_RESP**=0 and **GRP_AMT**=0, what was the missing value for **DONOR_AGE** replaced with?

a. 57

(b.) 64

c. 58

d. 65

16

3.03 Multiple Choice Poll – Correct Answer

Which of the following statements is false regarding Greenacre's method for collapsing levels of contingency tables?

a. The levels are hierarchically clustered based on the reduction in the chi-squared test of association.
b. Levels with similar marginal response rates are merged.
c. The method accounts for the sample size in each level.
d. The method is appropriate for any categorical input. (circled)

28

3.04 Multiple Choice Poll – Correct Answer

What is the optimum number of clusters for the cluster_code variable?

a. 3
b. 4
c. 5 (circled)
d. 6

32

3.06 Multiple Choice Poll – Correct Answer

How many clusters were in the final solution?

a. 25
b. 30
c. 32
d. 35

49

3.10 Multiple Choice Poll – Correct Answer

Which of the following statements is true regarding best subsets selection?

a. The models are ranked by the likelihood ratio chi-square.
b. The method uses a forward selection to find the best model.
c. The method is relatively efficient for a small number of variables (for example, less than 50).
d. None of the above.

72

3.11 Multiple Choice Poll – Correct Answer

What is the c statistic for the final model?

a. .610

b. .612

c. .613

d. .615

76

Chapter 4 Measuring Classifier Performance

4.1 Honest Assessment

Objectives

- Explain the optimism principle and the rationale for data splitting.
- Split the data into the training and validation data sets.
- Prepare the input variables and fit a logistic regression model on the training data set.

3

The Optimism Principle

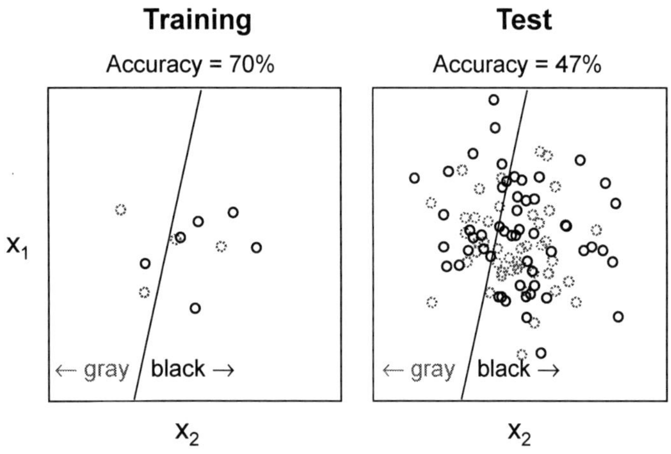

4

Evaluating the performance of a classifier on the same data used to train the classifier usually leads to an optimistically biased assessment.

For example, the above classifier was fit (or more properly *overfit*) to a 10-case data set. It correctly classified 70% of the cases. However, when the same classification rule was applied to 100 new cases from the same distribution, only 47% were correctly classified. This is called *overfitting*. The model was overly sensitive to peculiarities of the particular training data, in addition to true features of their joint distribution.

The more flexible the underlying model and the less plentiful the data, the more overfitting becomes a problem. When a relatively inflexible model like (linear) logistic regression is fitted to massive amounts of data, overfitting might not be a problem (Hand 1997). However, the chance of overfitting is increased by variable selection methods and supervised input preparation (such as collapsing levels of nominal variables based on associations with the target). It is prudent to assume that overfitting is a problem until proven otherwise.

Large differences between the performance on the training and test data sets usually indicate overfitting.

Data Splitting

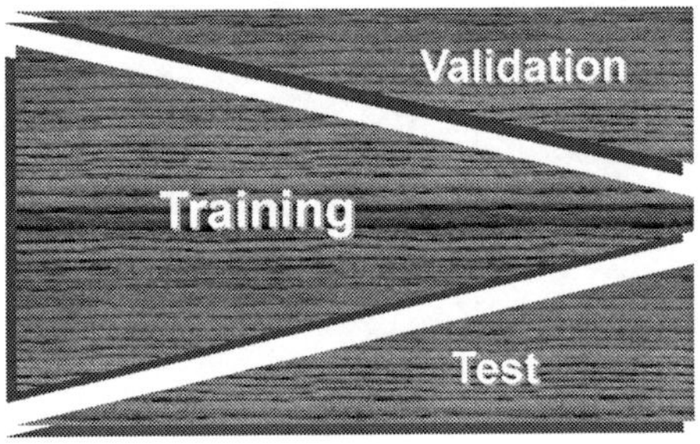

- Comparison
- Selection
- Tuning

- Final Assessment

5

The simplest strategy for correcting the optimism bias is to hold out a portion of the development data for assessment. The model is fit to the remainder (*training data set*) and performance is evaluated on the holdout portion (*test data set*). Usually from one-fourth to one-half of the development data is used as a test set (Picard and Berk 1990). After assessment, it is common practice to refit the final model on the entire undivided data set.

When the holdout data are used for comparing, selecting, and tuning models and the chosen model is assessed on the same data set that was used for comparison, then the optimism principle again applies. In this situation, the holdout sample is more correctly called a *validation data set*, not a test set. The test set is used for a final assessment of a fully specified classifier (Ripley 1996). If model tuning and a final assessment are both needed, then the data should be split three ways into training, validation, and test sets. In some applications, the test set is gathered from a different time or location.

Other Approaches

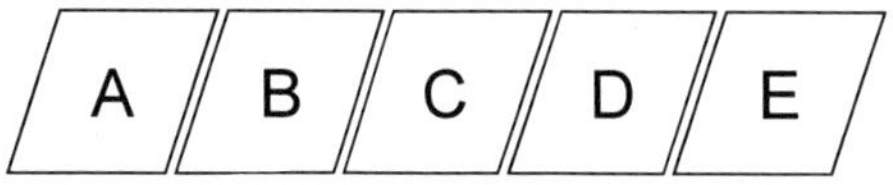

	Train	Validate
1)	BCDE	A
2)	ACDE	B
3)	ABDE	C
4)	ABCE	D
5)	ABCD	E

6

Data splitting is a simple but costly technique. When data are scarce, it is inefficient to use only a portion for training. Furthermore, when the test set is small, the performance measures might be unreliable because of high variability. For small and moderate data sets, v-fold cross-validation (Breiman et al. 1984; Ripley 1996; Hand 1997) is a better strategy. In 5-fold cross-validation, for example, the data would be split into five equal sets. The entire modeling process would be redone on each four-fifths of the data using the remaining one-fifth for assessment. The five assessments would then be averaged. In this way, all the data are used for both training and assessment.

Another approach that is frugal with the data is to assess the model on the same data set that was used for training but to penalize the assessment for optimism (Ripley 1996). The appropriate penalty can be determined theoretically or by using computationally intensive methods such as the bootstrap.

4.01 Poll

Do you have to deal with small data sets where data splitting is not feasible in your work as a predictive modeler?

- ❍ Yes
- ❍ No

7

Honest Model Assessment

Example: Split the data into training and validation data sets. Redo the input preparation and the model fitting on the training data set.

The validation data will be used for assessment. Consequently, it needs to be treated as if it were truly new data where the target variable value is unknown. The results of the analysis on the training data need to be applied to the validation data, not recalculated.

Several input-preparation steps can be done before the data are split. Creating missing indicator variables should be done on the full development data, because the results will not change.

```
/* pmlr04d01.sas */
%let pi1=0.02;

%let inputs=ACCTAGE DDA DDABAL DEP DEPAMT CASHBK
            CHECKS DIRDEP NSF NSFAMT PHONE TELLER
            SAV SAVBAL ATM ATMAMT POS POSAMT CD
            CDBAL IRA IRABAL LOC LOCBAL INV
            INVBAL ILS ILSBAL MM MMBAL MMCRED MTG
            MTGBAL CC CCBAL CCPURC SDB INCOME
            HMOWN LORES HMVAL AGE CRSCORE MOVED
            INAREA;

data develop(drop=i);
   set pmlr.develop;
   /* name the missing indicator variables */
   array mi{*} MIAcctAg MIPhone MIPOS MIPOSAmt
               MIInv MIInvBal MICC MICCBal
               MICCPurc MIIncome MIHMOwn MILORes
               MIHMVal MIAge MICRScor;
   /* select variables with missing values */
   array x{*} acctage phone pos posamt
              inv invbal cc ccbal
              ccpurc income hmown lores
              hmval age crscore;
   do i=1 to dim(mi);
      mi{i}=(x{i}=.);
   end;
run;
```

The SURVEYSELECT procedure can be used to select the records for the training and validation data sets. To create a stratified sample, the data must be sorted by the stratum variable. The SAMPRATE= option specifies what proportion of the **develop** data set should be selected. The default behavior of PROC SURVEYSELECT is to output the sample, not the entire data set, so the OUTALL option can be used to return the initial data set augmented by a flag to indicate selection in the sample. Of course, this flag indicates membership in the training and validation data sets in this context. PROC FREQ verifies the stratification. The SEED= option enables the user to control what series of pseudo-random numbers is generated to do the partitioning. A particular number, greater than zero, will produce the same split each time PROC SURVEYSELECT was run. If the seed were zero, then the data would be split differently each time the procedure was run.

```
proc sort data=develop out=develop;
   by ins;
run;

proc surveyselect noprint
                  data=develop
                  samprate=.6667
                  out=develop
                  seed=44444
                  outall;
   strata ins;
run;

proc freq data=develop;
   tables ins*selected;
run;
```

Notice that the proportion of responders is the same for both levels of selected, and the data have been partitioned into two-thirds for training and one-third for validation.

Frequency Percent Row Pct Col Pct	Table of Ins by Selected		
	Selected(Selection Indicator)		
Ins	0	1	Total
0	7028	14061	21089
	21.78	43.58	65.36
	33.33	66.67	
	65.36	65.36	
1	3724	7451	11175
	11.54	23.09	34.64
	33.32	66.68	
	34.64	34.64	
Total	10752	21512	32264
	33.33	66.67	100.00

The next DATA step creates the two data sets, **train** and **valid**. All other input-preparation steps are done after the split, on the training data only, because the validation data are treated as if they were truly new cases. This is imperative for supervised methods such as collapsing the levels of **Branch** based on its association with **Ins**. It could be argued that unsupervised methods, such as median imputation, could be done on **develop** because they do not involve **Ins**. This example presents a cautious approach and does not involve the validation data at all.

This conservative approach also permits the comparison of models based on different imputation schemes.

```
data train valid;
   set develop;
   if selected then output train;
   else output valid;
run;
```

PROC STDIZE imputes missing values. Here, as before, the median is used.

```
proc stdize data=train
            reponly
            method=median
            out=train1;
   var &inputs;
run;
```

PROC CLUSTER is used to perform Greenacre's correspondence analysis; this is the method used to reduce the cardinality of the nominal input **Branch**.

```
proc means data=train1 noprint nway;
   class branch;
   var ins;
   output out=level mean=prop;
run;

ods output clusterhistory=cluster;

proc cluster data=level method=ward outtree=fortree
     plots=(dendrogram(vertical height=rsq));
   freq _freq_;
   var prop;
   id branch;
run;
```

Cluster History						
Number of Clusters	Clusters Joined		Freq	Semipartial R-Square	R-Square	Tie
18	B17	B6	1497	0.0000	1.00	
17	B10	B19	368	0.0000	1.00	
16	B3	B8	2804	0.0000	1.00	
15	B18	B5	2212	0.0000	1.00	
14	CL16	B9	3162	0.0000	1.00	
13	B11	B7	1106	0.0000	1.00	
12	B12	CL18	1864	0.0001	1.00	
11	B13	CL14	3523	0.0001	1.00	
10	B1	B4	5629	0.0002	1.00	
9	CL11	CL15	5735	0.0004	.999	
8	CL13	B2	4672	0.0007	.999	
7	CL10	CL12	7493	0.0018	.997	
6	CL17	CL9	6103	0.0038	.993	
5	B15	B16	2517	0.0092	.984	
4	CL7	CL6	13596	0.0107	.973	
3	B14	CL5	3244	0.0231	.950	
2	CL4	CL8	18268	0.1408	.809	
1	CL2	CL3	21512	0.8091	.000	

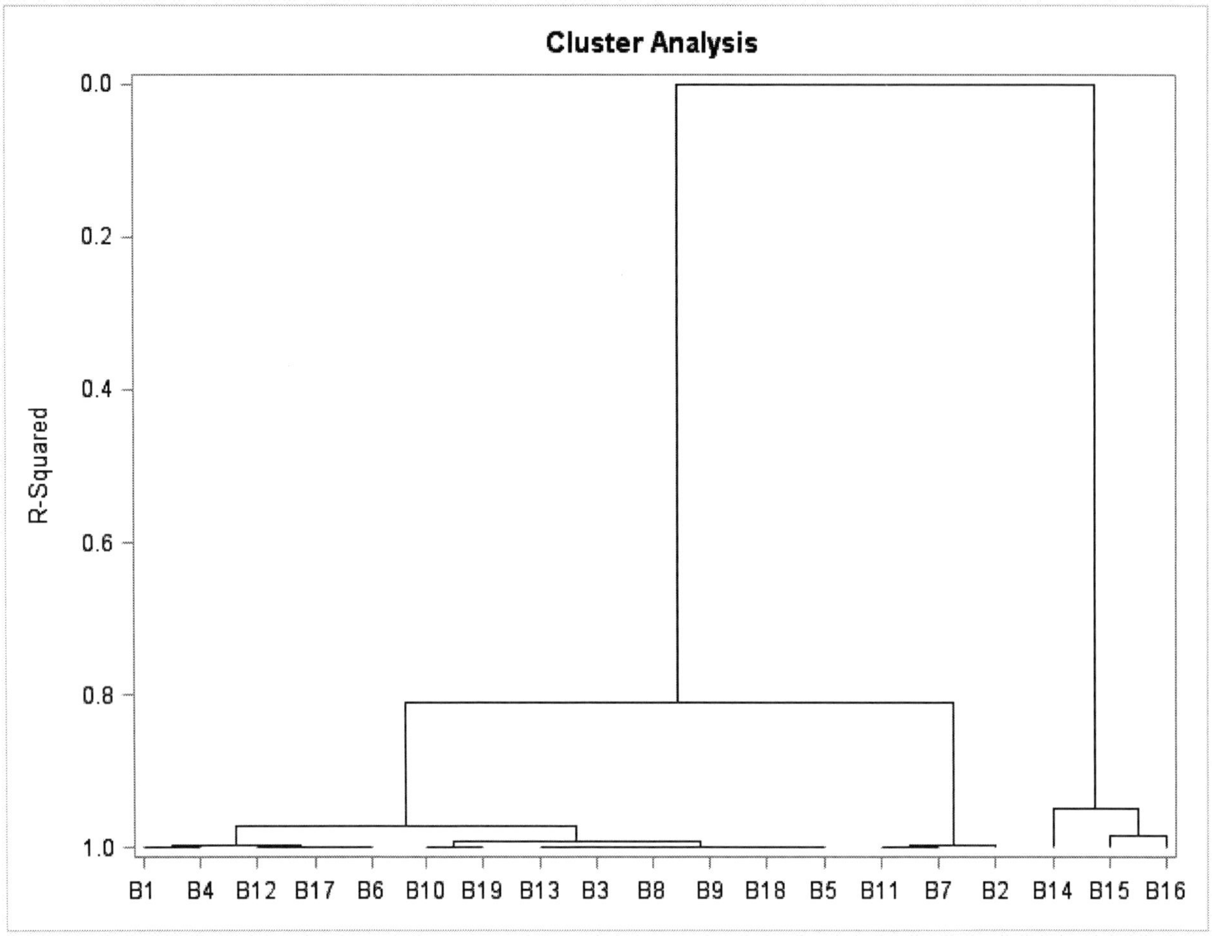


```
proc freq data=train1 noprint;
   tables branch*ins / chisq;
   output out=chi(keep=_pchi_) chisq;
run;

data cutoff;
   if _n_ = 1 then set chi;
   set cluster;
   chisquare=_pchi_*rsquared;
   degfree=numberofclusters-1;
   logpvalue=logsdf('CHISQ',chisquare,degfree);
run;

proc sgplot data=cutoff;
   scatter y=logpvalue x=numberofclusters
          / markerattrs=(color=blue symbol=circlefilled);
   xaxis label="Number of Clusters";
   yaxis label="Log of P-Value" min=-120 max=-90;
   title "Plot of the Log of the P-Value by Number of Clusters";
run;
```

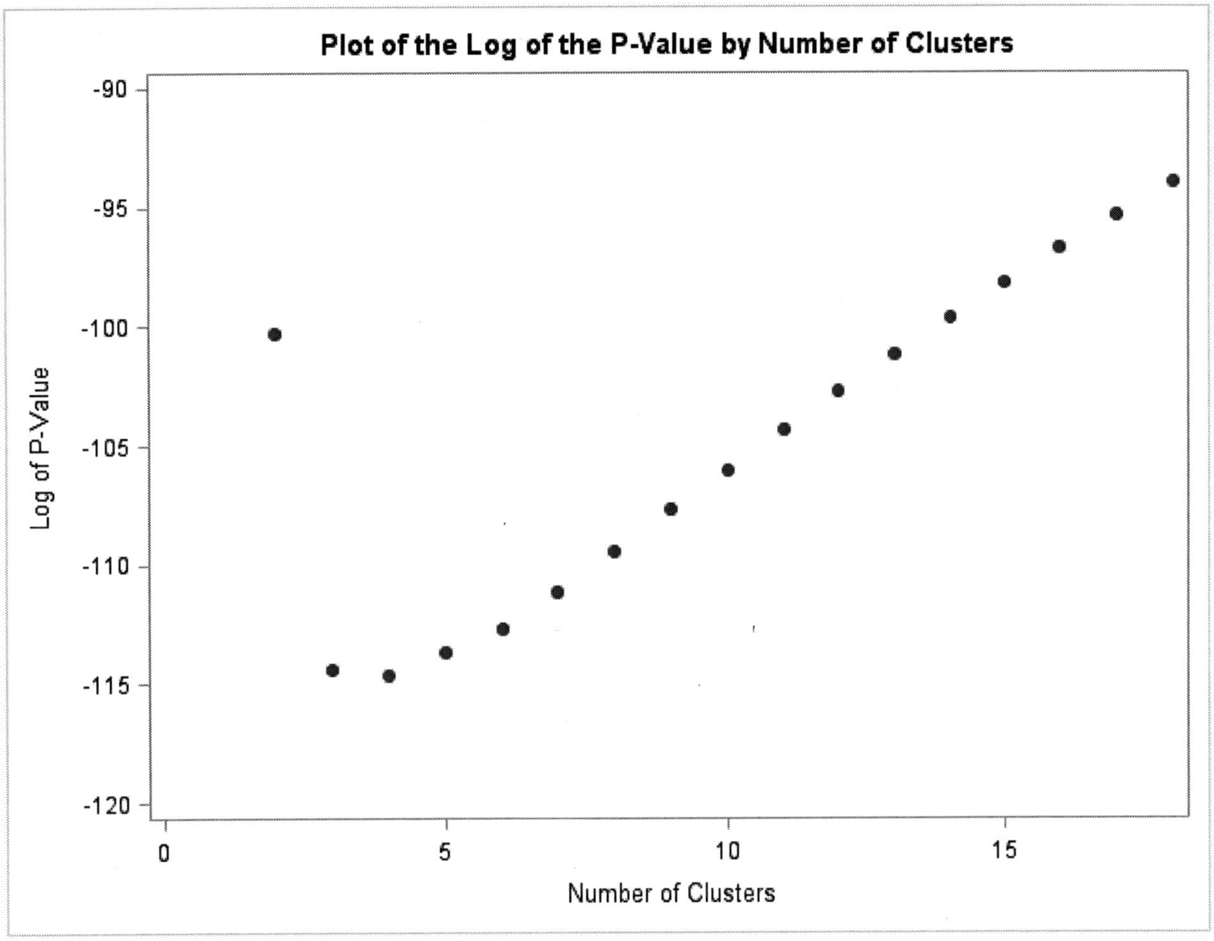

A macro variable is created using PROC SQL that contains the number of clusters associated with the smallest *p*-value. PROC TREE then creates a data set containing the information about that cluster solution.

```
proc sql;
   select NumberOfClusters into :ncl
   from cutoff
   having logpvalue=min(logpvalue);
quit;
```

Number of Clusters
4

```
ods html close;
proc tree data=fortree nclusters=&ncl out=clus;
   id branch;
run;
ods html;
```

```
proc sort data=clus;
   by clusname;
run;

title;
proc print data=clus;
   by clusname;
   id clusname;
run;
```

CLUSNAME	Branch	CLUSTER
B14	B14	4

CLUSNAME	Branch	CLUSTER
CL4	B17	1
	B6	1
	B10	1
	B19	1
	B3	1
	B8	1
	B18	1
	B5	1
	B9	1
	B12	1
	B13	1
	B1	1
	B4	1

CLUSNAME	Branch	CLUSTER
CL5	B15	3
	B16	3

CLUSNAME	Branch	CLUSTER
CL8	B11	2
	B7	2
	B2	2

Three dummy variables are created, and the cluster with the response rate closest to ρ_1 is made the reference level (this is the cluster consisting of branches B11, B7, and B2).

```
data train1;
   set train1;
   brclus1=(branch='B14');
   brclus2=(branch in ('B12','B5','B8',
                       'B3','B18','B19','B17',
                       'B4','B6','B10','B9',
                       'B1','B13'));
   brclus3=(branch in ('B15','B16'));
run;
```

PROC VARCLUS is used to group correlated inputs with one another. This allows variable reduction based on redundancy within the inputs.

```
ods html close;
ods output clusterquality=summary
           rsquare=clusters;

proc varclus data=train1
             maxeigen=.7
             short
             hi;
   var &inputs brclus1-brclus3 miacctag
       miphone mipos miposamt miinv
       miinvbal micc miccbal miccpurc
       miincome mihmown milores mihmval
       miage micrscor;
run;
ods listing;

data _null_;
   set summary;
   call symput('nvar',compress(NumberOfClusters));
run;

proc print data=clusters noobs;
   where NumberOfClusters=&nvar;
   var Cluster Variable RSquareRatio VariableLabel;
run;
```

Cluster	Variable	1-R**2 Ratio	Variable Label
Cluster 1	MIPhone	0.0000	
	MIPOS	0.0000	
	MIPOSAmt	0.0000	
	MIInv	0.0000	
	MIInvBal	0.0000	
	MICC	0.0000	
	MICCBal	0.0000	
	MICCPurc	0.0000	
Cluster 2	MIIncome	0.0074	
	MIHMOwn	0.0422	
	MILORes	0.0074	
	MIHMVal	0.0074	
	MIAge	0.0849	
Cluster 3	Teller	0.0000	Teller Visits
Cluster 4	MM	0.0890	Money Market
	MMBal	0.1053	Money Market Balance
	MMCred	0.4513	Money Market Credits
Cluster 5	Income	0.1626	Income
	HMVal	0.2372	Home Value
Cluster 6	ILS	0.0041	Installment Loan
	ILSBal	0.0041	Loan Balance
Cluster 7	LOC	0.2802	Line of Credit
	LOCBal	0.2974	Line of Credit Balance
Cluster 8	POS	0.0864	Number Point of Sale
	POSAmt	0.0858	Amount Point of Sale
Cluster 9	NSF	0.2494	Number Insufficient Fund
	NSFAmt	0.2464	Amount NSF
Cluster 10	CD	0.2875	Certificate of Deposit
	CDBal	0.3037	CD Balance

Cluster 11	Age	0.0000	Age
Cluster 12	CC	0.3523	Credit Card
	CCPurc	0.3321	Credit Card Purchases
Cluster 13	ATMAmt	0.0000	ATM Withdrawal Amount
Cluster 14	brclus2	0.2961	
	brclus3	0.3480	
Cluster 15	InvBal	0.0000	Investment Balance
Cluster 16	DDA	0.4446	Checking Account
	Dep	0.2571	Checking Deposits
	Checks	0.4117	Number of Checks
Cluster 17	CashBk	0.0000	Number Cash Back
Cluster 18	Moved	0.0000	Recent Address Change
Cluster 19	IRA	0.0000	Retirement Account
Cluster 20	CRScore	0.0000	Credit Score
Cluster 21	MIAcctAg	0.0000	
Cluster 22	IRABal	0.0000	IRA Balance
Cluster 23	MICRScor	0.0000	
Cluster 24	MTGBal	0.0000	Mortgage Balance
Cluster 25	AcctAge	0.0000	Age of Oldest Account
Cluster 26	SavBal	0.0000	Saving Balance
Cluster 27	DDABal	0.0000	Checking Balance
Cluster 28	SDB	0.0000	Safety Deposit Box
Cluster 29	InArea	0.0000	Local Address
Cluster 30	Sav	0.0000	Saving Account
Cluster 31	Phone	0.0000	Number Telephone Banking
Cluster 32	CCBal	0.0000	Credit Card Balance
Cluster 33	Inv	0.0000	Investment
Cluster 34	MTG	0.0000	Mortgage
Cluster 35	HMOwn	0.0000	Owns Home

Cluster 36	DepAmt	0.0000	Amount Deposited
Cluster 37	DirDep	0.0000	Direct Deposit
Cluster 38	ATM	0.0000	ATM
Cluster 39	brclus1	0.0000	
Cluster 40	LORes	0.0000	Length of Residence

A total of 40 clusters are formed.

A macro variable **reduced** is created with the names of the selected cluster representatives.

```
%let reduced=
MIPhone MIIncome Teller MM
Income ILS LOC POSAmt
NSFAmt CD LORes CCPurc
ATMAmt brclus2 Inv Dep
CashBk Moved IRA CRScore
MIAcctAg IRABal MICRScor MTGBal
AcctAge SavBal DDABal SDB
InArea Sav Phone CCBal
InvBal MTG HMOwn DepAmt
DirDep ATM brclus1 Age;
```

Using correlation coefficients, the list of potential inputs can be further screened. Recall that the purpose of this step is to eliminate poor performers, ***not*** select the top inputs.

```
ods html close;
ods output spearmancorr=spearman
           hoeffdingcorr=hoeffding;

proc corr data=train1 spearman hoeffding rank;
   var &reduced;
   with ins;
run;

ods html;

data spearman1(keep=variable scorr spvalue ranksp);
   length variable $ 8;
   set spearman;
   array best(*) best1--best&nvar;
   array r(*) r1--r&nvar;
   array p(*) p1--p&nvar;
   do i=1 to dim(best);
      variable=best(i);
      scorr=r(i);
      spvalue=p(i);
      ranksp=i;
      output;
   end;
run;
```

```
data hoeffding1(keep=variable hcorr hpvalue rankho);
   length variable $ 8;
   set hoeffding;
   array best(*) best1--best&nvar;
   array r(*) r1--r&nvar;
   array p(*) p1--p&nvar;
   do i=1 to dim(best);
      variable=best(i);
      hcorr=r(i);
      hpvalue=p(i);
      rankho=i;
      output;
   end;
run;

proc sort data=spearman1;
   by variable;
run;

proc sort data=hoeffding1;
   by variable;
run;

data correlations;
   merge spearman1 hoeffding1;
   by variable;
run;

proc sort data=correlations;
   by ranksp;
run;

proc print data=correlations label split='*';
   var variable ranksp rankho scorr spvalue hcorr hpvalue;
   label ranksp = 'Spearman rank*of variables'
         scorr = 'Spearman Correlation'
         spvalue = 'Spearman p-value'
         rankho = 'Hoeffding rank*of variables'
         hcorr = 'Hoeffding Correlation'
         hpvalue = 'Hoeffding p-value';
run;
```

Obs	variable	Spearman rank of variables	Hoeffding rank of variables	Spearman Correlation	Spearman p-value	Hoeffding Correlation	Hoeffding p-value
1	SavBal	1	1	0.25272	0.00000	0.010014	0.00001
2	CD	2	5	0.21013	0.00000	0.001984	0.00001
3	MM	3	9	0.15958	0.00000	0.001045	0.00001
4	Sav	4	4	0.15145	0.00000	0.002373	0.00001
5	Dep	5	2	-0.15102	0.00000	0.003463	0.00001
6	ATM	6	6	-0.12047	0.00000	0.001414	0.00001
7	Phone	7	11	-0.10721	0.00000	0.000639	0.00001
8	IRA	8	15	0.10603	0.00000	0.000177	0.00027
9	IRABal	9	19	0.10416	0.00000	0.000153	0.00066
10	Inv	10	21	0.09940	0.00000	0.000040	0.05602
11	brclus2	11	10	0.08566	0.00000	0.000673	0.00001
12	InvBal	12	29	0.07762	0.00000	-0.000028	0.99969
13	POSAmt	13	13	-0.07749	0.00000	0.000422	0.00001
14	CCPurc	14	17	0.07454	0.00000	0.000171	0.00034
15	DirDep	15	14	-0.07334	0.00000	0.000422	0.00001
16	SDB	16	18	0.07222	0.00000	0.000154	0.00064
17	NSFAmt	17	20	-0.07122	0.00000	0.000114	0.00292
18	MIPhone	18	16	-0.07046	0.00000	0.000176	0.00028
19	ATMAmt	19	7	-0.06790	0.00000	0.001336	0.00001
20	CCBal	20	12	0.06461	0.00000	0.000529	0.00001
21	InArea	21	24	-0.06090	0.00000	-0.000005	0.46212
22	brclus1	22	26	-0.05666	0.00000	-0.000021	0.92877
23	DDABal	23	3	0.05296	0.00000	0.003045	0.00001
24	DepAmt	24	8	-0.04935	0.00000	0.001214	0.00001
25	CashBk	25	32	-0.04212	0.00000	-0.000055	1.00000
26	ILS	26	34	-0.01885	0.00569	-0.000057	1.00000
27	Age	27	23	0.01501	0.02775	0.000003	0.31614
28	Teller	28	22	-0.01331	0.05091	0.000028	0.09305
29	Income	29	25	0.01305	0.05571	-0.000019	0.88381
30	MTGBal	30	37	-0.00814	0.23228	-0.000063	1.00000
31	MICRScor	31	39	0.00763	0.26310	-0.000065	1.00000
32	AcctAge	32	27	-0.00751	0.27048	-0.000021	0.94154
33	CRScore	33	28	0.00710	0.29760	-0.000021	0.94231
34	MTG	34	38	-0.00702	0.30299	-0.000063	1.00000
35	MIAcctAg	35	35	0.00597	0.38158	-0.000062	1.00000
36	LOC	36	36	-0.00540	0.42846	-0.000063	1.00000
37	LORes	37	30	0.00438	0.52027	-0.000040	1.00000
38	MIIncome	38	33	0.00398	0.55921	-0.000057	1.00000
39	Moved	39	40	0.00061	0.92861	-0.000066	1.00000
40	HMOwn	40	31	-0.00014	0.98360	-0.000052	1.00000

As before, a plot might be useful.

```
proc sql noprint;
   select min(ranksp) into :vref
   from (select ranksp
      from correlations
      having spvalue > .5);
   select min(rankho) into :href
   from (select rankho
      from correlations
      having hpvalue > .5);
run; quit;

proc sgplot data=correlations;
   refline &vref / axis=y;
   refline &href / axis=x;
   scatter y=ranksp x=rankho / datalabel=variable;
   yaxis label="Rank of Spearman";
   xaxis label="Rank of Hoeffding";
   title "Scatter Plot of the Ranks of Spearman vs. Hoeffding";
run;
```

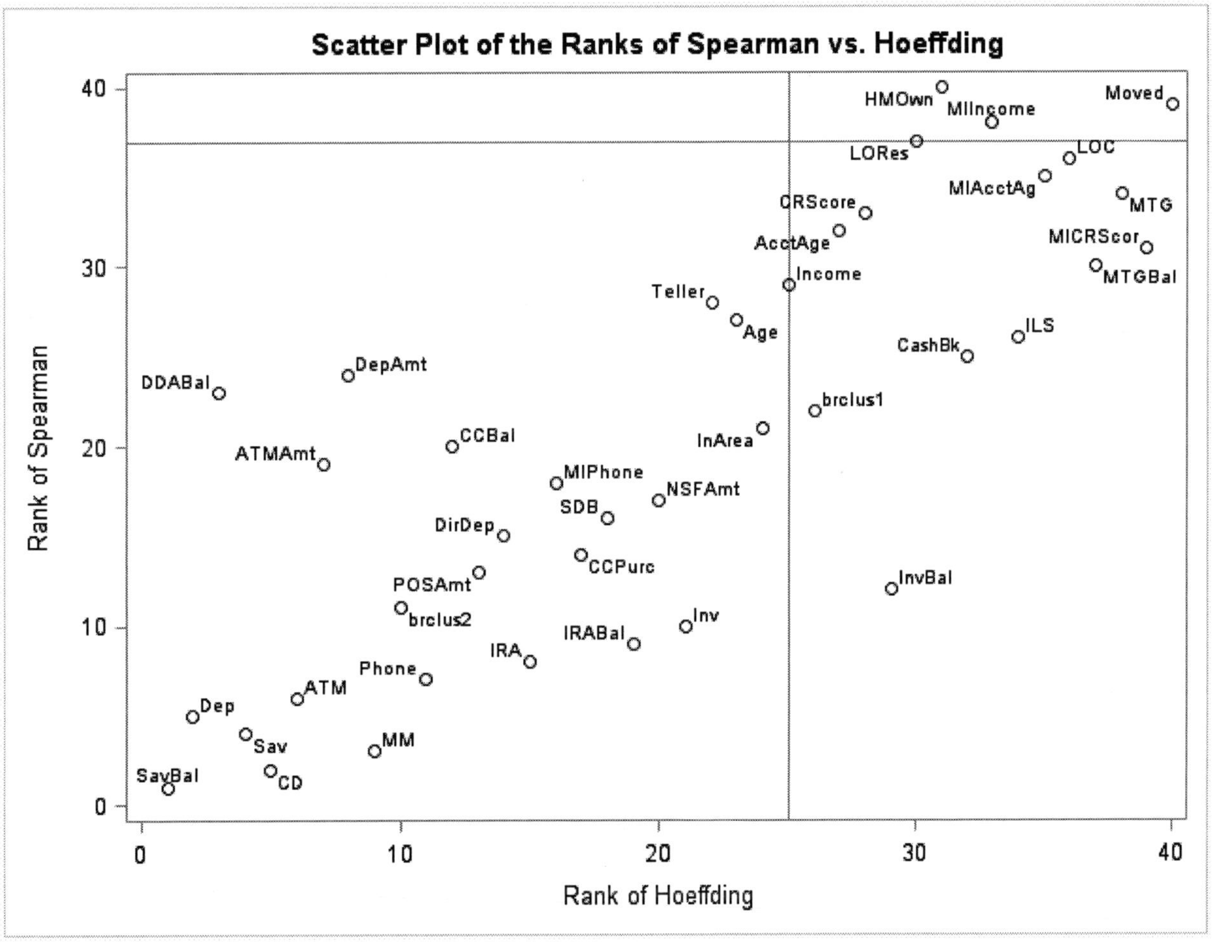

Dropping any variable that has both the Hoeffding and the Spearman *p*-value above .5 leaves 36 inputs.

Put their names into a macro variable named **screened**.

```
%let screened =
MIPhone Teller MM
Income ILS LOC POSAmt
NSFAmt CD CCPurc
ATMAmt brclus2 INV DEP
CashBk IRA CRScore
MIAcctAg IRABal MICRScor MTGBal
AcctAge SavBal DDABal SDB
InArea Sav Phone CCBal
INVBal MTG DEPAmt
DirDep ATM brclus1 Age;
```

Create logit plots and assess the linearity assumption for **DDABal**, a skewed input.[1] For illustrative purposes, also create a logit plot and assess the linearity assumption for **SavBal**. You can do this by running the code below, which generates plots for **DDABal**, and then re-running the code from the line after *****************. That second run will generate comparable plots for **SavBal**.

```
%let var=DDABal;
*****************
%let var = SavBal;
proc rank data=train1 groups=100 out=out;
   var &var;
   ranks bin;
run;

proc means data=out noprint nway;
   class bin;
   var ins &var;
   output out=bins sum(ins)=ins mean(&var)=&var;
run;

data bins;
   set bins;
   elogit=log((ins+(sqrt(_FREQ_ )/2))/
          (_FREQ_ -ins+(sqrt(_FREQ_ )/2)));
run;

proc sgplot data=bins;
   reg y=elogit x=&var /
       curvelabel="Linear Relationship?"
       curvelabelloc=outside
       lineattrs=(color=ligr);
   series y=elogit x=&var;
   title "Empirical Logit against &var";
run;
```

[1] You might also consider `DepAmt` and `ATMAmt` as skewed inputs.

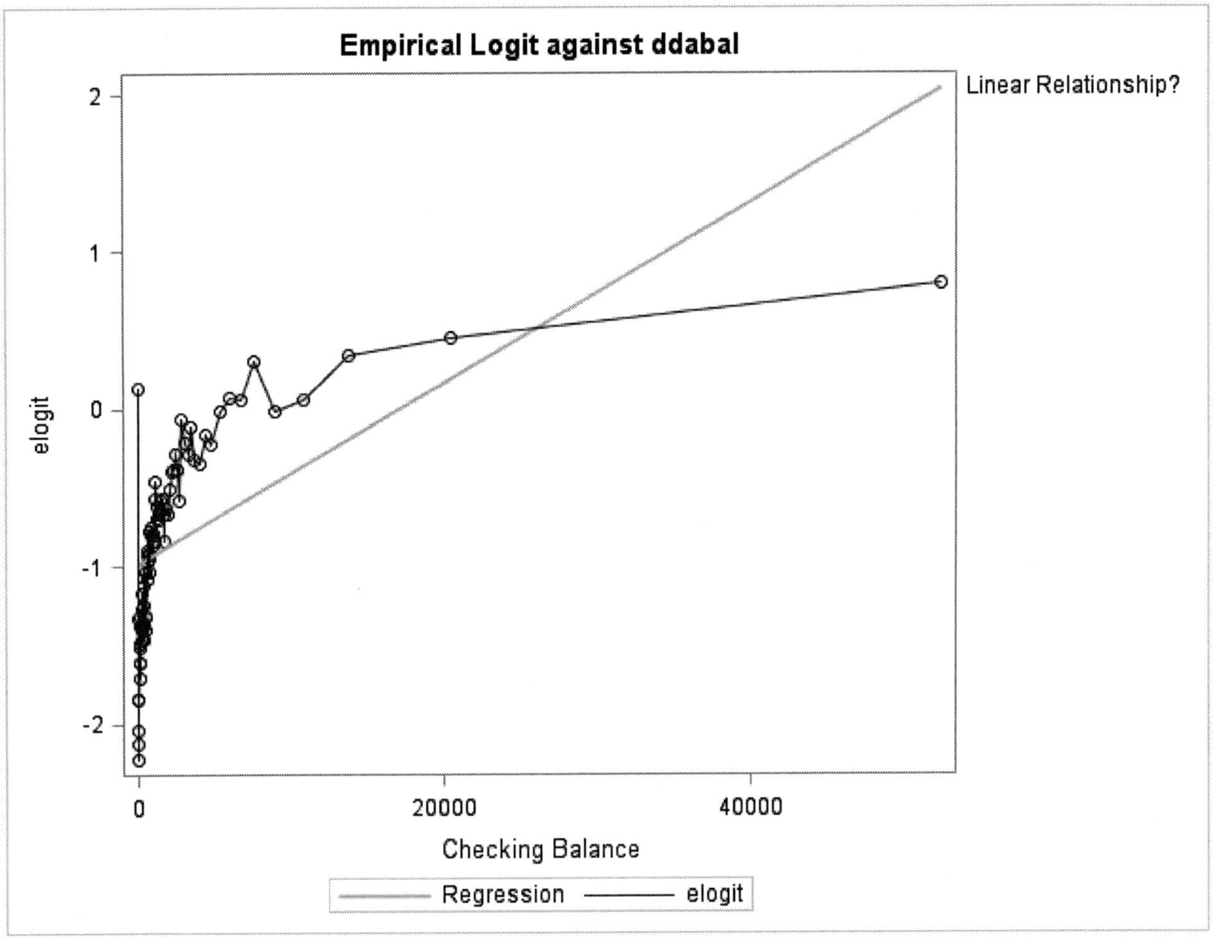


```
proc sgplot data=bins;
   reg y=elogit x=bin /
       curvelabel="Linear Relationship?"
       curvelabelloc=outside
       lineattrs=(color=ligr);
   series y=elogit x=bin;
   title "Empirical Logit against Binned &var";
run;
```

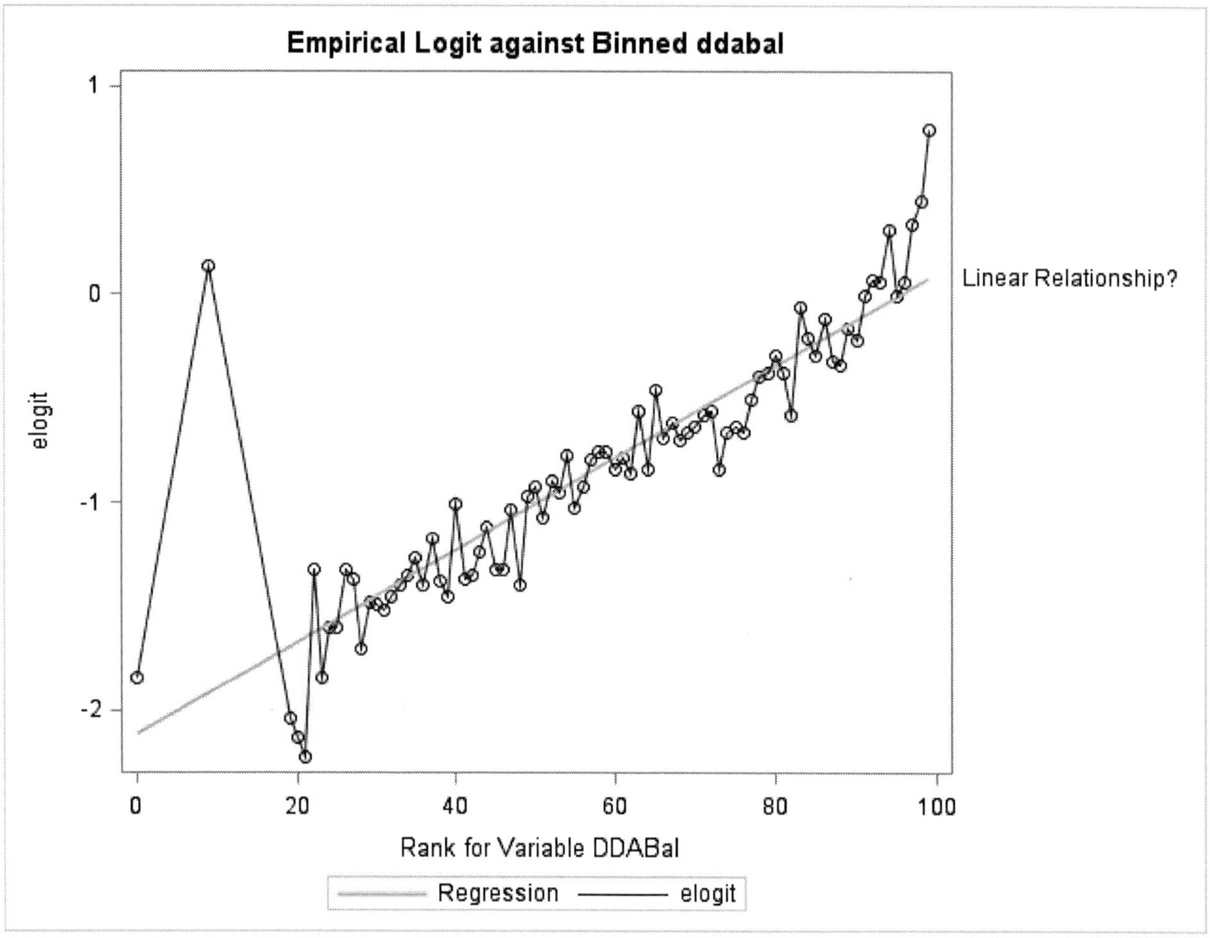

As before, the logical imputation of a $0 balance for customers without a **DDA** account will be replaced with mean imputation to account for the spike. Also, the rank-transformed **DDABal** looks like it has a more linear relationship with the target, so that is an attractive option.

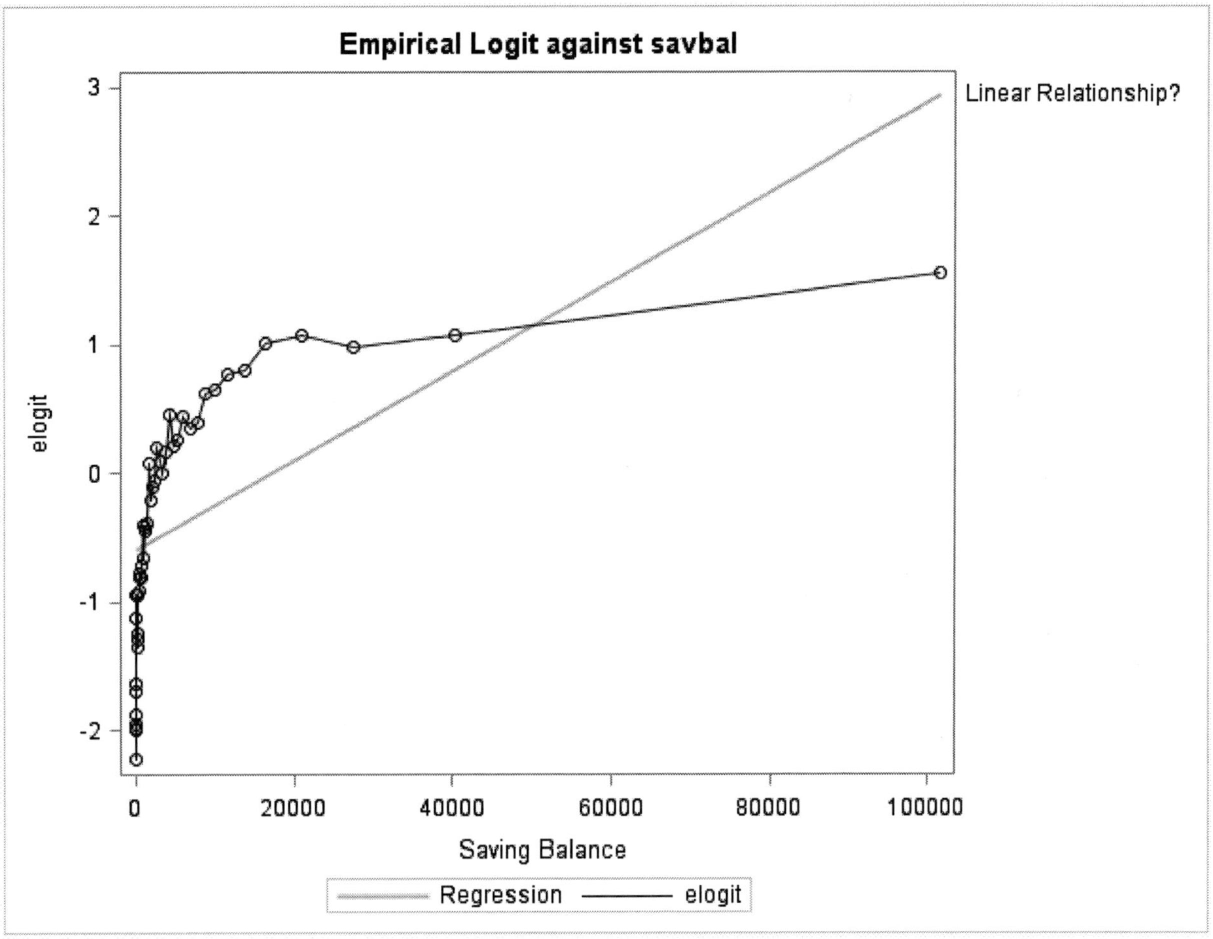
Empirical Logit against savbal
Linear Relationship?
elogit
3
2
1
0
-1
-2
0
20000
40000
60000
80000
100000
Saving Balance
Regression
elogit

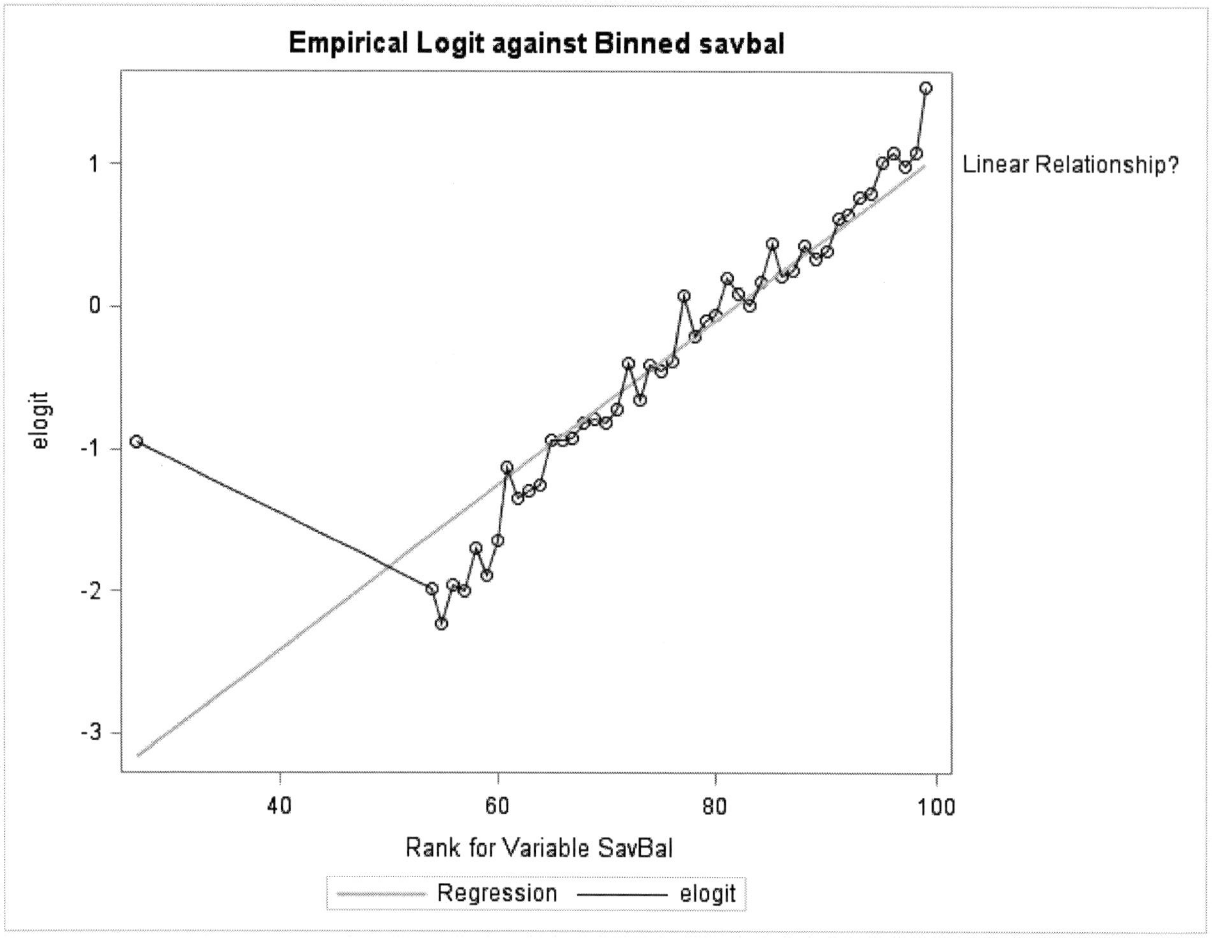

Performing a similar evaluation on **SavBal** reveals two things: the spike induced by logical imputation of $0 balances for customers without saving accounts is not as drastic as it was for **DDABal**, and the relationship would be (roughly) linear if the top 5% or 10% of individuals had their balances capped at the 95th or 90th percentile. Hence, a reasonable "transformation" of **SavBal** might be simply replacing every balance greater than some number with that number.

This capping could be handled using PROC UNIVARIATE (or PROC MEANS) to find the percentile and using macro variables to pass that information into DATA step processing, but rudimentary visual inspection indicates that the 95th percentile of savings balance is around $16,000. This appears to be a point where the relationship is turning a corner. Hence, it seems like a good value for the cap.

The binned savings balance does not have the overwhelming linear relationship that was seen in the earlier **DDABal** plots. Hence, the transformation for the **SavBal** input is probably best left at this capping.

To handle these transformations, first tend to the **DDABal** variable. Replace the $0 balances with the mean of the cases with nonzero account balances.

```
proc sql;
   select mean(ddabal) into :mean
   from train1 where dda;
quit;
```

2620.85

```
data train1;
   set train1;
   if not dda then ddabal = &mean;
run;
```

The rank-group or percentile transformation looks like it will help linearize the relationship between the logits and the predictor. PROC MEANS calculates the endpoints of the bins, and the DATA step is used to create DATA step code that will perform the rank-group transformation. The final DATA step uses the binning code to create **B_DDABal** and to truncate the larger values of **SavBal**.

```
proc rank data=train1 groups=100 out=out;
   var ddabal;
   ranks bin;
run;

proc means data=out noprint nway;
   class bin;
   var ddabal;
   output out=endpts max=max;
run;

filename rank "C:\temp\rank.sas";

data _null_;
   file rank;
   set endpts end=last;
   if _n_ = 1 then put "select;";
   if not last then do;
     put "  when (ddabal <= " max ") B_DDABal =" bin ";";
     end;
  else if last then do;
     put "otherwise B_DDABal =" bin ";";
     put "end;";
     end;
run;

data train1;
   set train1;
   %include rank /source2;
   if savbal > 16000 then savbal=16000;
run;
```

Now assess the linearity assumption for **b_ddabal** and **savbal**.

```
%let var=b_ddabal;

proc means data=train1 noprint nway;
   class &var;
   var ins &var;
   output out=bins sum(ins)=ins;
run;

data bins;
   set bins;
   elogit=log((ins+(sqrt(_FREQ_ )/2))/
          (_FREQ_ -ins+(sqrt(_FREQ_ )/2)));
run;

proc sgplot data=bins;
   reg y=elogit x=&var /
       curvelabel="Linear Relationship?"
       curvelabelloc=outside
       lineattrs=(color=ligr);
   series y=elogit x=&var;
   title "Empirical Logit against &var";
run;
```

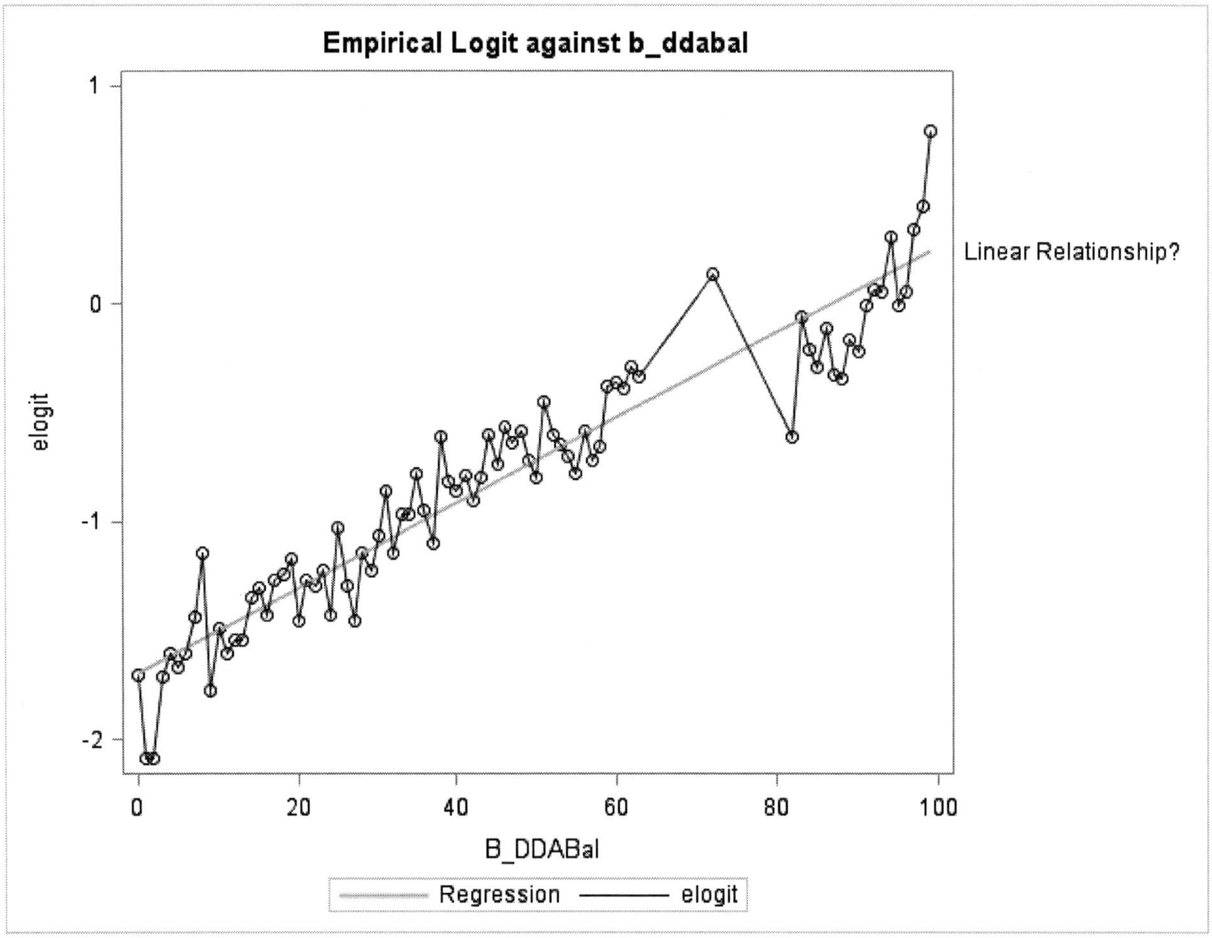

The input **B_DDABal** has a strong linear relationship with the target.

```
%let var = savbal;
proc rank data=train1 groups=100 out=out;
   var &var;
   ranks bin;
run;

proc means data=out noprint nway;
   class bin;
   var ins &var;
   output out=bins sum(ins)=ins mean(&var)=&var;
run;

data bins;
   set bins;
   elogit=log((ins+(sqrt(_FREQ_ )/2))/
          (_FREQ_ -ins+(sqrt(_FREQ_ )/2)));
run;

proc sgplot data=bins;
   reg y=elogit x=&var /
       curvelabel="Linear Relationship?"
       curvelabelloc=outside
       lineattrs=(color=ligr);
   series y=elogit x=&var;
   title "Empirical Logit against &var";
run;
```

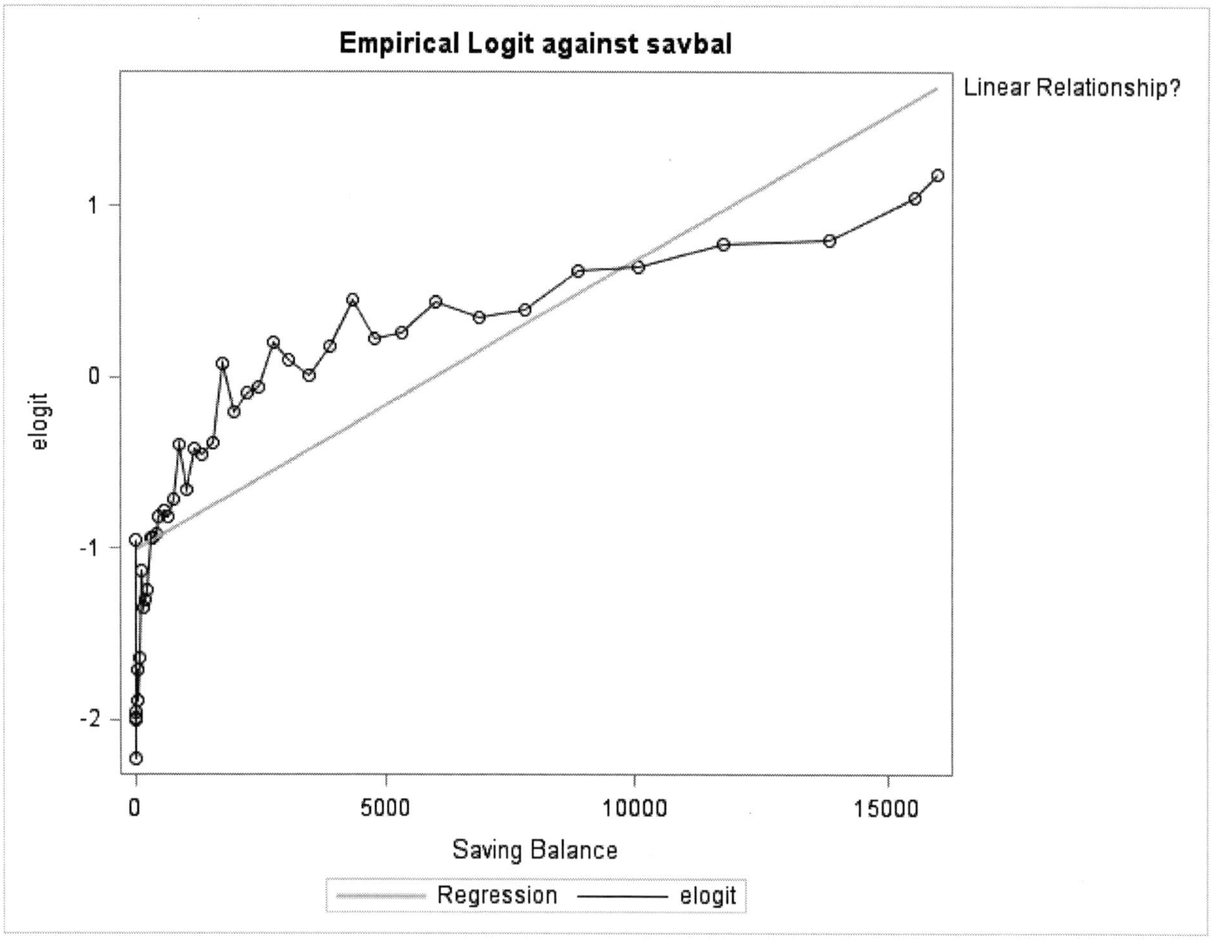

The input **SavBal** that is now capped at 16000 seems to have a stronger linear relationship with the target than the uncapped **SavBal**. Adding a quadratic term might also lead to a better fit in the logistic model.

After performing the transformation, replace **DDABal** with the transformed input **B_DDABal** in the **screened** macro variable.

```
%let screened =
MIPhone Teller MM
Income ILS LOC POSAmt
NSFAmt CD CCPurc
ATMAmt brclus2 INV DEP
CashBk IRA CRScore
MIAcctAg IRABal MICRScor MTGBal
AcctAge SavBal B_DDABal SDB
InArea Sav Phone CCBal
INVBal MTG DEPAmt
DirDep ATM brclus1 Age;
```

The best subsets selection method is used to find the subset of variables that minimizes the Bayesian information criterion (BIC).

```
title;

data train1;
  set train1;
  resr=(res='R');
  resu=(res='U');
run;

ods html close;
ods output bestsubsets=score;

proc logistic data=train1;
   model ins(event='1')=&screened resr resu
   / selection=score best=1;
run;

proc sql noprint;
  select variablesinmodel into :inputs1 - :inputs999
  from score;
  select NumberOfVariables into :ic1 - :ic999
  from score;
quit;

%let lastindx = &SQLOBS;

%macro fitstat( );

%do model_indx=1 %to &lastindx;

%let im=&&inputs&model_indx;
%let ic=&&ic&model_indx;

ods output scorefitstat=stat&ic;
proc logistic data=train1;
  model ins(event='1')=&im;
  score data=train1 out=scored fitstat
        priorevent=&pi1;
run;

proc datasets
   library=work
   nodetails
   nolist;
   delete scored;
run;
quit;

%end;
%mend fitstat;
```

```
%fitstat( );

data modelfit;
   set stat1 - stat&lastindx;
   model = _n_;
run;

proc sort data = modelfit;
   by bic;
run;

ods html;
proc print data=modelfit;
   var model auc aic bic misclass adjrsquare brierscore;
   title "Fit Statistics from Models selected from Best-Subsets";
run;
```

Fit Statistics from Models selected from Best-Subsets

Obs	model	AUC	AIC	BIC	MisClass	AdjRSquare	BrierScore
1	24	0.785453	50463.64	50663.05	0.3453	0.283223	0.307591
2	23	0.785278	50471.91	50663.34	0.3454	0.282894	0.307636
3	25	0.785495	50457.39	50664.78	0.3451	0.28346	0.307552
4	21	0.784845	50489.64	50665.12	0.3453	0.282344	0.307731
5	22	0.785036	50484.14	50667.6	0.3453	0.282567	0.307718
6	26	0.785667	50452.58	50667.94	0.3452	0.283674	0.307542
7	20	0.784612	50502.64	50670.15	0.3454	0.282041	0.307816
8	27	0.785693	50451.98	50675.32	0.3452	0.283843	0.307554
9	18	0.784222	50524.56	50676.12	0.3454	0.280834	0.307825
10	19	0.784371	50518.24	50677.77	0.3454	0.281479	0.307877
11	17	0.784022	50538.18	50681.75	0.3453	0.280367	0.307893
12	28	0.785736	50451.61	50682.93	0.3453	0.283907	0.307555
13	29	0.785768	50448.56	50687.85	0.3453	0.284001	0.307522
14	30	0.78582	50448.31	50695.58	0.3453	0.284114	0.307527
15	16	0.783734	50561.69	50697.29	0.3454	0.279732	0.308032

16	31	0.785853	50448.37	50703.61	0.3452	0.284177	0.30752
17	15	0.783411	50576.96	50704.58	0.3455	0.279035	0.308026
18	32	0.785845	50448.42	50711.64	0.3452	0.284238	0.307508
19	33	0.78584	50449.27	50720.47	0.3452	0.28426	0.307497
20	34	0.785844	50450.96	50730.13	0.3452	0.284269	0.307496
21	35	0.78586	50451.91	50739.05	0.3452	0.284284	0.307488
22	14	0.783089	50624.25	50743.89	0.3458	0.277958	0.308382
23	36	0.785873	50453.58	50748.71	0.3452	0.284293	0.307488
24	37	0.785875	50455.48	50758.58	0.3453	0.284298	0.30749
25	38	0.785874	50457.47	50768.55	0.3453	0.284298	0.30749
26	13	0.782294	50658.56	50770.23	0.3457	0.276988	0.308492
27	12	0.781776	50694.38	50798.07	0.3457	0.275958	0.308637
28	10	0.780442	50738.78	50826.52	0.3455	0.272839	0.308357
29	11	0.780946	50734.96	50830.67	0.3458	0.274637	0.308757
30	9	0.779745	50802.89	50882.66	0.3455	0.27103	0.308668
31	8	0.778427	50888.51	50960.3	0.3457	0.26891	0.309058
32	7	0.777387	50962.73	51026.54	0.3459	0.26659	0.309336
33	6	0.776043	51068.5	51124.34	0.3461	0.263003	0.309672
34	5	0.773762	51210.97	51258.83	0.3462	0.258369	0.310102
35	4	0.770288	51477.45	51517.33	0.3462	0.250044	0.31114
36	3	0.758302	52004.31	52036.22	0.3464	0.23354	0.312458
37	2	0.740536	53014.46	53038.39	0.3464	0.202105	0.315915
38	1	0.640517	55131.94	55147.9	0.3464	0.123794	0.320301

```
proc sql;
   select VariablesInModel into :selected
   from score
   where numberofvariables=24;
quit;
```

Variables Included in Model
MIPhone Teller MM ILS LOC NSFAmt CD ATMAmt brclus2 Inv Dep IRA MIAcctAg MTGBal AcctAge SavBal B_DDABal Sav Phone CCBal MTG DirDep ATM brclus1

A total of 24 inputs were selected.

Fit a logistic regression model on the selected subset of variables. Use the OFFSET = option in the MODEL statement to correct for oversampling. The formula for the offset variable was shown in chapter 2. The only difference between the parameter estimates with and without the offset variable is the intercept term.

```
proc sql noprint;
  select mean(INS) into :rho1 from pmlr.develop;
quit;

data train1;
   set train1;
   off=log(((1-&pi1)*&rho1)/(&pi1*(1-&rho1)));
run;

proc logistic data=train1 plots(only)=
     (oddsratio (type=horizontalstat));
   model ins(event='1') = &selected / clodds=pl offset=off;
   title "Model with Lowest BIC";
run;
```

Model with Lowest BIC

The LOGISTIC Procedure

Model Information	
Data Set	WORK.TRAIN1
Response Variable	Ins
Number of Response Levels	2
Offset Variable	off
Model	binary logit
Optimization Technique	Fisher's scoring

Number of Observations Read	21512
Number of Observations Used	21512

Response Profile		
Ordered Value	**Ins**	**Total Frequency**
1	0	14061
2	1	7451

Probability modeled is Ins=1.

Intercept-Only Model Convergence Status
Convergence criterion (GCONV=1E-8) satisfied.

Model Convergence Status
Convergence criterion (GCONV=1E-8) satisfied.

Model Fit Statistics		
Criterion	Intercept Only	Intercept and Covariates
AIC	27759.675	22864.790
SC	27767.651	23064.199
-2 Log L	27757.675	22814.790

Testing Global Null Hypothesis: BETA=0			
Test	Chi-Square	DF	Pr > ChiSq
Likelihood Ratio	4942.8853	24	<.0001
Score	4675.3068	24	<.0001
Wald	3626.6270	24	<.0001

Analysis of Maximum Likelihood Estimates					
Parameter	DF	Estimate	Standard Error	Wald Chi-Square	Pr > ChiSq
Intercept	1	-5.2340	0.0582	8095.7327	<.0001
MIPhone	1	-0.3602	0.0619	33.8464	<.0001
Teller	1	0.0550	0.00808	46.2727	<.0001
MM	1	0.7931	0.0496	255.2380	<.0001
ILS	1	-0.2029	0.0805	6.3426	0.0118
LOC	1	-0.2712	0.0707	14.7304	0.0001
NSFAmt	1	0.00320	0.00129	6.1485	0.0132
CD	1	0.9622	0.0473	413.2725	<.0001
ATMAmt	1	0.000026	5.564E-6	22.6785	<.0001
brclus2	1	0.2584	0.0366	49.7263	<.0001
Inv	1	0.5411	0.1014	28.4533	<.0001
Dep	1	-0.0738	0.0139	28.0470	<.0001
IRA	1	0.3179	0.0714	19.8243	<.0001
MIAcctAg	1	-0.2072	0.0671	9.5343	0.0020
MTGBal	1	-3.01E-6	8.789E-7	11.7310	0.0006
AcctAge	1	-0.0206	0.00271	58.1726	<.0001
SavBal	1	0.000130	4.97E-6	687.3814	<.0001
B_DDABal	1	0.0182	0.000635	818.6636	<.0001
Sav	1	0.2425	0.0395	37.7108	<.0001
Phone	1	-0.0706	0.0190	13.8114	0.0002
CCBal	1	2.973E-6	8.858E-7	11.2678	0.0008
MTG	1	-0.2248	0.0842	7.1343	0.0076
DirDep	1	-0.1704	0.0402	17.9608	<.0001
ATM	1	-0.1520	0.0405	14.0939	0.0002
brclus1	1	-0.3889	0.1172	11.0024	0.0009
off	1	1.0000	0	.	.

Association of Predicted Probabilities and Observed Responses			
Percent Concordant	78.4	Somers' D	0.571
Percent Discordant	21.3	Gamma	0.572
Percent Tied	0.2	Tau-a	0.259
Pairs	104768511	c	0.785

Odds Ratio Estimates and Profile-Likelihood Confidence Intervals				
Effect	Unit	Estimate	95% Confidence Limits	
MIPhone	1.0000	0.698	0.617	0.787
Teller	1.0000	1.056	1.040	1.073
MM	1.0000	2.210	2.006	2.436
ILS	1.0000	0.816	0.696	0.955
LOC	1.0000	0.762	0.663	0.875
NSFAmt	1.0000	1.003	1.001	1.006
CD	1.0000	2.617	2.386	2.872
ATMAmt	1.0000	1.000	1.000	1.000
brclus2	1.0000	1.295	1.205	1.391
Inv	1.0000	1.718	1.409	2.098
Dep	1.0000	0.929	0.904	0.954
IRA	1.0000	1.374	1.195	1.581
MIAcctAg	1.0000	0.813	0.712	0.927
MTGBal	1.0000	1.000	1.000	1.000
AcctAge	1.0000	0.980	0.974	0.985
SavBal	1.0000	1.000	1.000	1.000
B_DDABal	1.0000	1.018	1.017	1.020

Sav	1.0000	1.274	1.180	1.377
Phone	1.0000	0.932	0.897	0.966
CCBal	1.0000	1.000	1.000	1.000
MTG	1.0000	0.799	0.676	0.941
DirDep	1.0000	0.843	0.779	0.912
ATM	1.0000	0.859	0.793	0.930
brclus1	1.0000	0.678	0.537	0.851

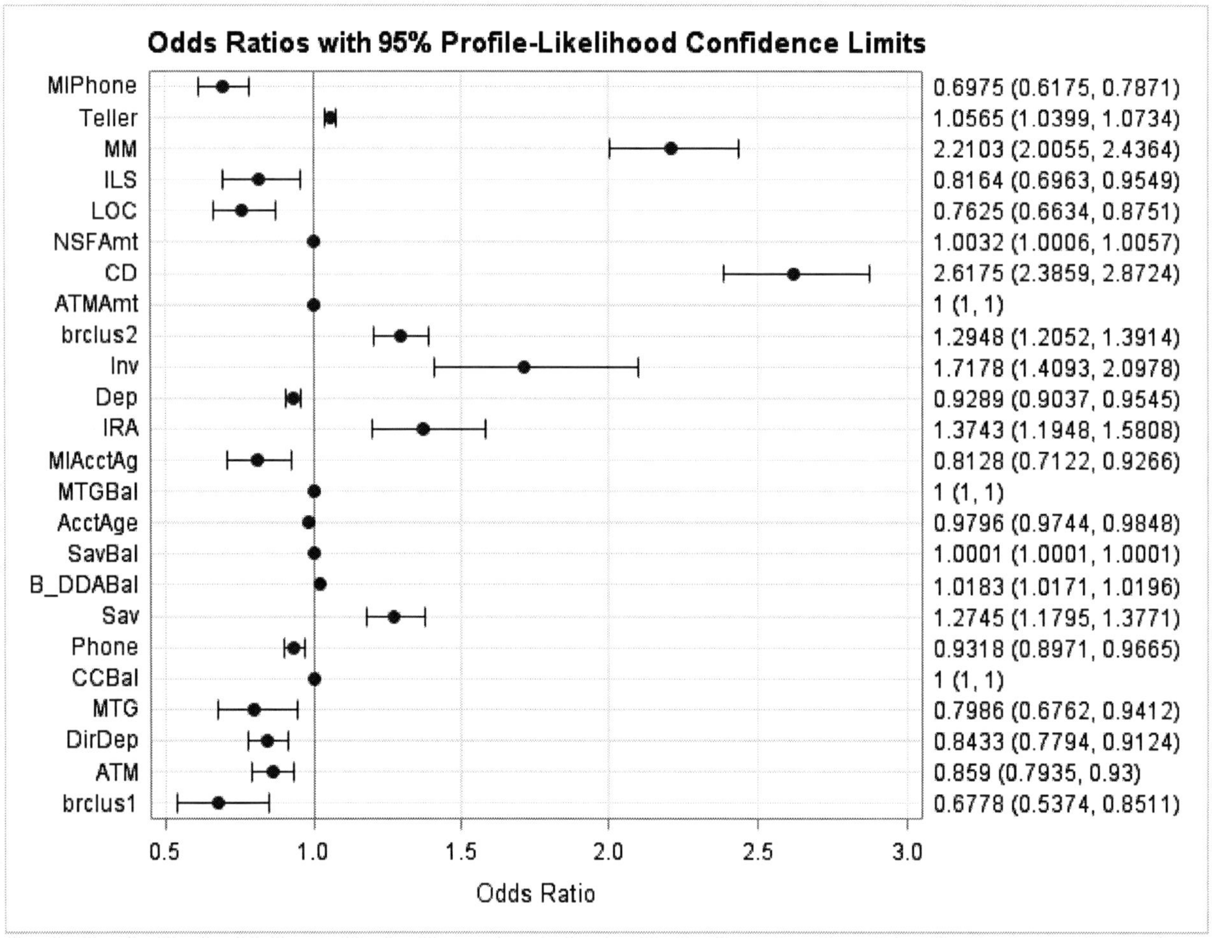

To assess the model generalization performance, the validation data need to be prepared for scoring the same way that the training data were prepared for model building. Missing values need to be imputed, new inputs need to be created, and any transformations need to be applied. PROC MEANS can be used to see which inputs need imputation on this **valid** data set.

```
proc means data = valid nmiss;
   var Teller MM ILS LOC NSFAmt CD ATMAmt Inv Dep IRA
       MTGBal AcctAge SavBal Sav Phone CCBal MTG DirDep ATM;
run;
```

Variable	Label	N Miss
Teller	Teller Visits	0
MM	Money Market	0
ILS	Installment Loan	0
LOC	Line of Credit	0
NSFAmt	Amount NSF	0
CD	Certificate of Deposit	0
ATMAmt	ATM Withdrawal Amount	0
Inv	Investment	1369
Dep	Checking Deposits	0
IRA	Retirement Account	0
MTGBal	Mortgage Balance	0
AcctAge	Age of Oldest Account	687
SavBal	Saving Balance	0
Sav	Saving Account	0
Phone	Number Telephone Banking	1369
CCBal	Credit Card Balance	1369
MTG	Mortgage	0
DirDep	Direct Deposit	0
ATM	ATM	0

In the validation data set, missing values should be replaced with the medians from the training data set. Because the variables **Inv**, **AcctAge**,**Phone**, and **CCBal** have missing values, PROC UNIVARIATE is used to create an output data set with the medians of those variables. The PCTLPTS option requests the 50th percentile and the PCTLPRE option specifies the prefix for the variable names in the output data set.

```
proc univariate data=train1 noprint;
   var acctage inv phone ccbal;
   output out=medians
          pctlpts=50
          pctlpre=acctage inv phone ccbal;
run;
```

The DATA step first combines values from a single observation in one data set (**medians**) with all of the observations in another data set (**valid1**). Array **X** contains the variables with missing values and array **med** contains the variables with the medians. The DO loop replaces the missing values with the medians. The necessary **brclus1** and **brclus2** variables, the **B_DDABal** rank-transformed input, and the truncated **SavBal** are all added at this stage.

```
data valid1(drop=acctage50 inv50 phone50 ccbal50 i);
   if _N_ = 1 then set medians;
   set valid;
   array x(*) acctage inv phone ccbal;
   array med(*) acctage50 inv50 phone50 ccbal50;
      do i = 1 to dim(x);
         if x(i)=. then x(i)=med(i);
      end;
   if not dda then ddabal = &mean;
   brclus1=(branch='B14');
   brclus2=(branch in ('B12','B5','B8',
                        'B3','B18','B19','B17',
                        'B4','B6','B10','B9',
                        'B1','B13'));
   brclus3=(branch in ('B15','B16'));
   %include rank;
   if savbal > 16000 then savbal=16000;
run;
```

The variable **brclus3** is not used by this model, but if you are considering several possible models, it might be easier to create one validation data set that has received exactly the same treatment as the training data set so that assessing model performance is simplified.

Now that the validation data are prepared for scoring, you could use any of the techniques discussed in Chapter 2 to score it. However, this begs a question: what metrics can you use to measure model performance? This question and the related question of optimal use of a model are the foci of the following sections.

Imputation for All Inputs

Instead of using PROC UNIVARIATE to impute missing variables for selected variables, as above, it is possible to automate the imputation step without having to check which particular variables have missing values. PROC STDIZE can be used to output a data set that contains the relevant information about the imputed values for every input. In addition, PROC STDIZE can also be used to take that information and use it to impute the training data set values in the validation data set. An example follows.

As before, use PROC STDIZE with the REPONLY option to impute missing values on the training data. In addition, specify the OUTSTAT= option to save the imputed values in a separate data set, called **med**.

```
proc stdize data=train out=train2
            method=median reponly
            OUTSTAT=med;
   var &inputs;
run;
```

After the **med** data set has been created, it can be used to impute for missing values in a different data set. The code below creates a data set, **valid2**, based on the unimputed **valid** data, with the medians from the imputed training data. The option to specify the data set with the median information is METHOD=IN(*data-set-name*).

```
proc stdize data=valid out=valid2
            reponly method=in(med);
   var &inputs;
run;
```

To see that the values imputed for **AcctAge**, **Inv**, **Phone**, **and CCbal** are the same in **valid1** (created above) as in **valid2** (created here) you can use the COMPARE procedure.

```
proc compare base= valid1 compare=valid2;
   var acctage inv phone ccbal;
run;
```

```
                         The COMPARE Procedure
               Comparison of WORK.VALID1 with WORK.VALID2
                            (Method=EXACT)

                           Data Set Summary

Dataset                 Created          Modified  NVar    NObs

WORK.VALID1  12MAR12:17:49:07  12MAR12:17:49:07    70   10752
WORK.VALID2  12MAR12:17:52:04  12MAR12:17:52:04    66   10752


                           Variables Summary

Number of Variables in Common: 66.
Number of Variables in WORK.VALID1 but not in WORK.VALID2: 4.
Number of VAR Statement Variables: 4.
```

```
                         Observation Summary

                    Observation      Base  Compare

                    First Obs           1        1
                    Last  Obs       10752    10752

Number of Observations in Common: 10752.
Total Number of Observations Read from WORK.VALID1: 10752.
Total Number of Observations Read from WORK.VALID2: 10752.

Number of Observations with Some Compared Variables Unequal: 0.
Number of Observations with All Compared Variables Equal: 10752.

NOTE: No unequal values were found. All values compared are exactly equal.
```

The **train2** and **valid2** data sets will be used in a later section. In order to generate a series of models, you probably want to impute for all inputs first. In this way, you can evaluate model performance on the validation data without having to intervene by hand to impute for missing values.

4.2 Misclassification

Objectives

- Discuss several model performance measures.
- Adjust the confusion matrix for oversampling.
- Create ROC curves and lift charts on the validation data set.

11

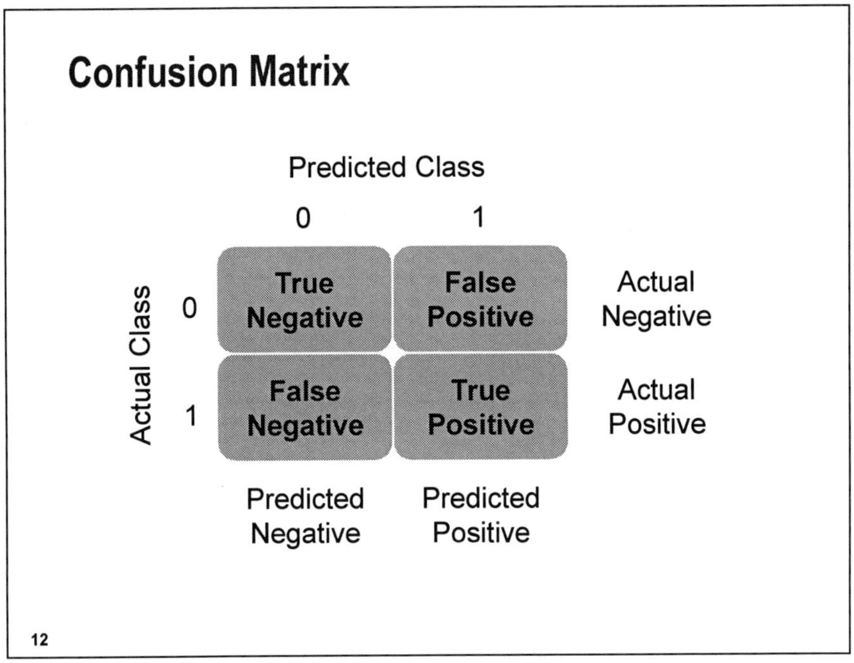

Supervised classification does not usually end with an estimate of the posterior probability. An allocation rule corresponds to a threshold value (cutoff) of the posterior probability. For example, all cases with probabilities of default greater than .04 might be rejected for a loan. For a given cutoff, how well does the classifier perform?

The fundamental assessment tool is the confusion matrix. The *confusion matrix* is a crosstabulation of the actual and predicted classes. It quantifies the confusion of the classifier. The event of interest, whether it is unfavorable (like fraud, churn, or default) or favorable (like response to offer), is often called a positive, although this convention is arbitrary. The simplest performance statistics are *accuracy*

(true positives and negatives) / (total cases)

and *error rate*

(false positives and negatives) / (total cases).

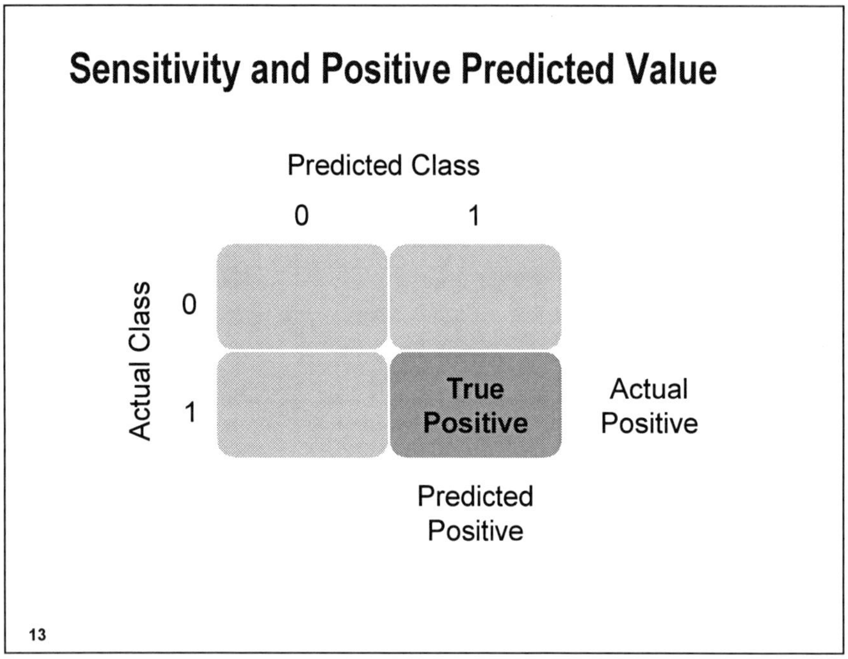

Two specialized measures of classifier performance are *sensitivity*

(true positives) / (total actual positives)

and *positive predicted value* (PV+)

(true positives) / (total predicted positives).

The analogs to these measures for true negatives are *specificity*

(true negatives) / (total actual negatives)

and *negative predicted value* (PV–)

(true negatives) / (total predicted negatives).

Large sensitivities do not necessarily correspond to large values of PV+. Ideally, one would like large values of all these statistics. The context of the problem determines which of these measures is the primary concern. For example, a database marketer might be most concerned with PV+ because it gives the response rate for the customers that receive an offer. In contrast, a fraud investigator might be most concerned with sensitivity because it gives the proportion of frauds that would be detected.

ROC Curve

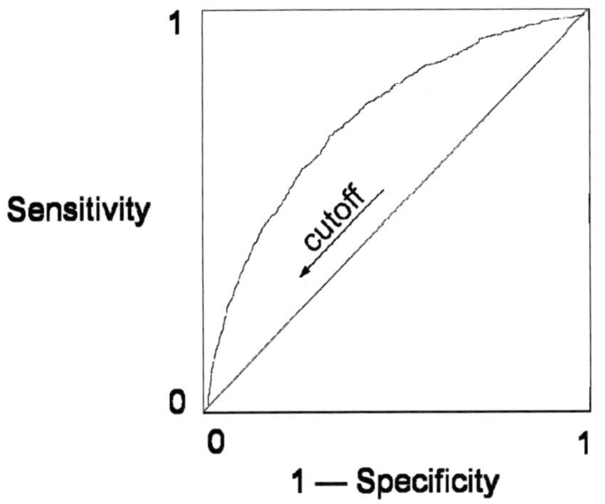

14

The *receiver operating characteristic* (ROC) curve was adapted from signal detection theory for the assessment of classifiers. The ROC curve displays the sensitivity and specificity for the entire range of cutoff values. As the cutoff decreases, more and more cases are allocated to class 1. Hence, the sensitivity increases and specificity decreases. As the cutoff increases, more and more cases are allocated to class 0. Hence, the sensitivity decreases and specificity increases. Consequently, the ROC curve intersects (0,0) and (1,1). If the posterior probabilities were arbitrarily assigned to the cases, then the ratio of false positives to true positives would be the same as the ratio of the total actual negatives to the total actual positives. Consequently, the baseline (random) model is a 45° angle going through the origin. As the ROC curve bows above the diagonal, the predictive power increases. A perfect model would reach the (0,1) point where both sensitivity and specificity equal 1.

Gains Chart

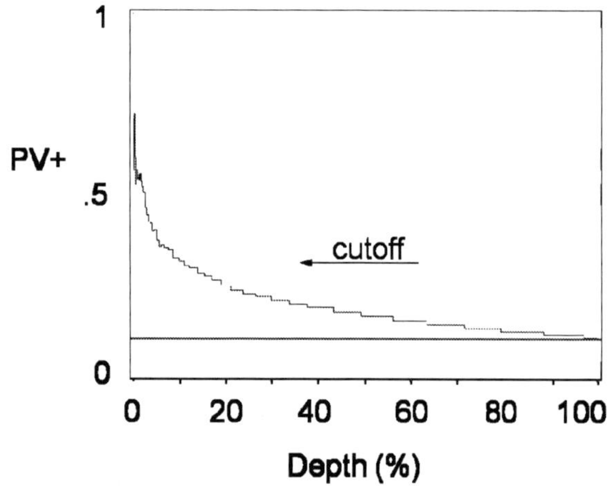

15

The *depth* of a classification rule is the total proportion of cases that were allocated to class 1. The (cumulative) *gains chart* displays the positive predicted value and depth for a range of cutoff values. As the cutoff decreases, more and more cases are allocated to class 1; hence, the depth increases and the PV+ approaches the marginal event rate. When the cutoff is minimum, then 100% of the cases are selected and the response rate is ρ_1. As the cutoff increases the depth decreases. A model with good predictive power would have increasing PV+ (response rate) as the depth decreases. If the posterior probabilities were arbitrarily assigned to the cases, then the gains chart would be a horizontal line at ρ_1.

The gains chart is widely used in database marketing to decide how deep in a database to go with a promotion. The simplest way to construct this curve is to sort and bin the predicted posterior probabilities (for example, deciles). The gains chart is easily augmented with revenue and cost information. The *lift* is PV+/ρ_1, so for a given depth, there are (lift)× more responders targeted by the model than by random chance.

A plot of sensitivity versus depth is sometimes called a *Lorentz* curve, *concentration* curve, or a lift curve (although lift value is not explicitly displayed).

Oversampled Test Set

Sample

Actual \ Predicted	0	1	
0	29	21	50
1	17	33	50
	46	54	

Population

Actual \ Predicted	0	1	
0	56	41	97
1	1	2	3
	57	43	

16

If the holdout data were obtained by splitting oversampled data, then they are oversampled as well. If the proper adjustments were made when the model was fitted, then the predicted posterior probabilities are correct. However, the confusion matrices would be incorrect (with regard to the population) because the event cases are over-represented. Consequently, PV+ (response rate) might be badly overestimated. Sensitivity and specificity, however, are not affected by separate sampling because they do not depend on the proportion of each class in the sample.

Adjustments for Oversampling

		Predicted Class 0	Predicted Class 1	
Actual Class	0	$\pi_0 \cdot Sp$	$\pi_0(1-Sp)$	π_0
	1	$\pi_1(1-Se)$	$\pi_1 \cdot Se$	π_1

17

Knowing sensitivity, specificity, and the priors is sufficient for adjusting the confusion matrix for oversampling. For example, if the sample represented the population, then $n\pi_1$ cases are in class 1. The proportion of those that were allocated to class 1 is *Se*. Thus, there are $n\pi_1 \cdot Se$ true positives. Note that these adjustments are equivalent to multiplying the cell counts by their sample weights, for example

$$\text{TP}_{\text{sample}} \cdot wt_1 = \text{TP}_{\text{sample}} \frac{\pi_1}{\rho_1} = \text{TP}_{\text{sample}} \cdot \pi_1 \frac{n}{\text{Tot Pos}_{\text{sample}}} = n \cdot \pi_1 \cdot Se$$

where **TP** is the proportion of true positives, and sample weights are defined as π_i / ρ_i for Class *i*.

4.02 Multiple Choice Poll

What is the formula for sensitivity?

a. true positives / total actual positives
b. true positives / total predicted positives
c. true negatives / total actual negatives
d. true negatives / total predicted negatives

18

Assessing Classifier Performance

Example: Calculate performance measures on the validation data set. Use the SCORE statement in PROC LOGISTIC to score the validation data set with the model fit on the training data set and use the OUTROC= option to create a data set with many of the statistics necessary for assessment. When you specify the OUTROC= option in the SCORE statement, the ROC curve for the scored data set is displayed. Use the FITSTAT option to generate model fit statistics.

The OUTROC= option creates an output data set with sensitivity (**_SENSIT_**) and one minus specificity (**_1MSPEC_**) calculated for a full range of cutoff probabilities (**_PROB_**). The other statistics in the OUTROC= data set are not useful when the data are oversampled. The two variables **_SENSIT_** and **_1MSPEC_** in the OUTROC= data set are correct whether the validation data are oversampled. The variable **_PROB_** is correct, provided the PRIOREVENT= was set to π_1. If they were not corrected, then **_PROB_** needs to be adjusted using the formula

$$\hat{p}_i = \frac{\hat{p}_i^* \rho_0 \pi_1}{(1-\hat{p}_i^*)\rho_1\pi_0 + \hat{p}_i^* \rho_0 \pi_1}$$

where $\hat{p}_i^*$ is the unadjusted estimate of the posterior probability (**_PROB_**). The **scoval** (scored validation) data set will be used later.

```
/* pmlr04d02.sas  */
ods select roccurve scorefitstat;
proc logistic data=train1;
   model ins(event='1')=&selected;
   score data=valid1 out=scoval
         priorevent=&pi1 outroc=roc fitstat;
run;
```

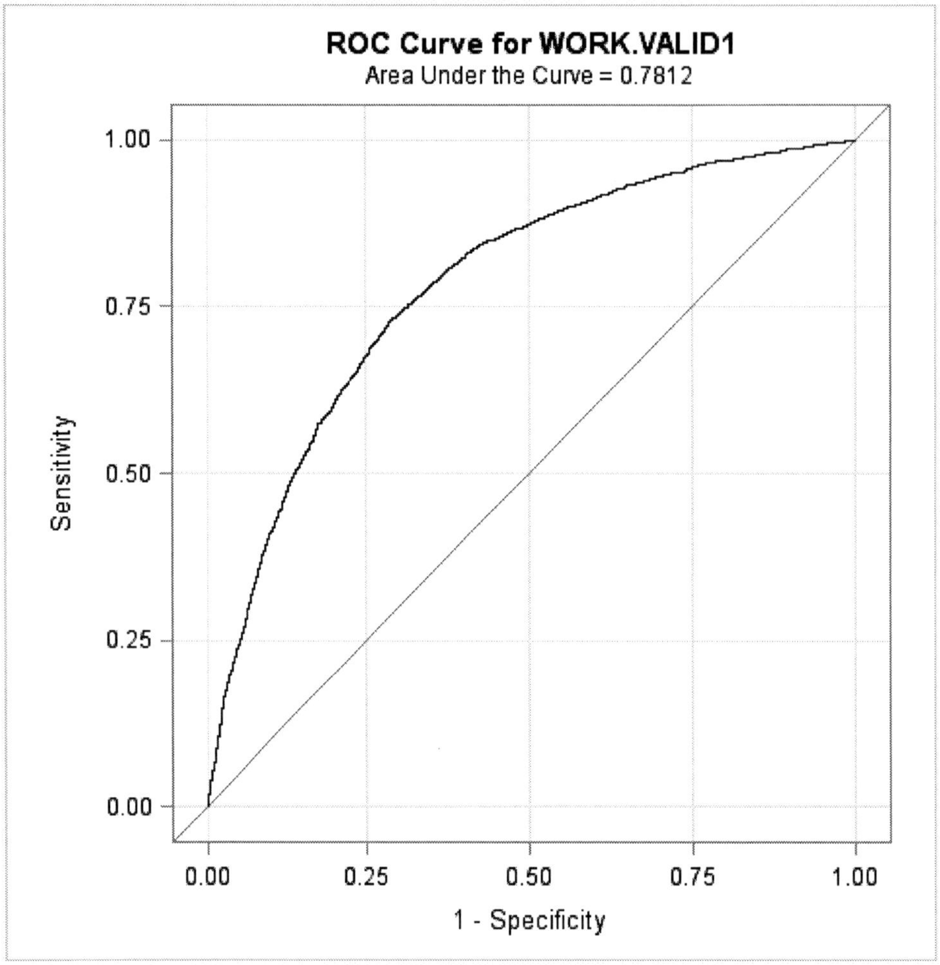

Fit Statistics for SCORE Data											
Data Set	Total Frequency	Log Likelihood	Error Rate	AIC	AICC	BIC	SC	R-Square	Max-Rescaled R-Square	AUC	Brier Score
WORK.VALID1	10752	-12593.8	0.3448	25237.63	25237.75	25419.7	25419.7	-1.86417	-2.57192	0.781153	0.307536

The c statistic for the training data set was 0.785, which is not much higher than 0.781. This small difference in the c statistics between the training and validation data sets indicates that this model will generalize very well to new data.

```
proc print data=roc(obs=10);
   var _prob_ _sensit_ _1mspec_;
run;
```

Obs	_PROB_	_SENSIT_	_1MSPEC_
1	0.99995	.000268528	.000000000
2	0.76854	.000537057	.000000000
3	0.74763	.000805585	.000000000
4	0.69819	.001074114	.000000000
5	0.68969	.001074114	.000142288
6	0.68380	.001342642	.000142288
7	0.67272	.001611171	.000142288
8	0.65789	.001879699	.000142288
9	0.61134	.002148228	.000142288
10	0.61001	.002148228	.000284576

Knowledge of the population priors and sensitivity and specificity is sufficient to fill in the confusion matrices. Several additional statistics can be calculated in a DATA step:

- TP = proportion of true positives
- FN = proportion of false negatives
- TN = proportion of true negatives
- FP = proportion of false positives
- POSPV = positive predicted value
- NEGPV = negative predicted value
- ACC = accuracy
- DEPTH = proportion allocated to class 1
- LIFT = positive predicted value/π_1.

Each row in the OUTROC= data set corresponds to a cutoff (**_PROB_**). The selected cutoffs occur where values of the estimated posterior probability change, provided the posterior probabilities are more than .0001 apart, otherwise they are grouped. Consequently, the maximum number of rows in the OUTROC= data set is 9999, but it is usually much less. The grouping can be made coarser by using the ROCEPS= option in the MODEL statement.

```
data roc;
   set roc;
   cutoff=_PROB_;
   specif=1-_1MSPEC_;
   tp=&pi1*_SENSIT_;
   fn=&pi1*(1-_SENSIT_);
   tn=(1-&pi1)*specif;
   fp=(1-&pi1)*_1MSPEC_;
   depth=tp+fp;
   pospv=tp/depth;
   negpv=tn/(1-depth);
   acc=tp+tn;
   lift=pospv/&pi1;
   keep cutoff tn fp fn tp
        _SENSIT_ _1MSPEC_ specif depth
        pospv negpv acc lift;
run;
```

Example: Create a lift chart by plotting **lift** against **depth**. Add a reference line at the baseline (a lift of 1) and restrict the focus to the region where depth is greater than 0.5% (less erratic) and less than 50%.

```
proc sgplot data=roc;
   where 0.005 <= depth <= 0.50;
   title "Lift Chart for Validation Data";
   series y=lift x=depth;
   refline 1.0 / axis=y;
   yaxis values=(0 to 8 by 1);
run; quit;
```

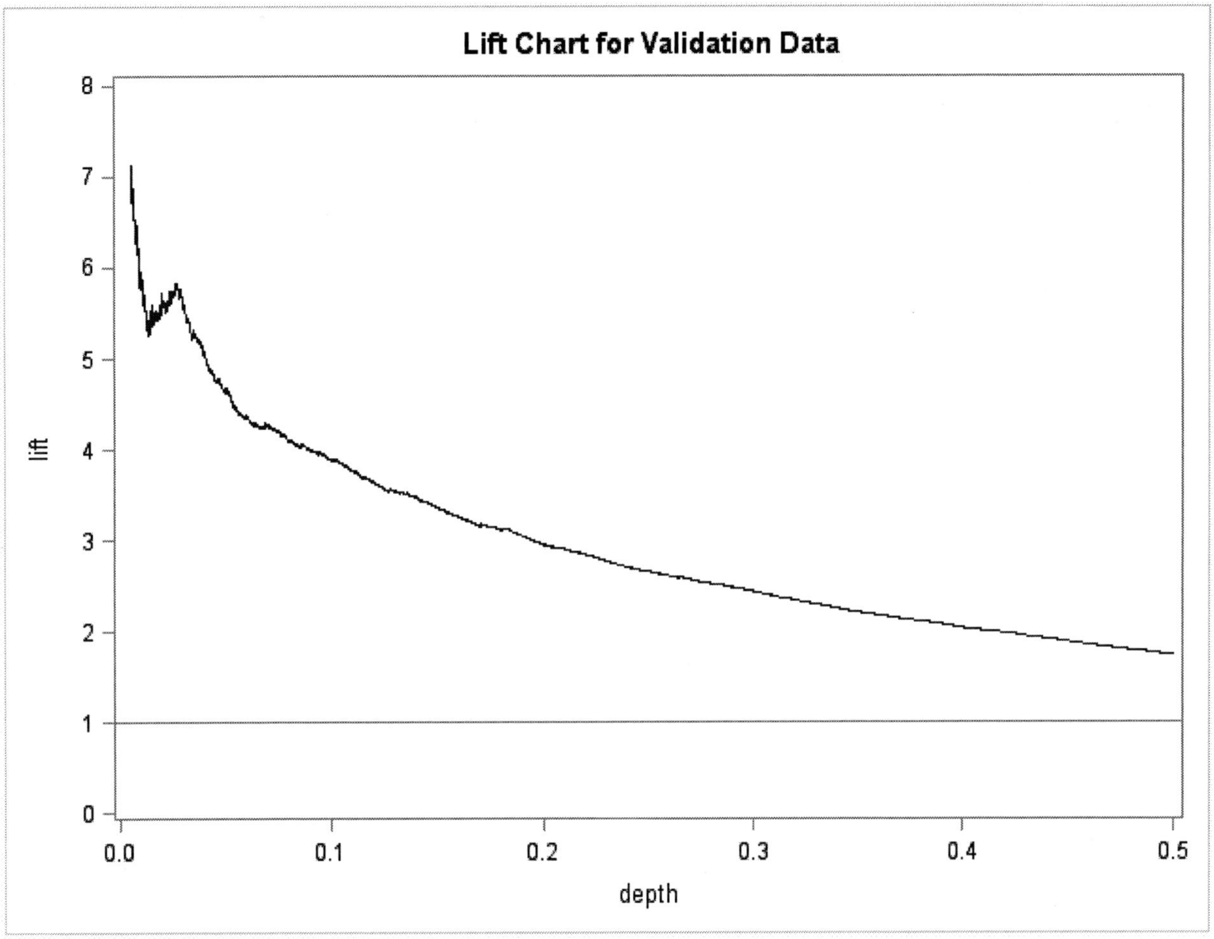

The lift chart shows that at a depth of 0.1, the lift would be approximately 4.0. This means that if you targeted the top 10% of your customers based on the predicted probabilities, you would get 4 times as many responses compared to targeting a random sample of 10%.

Exercises

1. Model Assessment

a. Use PROC SURVEYSELECT to split the imputed data set (**pva1**) into training and validation data sets. If **pva1** does not exist, submit programs **pmlr00d01.sas** and **pmlr03s01.sas**. Use 50% of the data for each data set role. Stratify on the target variable and use a seed of 27513.

1) How many observations are on the training data set?

b. Fit a logistic regression model on the training data set using **TARGET_B** as the target variable and the macro variable **EX_SELECTED** as the input variables. Use the event= option to model the probability that **TARGET_B**=1. Use the SCORE statement to score the validation data set adjusting for oversampling. Use the OUTROC= option to create a data set and an ROC curve for the validation data set. Use the FITSTAT option to generate model fit statistics.

1) What is the c statistic for the validation data set?

c. Using the OUTROC= data set, write a DATA step to compute the proportion of true positives, the proportion of false negatives, the proportion of true negatives, the proportion of false positives, the positive predicted value, the negative predicted value, the accuracy, the proportion allocated to class 1 (depth), and the lift. Then use PROC SGPLOT to create a lift chart. Add a reference line at a lift of 1 and restrict the focus to the region where depth is greater than 0.5% and less than 50%. Also restrict the Y-axis from 0 to 4 by 1.

1) What is the lift at a depth of 10%?

4.03 Multiple Choice Poll

What is the lift at a depth of 10%?

a. 1.5
b. 1.9
c. 2.3
d. 2.7

22

4.3 Allocation Rules

Objectives

- Illustrate the decision rule that maximizes the expected profit.
- Explain the profit matrix and how to use it to estimate the profit per scored customer.
- Graph the average validation profit against different cutoffs and different depths.

26

Cutoffs

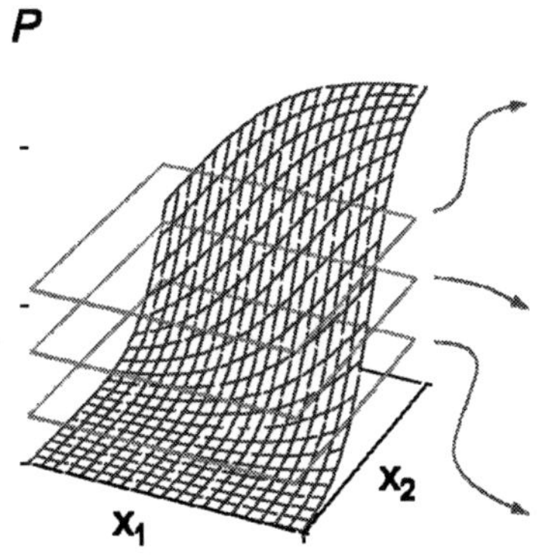

0	1	Se	Sp
70	5	.64	.93
9	16		
66	9	.84	.88
4	21		
57	18	.96	.76
1	24		

27

Different cutoffs produce different allocations and different confusion matrices. To determine the optimal cutoff, a performance criterion needs to be defined. If the goal were to increase the sensitivity of the classifier, then the optimal classifier would allocate all cases to class 1. If the goal were to increase specificity, then the optimal classifier would be to allocate all cases to class 0. For realistic data, there is a trade-off between sensitivity and specificity. Higher cutoffs decrease sensitivity and increase specificity. Lower cutoffs decrease specificity and increase sensitivity.

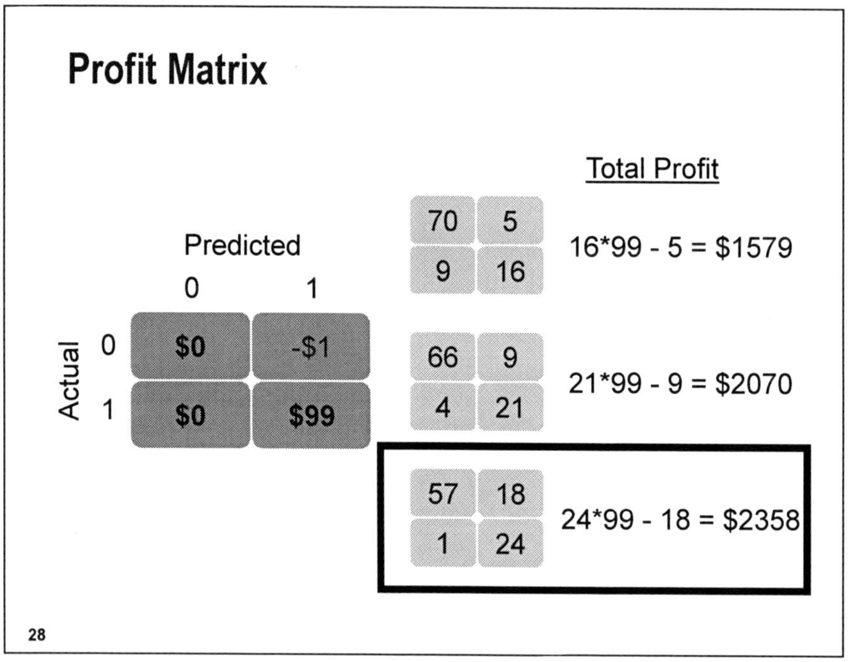

A formal approach to determining the optimal cutoff uses statistical decision theory (McLachlan 1992, Ripley 1996, Hand 1997). The decision-theoretic approach starts by assigning profit margins to true positives and loss margins to false positives. The optimal decision rule maximizes the total expected profit.

The profit matrix in the above slide is consistent with a marketing effort that costs $1, and, when successful, garners revenue of $100. Hence, the profit for soliciting a non-responder is -$1, and the profit for soliciting a responder is $100-$1 = $99. Given that each individual has a posterior probability p_i, you can resort to simple algebra to find the optimum cutoff.

A typical decision rule would be: Solicit if the expected profit for soliciting, given the posterior probability, is higher than the expected profit for ignoring the customer.

Solicit if:

$$
\begin{aligned}
E(\text{Profit} \mid p_i, \text{solicit}) &> E(\text{Profit} \mid p_i, \text{do not solicit}) \\
p_i*99 + (1-p_i)*(-1) &> p_i*0 + (1-p_i)*(0) \\
99*p_i - 1 + p_i &> 0 \\
100*p_i - 1 &> 0 \\
p_i &> 0.01.
\end{aligned}
$$

This cutoff of 0.01 can be used to calculate the expected profit of using this rule with the current model.

Profit Matrix

Actual Class \ Decision	0	1
0	δ_{TN}	δ_{FP}
1	δ_{FN}	δ_{TP}

Bayes Rule:

Decision 1 if

$$P > \frac{1}{1+\left(\frac{\delta_{\mathrm{TP}}-\delta_{\mathrm{FN}}}{\delta_{\mathrm{TN}}-\delta_{\mathrm{FP}}}\right)}$$

29

The *Bayes rule* is the decision rule that maximizes the expected profit. In the two-class situation, the Bayes rule can be determined analytically. Using the symbols in the above profit matrix, if a customer is solicited then the expected profit is

$$p(\delta_{TP})+(1-p)\,(\delta_{FP})$$

where p is the true posterior probability that a case belongs to class 1. If a customer is not solicited, then the expected profit is

$$p(\delta_{FN})+(1-p)(\delta_{TN})$$

Therefore, the optimal rule allocates a case to class 1 if

$$p(\delta_{TP})+(1-p)\,(\delta_{FP}) > p(\delta_{FN})+(1-p)(\delta_{TN})$$

otherwise allocate the case to class 0. Solving for p gives the optimal cutoff probability. Because p must be estimated from the data, the *plug-in Bayes rule* is used in practice

$$\hat{p} > \frac{1}{1+\left(\frac{\delta_{TP}-\delta_{FN}}{\delta_{TN}-\delta_{FP}}\right)}$$

Consequently, the plug-in Bayes rule might not achieve the maximum profit if the estimate of the posterior probability is poorly estimated.

Using the profit matrix defined earlier, the optimal cutoff becomes

$$\hat{p} > \frac{1}{1+\left(\frac{99-0}{0-(-1)}\right)} \text{ or } 0.01.$$

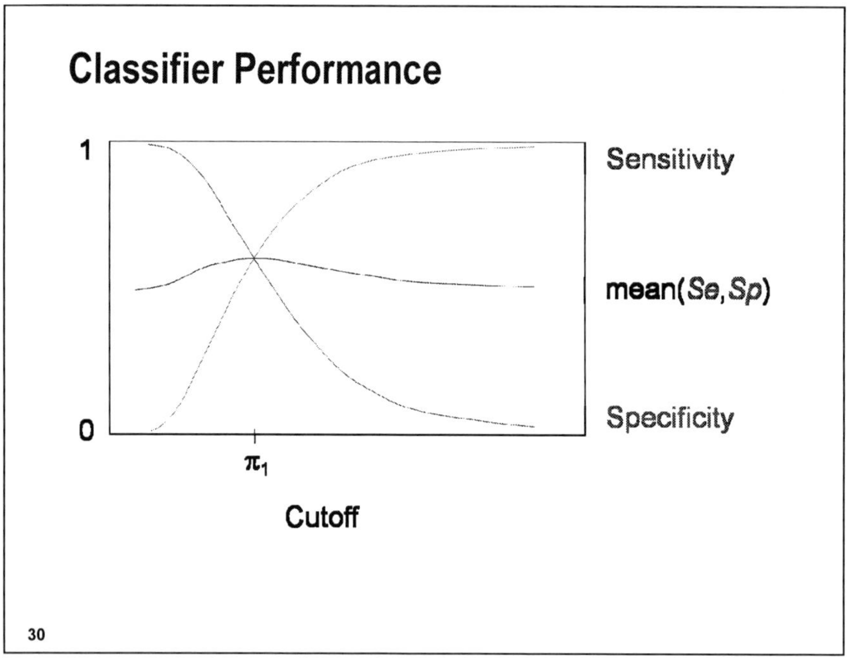

In many situations, gathering profit information can be difficult. One recommendation is to use a cutoff of π_1. The central cutoff, π_1, tends to maximize the mean of sensitivity and specificity. Because increasing sensitivity usually corresponds to decreasing specificity, the central cutoff tends to equalize sensitivity and specificity.

If separate samples were taken with equal allocation (50% events and 50% nonevents), then using the unadjusted cutoff of 0.5 on the biased sample is equivalent to using the central cutoff, π_1, on the population.

Using Profit to Assess Fit

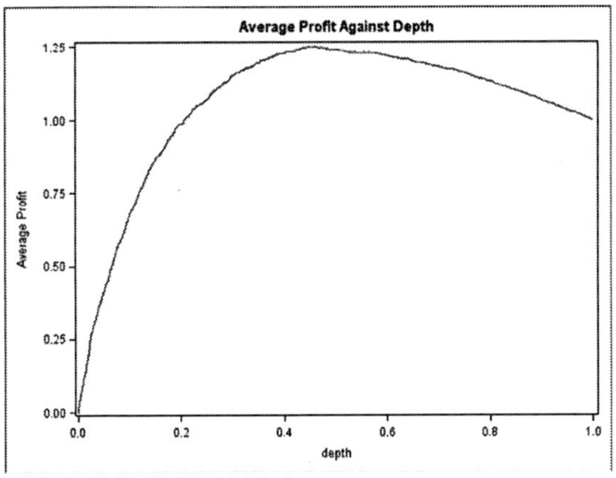

31

Defining a *profit matrix* can create a useful statistic for measuring classifier performance. The model yields posterior probabilities, and those probabilities (in conjunction with a profit matrix) classify individuals into likely positives and likely negatives. On the validation data, the behavior of these individuals is known. Hence, it is feasible to calculate each individual's expected profit, and hence it is also feasible to calculate a total profit. This total profit can be used as a model selection and assessment criterion.

If profit information can be used, it permits a more familiar scale for comparing models. Consumers of models might not have a feel for what type of lift they expect, or what constitutes a good value for sensitivity. Using total or average profit as an assessment statistic might skirt those issues.

4.04 Multiple Choice Poll

If the profit margin of true positives is 9 times higher than the loss margins of false positives, then according to Bayes rule what is the cutoff that maximizes the expected profit (assuming 0 profit and loss for true negatives and false negatives)?

a. 0.90
b. 0.09
c. 1/9
d. 0.10

32

Using Profit to Assess Fit

Example: Use a cutoff of 0.01 and the profit matrix of -\$1 for soliciting a non-responder and \$99 for soliciting a responder to calculate profit per individual. Use PROC MEANS to sum and average the profits and use the WEIGHT statement to account for oversampling.

In order to calculate total and average profit comparable to what would be achieved in the population, weights must be calculated. Sampling weights adjust the data so that it better represents the true population. When a rare target event has been oversampled, class 0 is under-represented in the sample. Consequently, a class-0 case should actually count more in the analysis than a class-1 case.

$$weight_i = \begin{cases} \dfrac{\pi_1}{\rho_1} & \text{if } y_i = 1 \\ \dfrac{\pi_0}{\rho_0} & \text{if } y_i = 0 \end{cases}$$

The weights adjust the number of cases in the sample to be $n\pi_0$ and $n\pi_1$, in class 0 and 1 respectively. The classes now are in the same proportion in the adjusted sample as they are in the population.

The macro variables for the proportion of events in the population and sample were created earlier. The decision variable is created as a flag indicating whether the predicted probability is greater than the cutoff, 0.01. Using the information about decision and response, the profit per individual is calculated.

```
/* pmlr04d03.sas */
data scoval;
   set scoval;
   sampwt = (&pi1/&rho1)*(INS)
              + ((1-&pi1)/(1-&rho1))*(1-INS);
   decision = (p_1 > 0.01);
   profit = decision*INS*99
              - decision*(1-INS)*1;
run;

proc means data=scoval sum mean;
   weight sampwt;
   var profit;
   title "Total and Average Profit";
run;
```

Total and Average Profit

The MEANS Procedure

Analysis Variable : profit	
Sum	**Mean**
13332.95	1.2400313

Using this model to score a population of, say, 1,000,000 individuals and soliciting only those with p_i greater than 0.01 would yield a total expected profit of $1,240,031.30. With the above profit matrix and π_1=0.02, the "solicit everyone" rule generates a profit of 1,000,000*0.02*99-1,000,000*.98*1= $1,000,000. Using the model and some elementary decision theory leads to better decisions and more profit. Other models can be compared to this current model with this statistic.

Example: To see how other cutoffs fare, use the information in the **ROC** data set to draw a plot of how average profit changes as a function of the solicited depth and the cutoff. For the plot showing the cutoff, restrict the plot to the region around the cutoff of 0.01.

Using the true positive and false positive rates calculated earlier, you can calculate the average profit for each of the cutoffs considered in the **ROC** data set. A false positive (**fp**) is an individual who is solicited but does not respond. Hence, the cost of soliciting the false positives, on average, is the $1 solicitation cost times the false positive rate. Likewise, the profit associated with individuals who are solicited and respond is $99 times the true positive rate, **tp**. The difference of these two terms is the average profit.

```
data roc;
   set roc;
   AveProf = 99*tp - 1*fp;
run;

title "Average Profit Against Depth";
proc sgplot data=roc;
   series y=aveProf x=depth;
   yaxis label="Average Profit";
run;
```

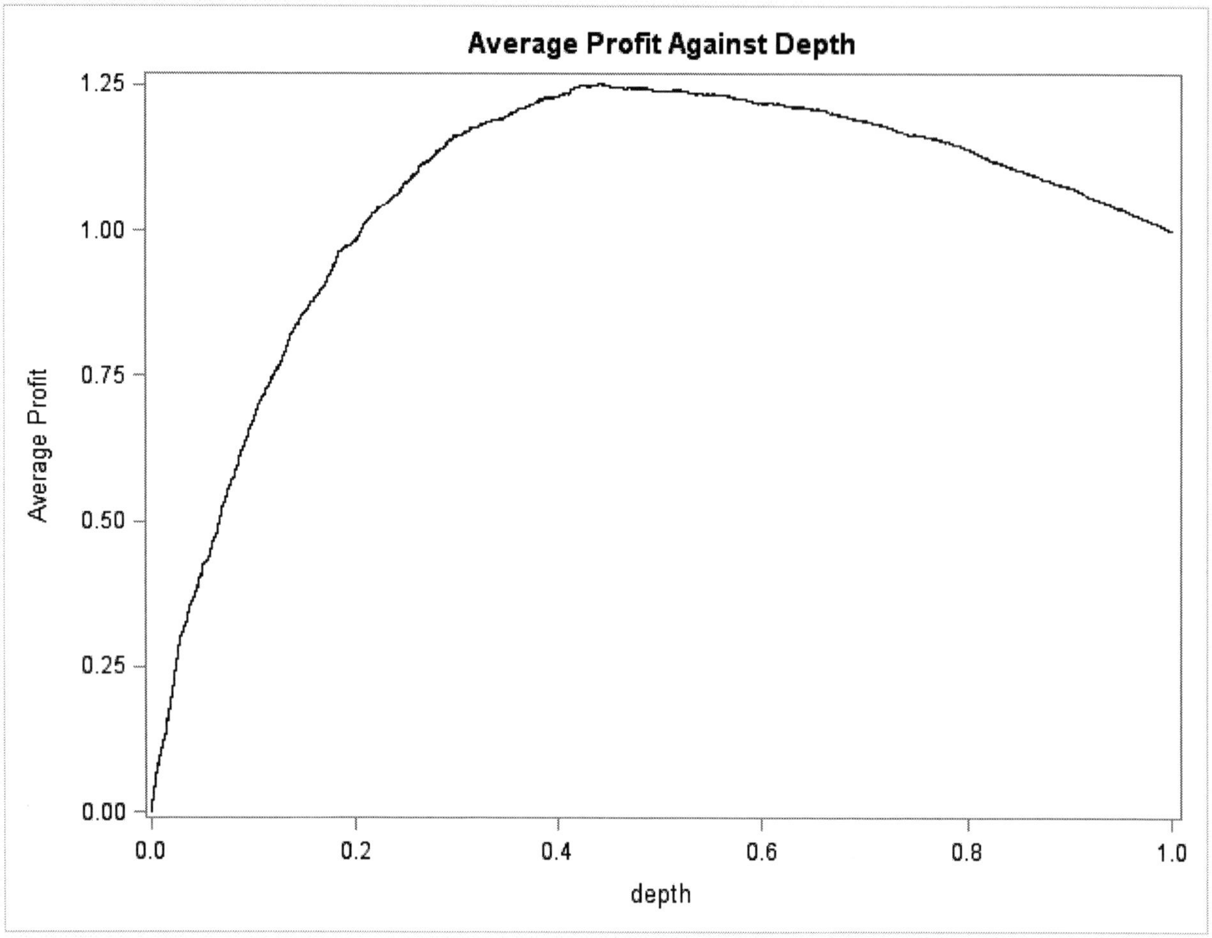

The plot shows that the highest average profit would occur at a solicited depth of 45-50%.

```
title "Average Profit Against Cutoff";
proc sgplot data=roc;
   where cutoff le 0.05;
   refline .01 / axis=x;
   series y=aveProf x=cutoff;
   yaxis label="Average Profit";
run;
```

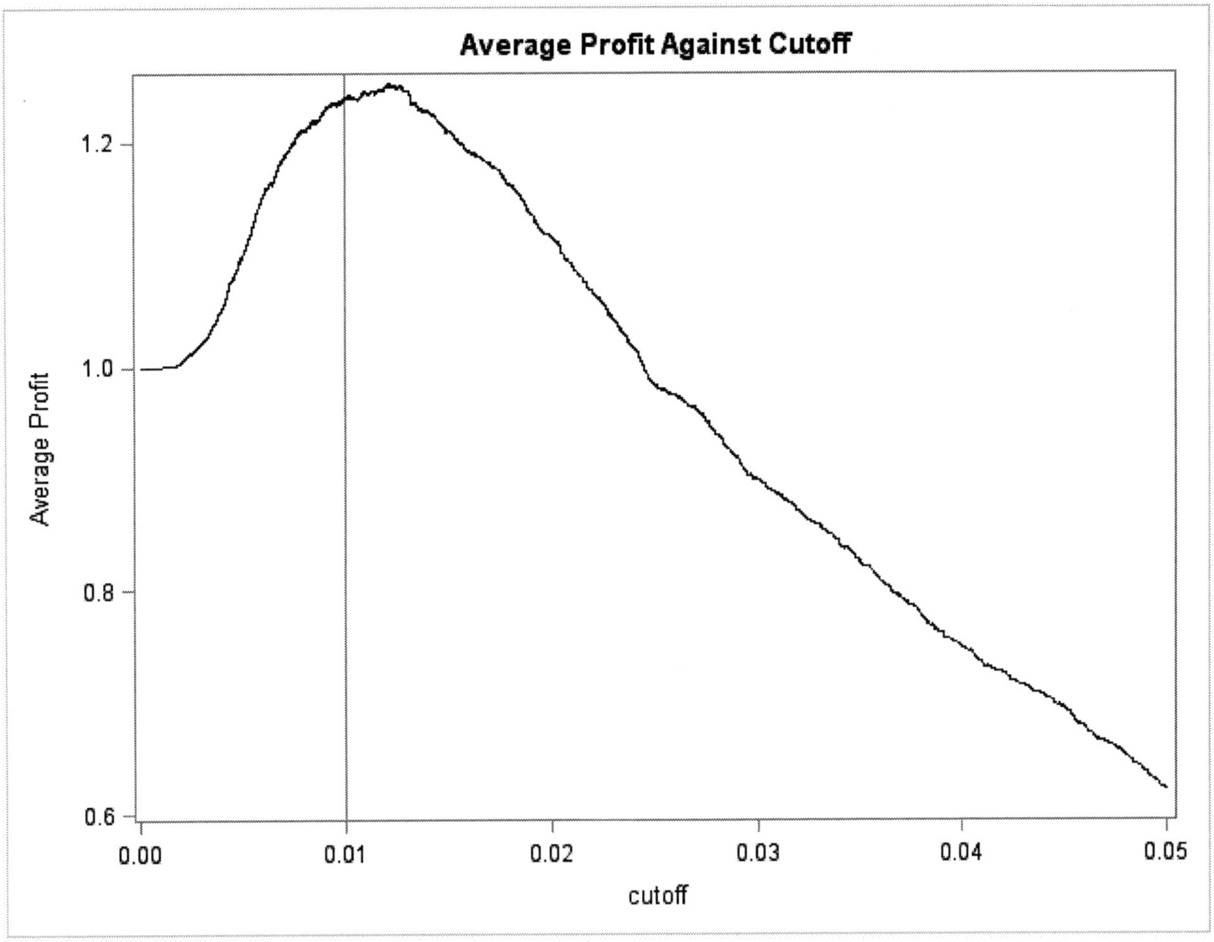

The plot shows that the highest average profit would occur at a cutoff around 0.012.

4.4 Overall Predictive Power

Objectives

- Discuss the utility of the Kolmogorov-Smirnov statistic.
- Compute the Kolmogorov-Smirnov statistic in PROC NPAR1WAY.

37

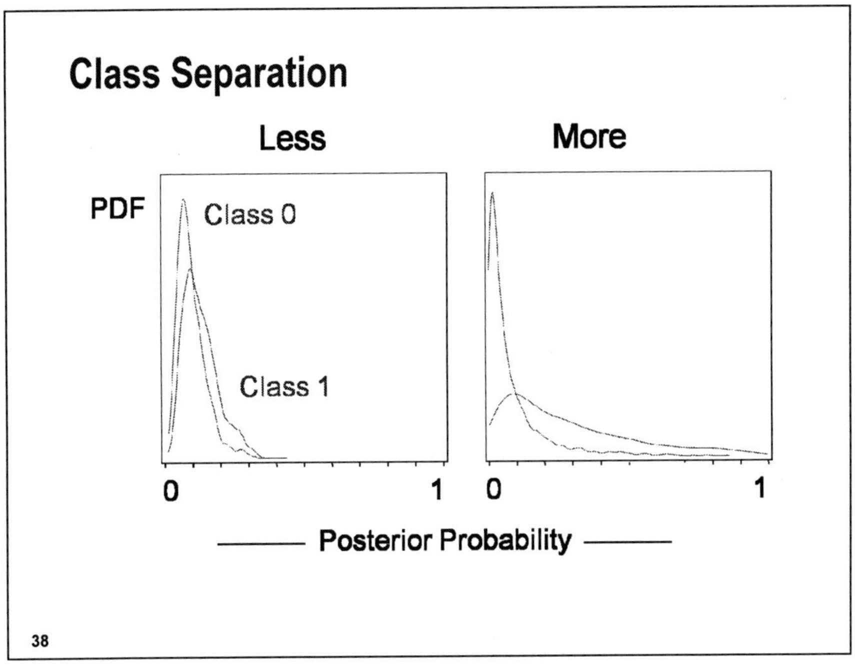

Statistics such as sensitivity, positive predictive value, and risk depend on the choice of cutoff value. Statistics that summarize the performance of a classifier across a range of cutoffs can also be useful for assessing global discriminatory power. One approach is to measure the separation between the predicted posterior probabilities for each class. The more that the distributions overlap, the weaker the model is.

The simplest statistics are based on the difference between the means of the two distributions. In credit scoring, the *divergence* statistic is a scaled difference between the means (Nelson 1997). Hand (1997) discusses several summary measures based on the difference between the means.

The well-known *t*-test for comparing two distributions is based on the difference between the means. The *t*-test has many optimal properties when the two distributions are symmetric with equal variance (and have light tails). However, the distributions of the predicted posterior probabilities are typically asymmetric with unequal variance. Many other two-sample tests have been devised for nonnormal distributions (Conover 1980).

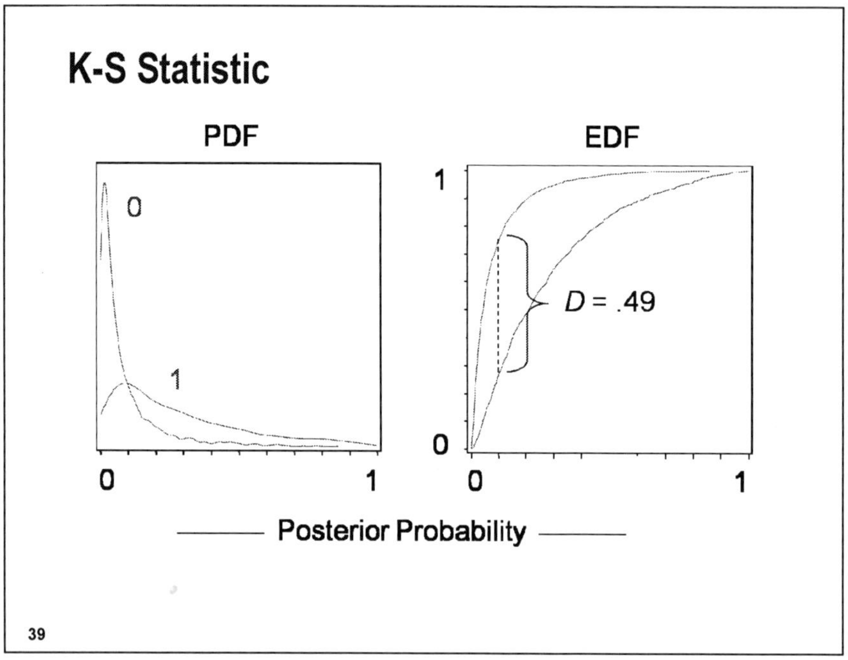

The Kolmogorov-Smirnov two-sample test is based on the distance between the empirical distribution functions (Conover 1980). The test statistic, D, is the maximum vertical difference between the cumulative distributions. If D equals zero, the distributions are everywhere identical. If D>0, then there is some posterior probability where the distributions differ. The maximum value of the K-S statistic, 1, occurs when the distributions are perfectly separated. Use of the K-S statistic for comparing predictive models is popular in credit risk modeling.

An oversampled validation data set does not affect D because the empirical distribution function is unchanged if each case represents more than one case in the population. Furthermore, when you use the central cutoff, π_1, you maximize the D statistic.

Area under the ROC Curve

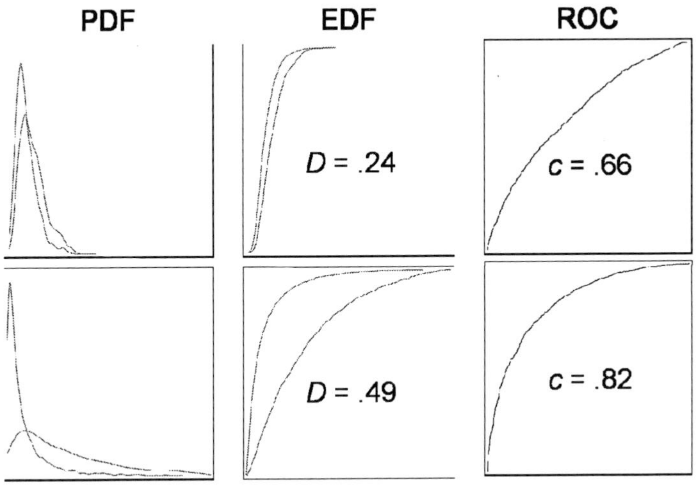

40

The Kolmogorov-Smirnov two-sample test is sensitive to all types of differences between the distributions – location, scale, and shape. In the predictive modeling context, it could be argued that location differences are paramount. Because of its generality, the K-S test is not particularly powerful at detecting location differences. The most powerful nonparametric two-sample test is the Wilcoxon-Mann-Whitney test. Remarkably, the Wilcoxon-Mann-Whitney test statistic is also equivalent to the area under the ROC curve (Hand 1997).

The Wilcoxon version of this popular two-sample test is based on the ranks of the data. In the predictive modeling context, the predicted posterior probabilities would be ranked from smallest to largest. The test statistic is based on the sum of the ranks in the classes. The area under the ROC curve, c, can be determined from the rank-sum in class 1.

$$c = \frac{\sum_{\{i|y=1\}}^{n_1} R_i - \tfrac{1}{2} n_1 (n_1 + 1)}{n_1 \cdot n_0}$$

The first term in the numerator is the sum of the ranks in class 1.

A perfect ROC curve would be a horizontal line at one – that is, sensitivity and specificity would both equal one for all cutoffs. In this case, the c statistic would equal one. The c statistic technically ranges from zero to one, but in practice, it should not get much lower than one-half. A perfectly random model, where the posterior probabilities were assigned arbitrarily, would give a 45° angle straight ROC curve that intersects the origin. Hence, it would give a c statistic of 0.5.

Oversampling does not affect the area under the ROC curve because sensitivity and specificity are unaffected. The area under the ROC curve is also equivalent to the Gini coefficient, which is used to summarize the performance of a Lorentz curve (Hand 1997).

Calculating the K-S Statistic

Example: Calculate the K-S statistic on the scored validation data set using PROC NPAR1WAY. Also create an empirical distribution function plot.

The K-S statistic can be computed in the NPAR1WAY procedure using the scored validation data set. The EDF option in PROC NPAR1WAY requests the Kolmogorov-Smirnov test. The test compares the values of the variable listed in the VAR statement between the groups listed in the CLASS statement.

```
/* pmlr04d04.sas */
proc npar1way edf data=scoval;
   class ins;
   var p_1;
   title "K-S Statistic for the Validation Data Set";
run;
```

Partial Output

K-S Statistic for the Validation Data Set

The NPAR1WAY Procedure

Kolmogorov-Smirnov Test for Variable P_1 Classified by Variable Ins			
Ins	N	EDF at Maximum	Deviation from Mean at Maximum
0	7028	0.710729	12.800721
1	3724	0.269871	-17.585126
Total	****	0.558036	
Maximum Deviation Occurred at Observation 2578			
Value of P_1 at Maximum = 0.018131			

Kolmogorov-Smirnov Two-Sample Test (Asymptotic)			
KS	0.209763	D	0.440857
KSa	21.750750	Pr > KSa	<.0001

The results show that the two-sample Kolmogorov statistic D is 0.44, which represents the largest separation between the two cumulative distributions.

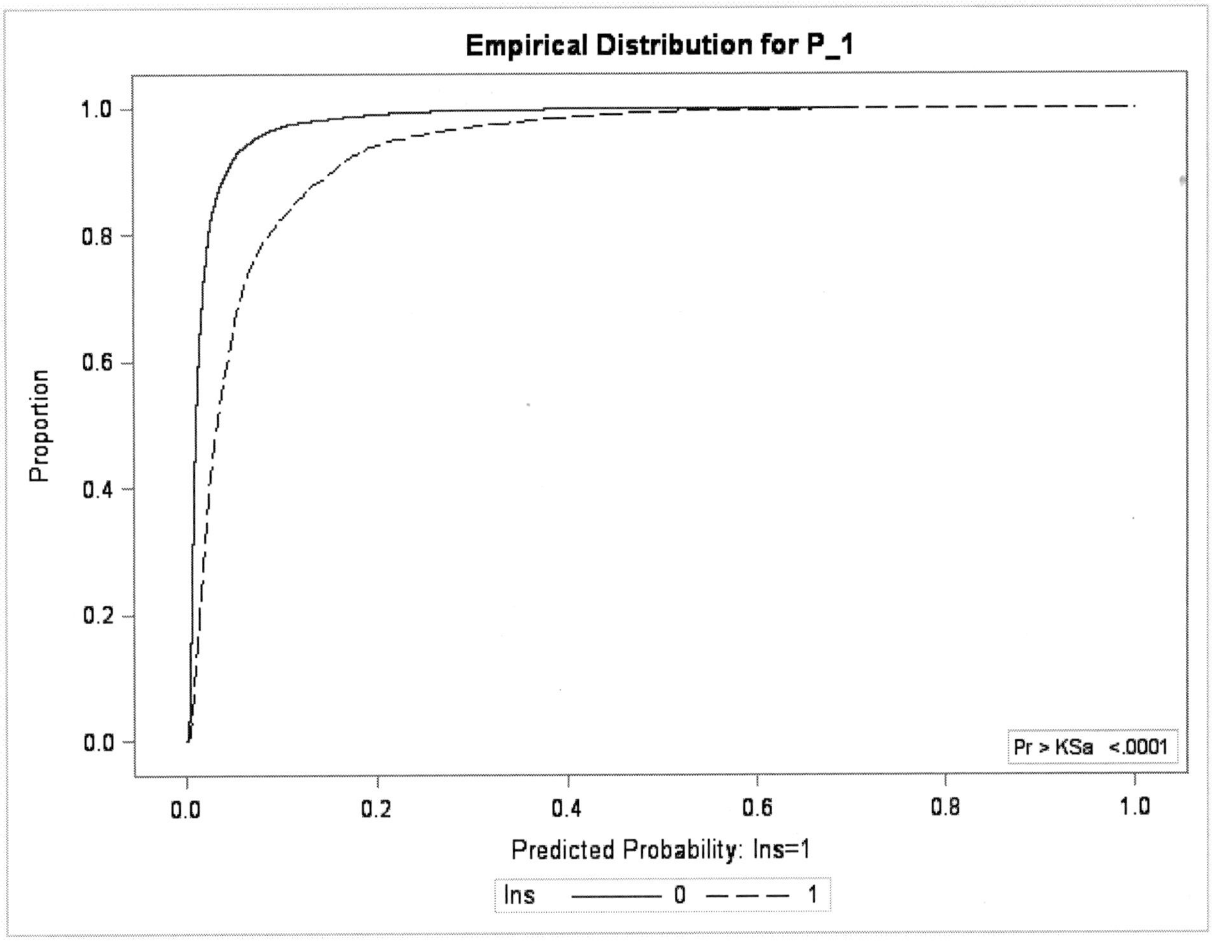

The empirical distribution function plot shows the proportion of observations less than a given probability for the responders and nonresponders. The D statistic is the maximum vertical difference between the two distributions.

4.05 Multiple Choice Poll

Which of the following statements is false regarding the K-S statistic?

a. The test statistic, D, is the maximum vertical distance between the cumulative distributions.
b. An oversampled validation data set does not affect the test statistic D.
c. The K-S statistic is statistically equivalent to the area under the ROC curve.
d. The K-S statistic is not as powerful at detecting location differences as the Wilcoxon-Mann-Whitney test.

41

4.5 Model Selection Plots

Objectives

- Discuss the utility of comparing the training and validation data fit statistics versus model complexity.
- Illustrate the ROC and ROCCONTRAST statements in PROC LOGISTIC.
- Use the ASSESS and FITANDSCORE macros to generate and evaluate many models.

46

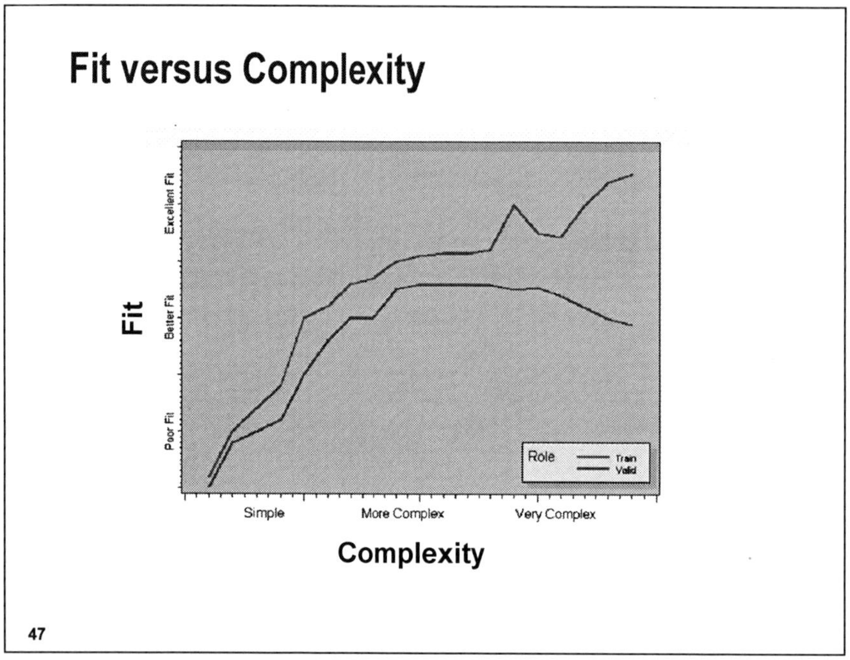

To compare many models, an appropriate fit statistic (or statistics) must be selected. For statistics like average profit, c, and Kolmogorov-Smirnov's D, higher values mean better fitting models. Because the goal of most predictive modeling efforts is a model that generalizes well, these statistics are typically measured on the validation data set. For a series of models, which could be generated by an automatic selection routine, it is conceivable to plot a fit measure against some index of complexity. For standard logistic regression models, this index is likely equivalent to the degrees of freedom in the model.

Typically, model performance follows a fairly straightforward trend. As the complexity increases (that is, as terms are added) the fit on the training data gets better. After a point, the fit might plateau, but on the training data, the fit gets better as model complexity increases. Some of this increase is attributable to the model capturing relevant trends in the data. Detecting these trends is the goal of modeling. Some of the increase, however, is due to the model identifying vagaries of the training data set. This behavior has been called overfitting. Because these vagaries are not likely to be repeated, in the validation data or in future observations, it is reasonable to want to eliminate those models. Hence, the model fit on the validation data, for models of varying complexity, is also plotted. The typical behavior of the validation fit line is an increase (as more complex models detect more usable patterns) followed by a plateau, which might finally result in a decline[2] in performance. The decline in performance is due to overfitting. The plateau just indicates more complicated models that have no fit-based arguments for their use. A reasonable rule would be to select the model associated with the complexity that has the highest validation fit statistic.

Plotting the training and validation results together permits a further assessment of the model's generalizing power. Typically, the performance will deteriorate from the training data to the validation data. This phenomenon, sometimes known as *shrinkage*, is an additional statistic that some modelers use to get a measure of the generalizing power of the selected model. For example, the rule used to select a model from the many different models plotted might be: "Choose the simplest model that has the highest validation fit measure, with no more than 10% shrinkage from the training to the validation results."

---

[2] This behavior is sometimes called *peaking*.

If the measure of model fit is some sort of error rate, then the plot looks like the one in the previous slide but flipped about the horizontal axis. In the absence of profit or cost information, the Mean Squared Error (MSE) is one such fit statistic that measures how poorly a model fits. That is, smaller is better.

ROC and ROCCONTRAST Statements

General form of the ROC and ROCCONTRAST statements:

```
ROC <'label'> <specification> </ options>;
ROCCONTRAST <'label'><contrast></ options>;
```

48

You can use the ROC and ROCCONTRAST statements if you want to compare ROC curves from several models. The ROC statements specify models to be used in the ROC comparisons. You can specify more than one ROC statement. ROC statements are identified by their label. The specification can be either a list of effects that have previously been specified in the MODEL statement, or PRED=variable, where the variable does not have to be specified in the MODEL statement. The PRED= option enables you to input a criterion produced outside PROC LOGISTIC.

The ROCCONTRAST statement compares the different ROC models. You can specify only one ROCCONTRAST statement.

ASSESS and FITANDSCORE Macros

- Macros take a series of models generated by the best subsets logistic regression and compares them on the validation data performance.
- Plots of the results can be generated, which shows the performance gains as a function of model complexity, which should be a very useful tool for final model selection.

49

The process of selecting inputs for a model, fitting that model, and evaluating that model's fit on the validation data set can be automated with macro programming. This will enable you to consider many candidate models in a small time frame, which should lead to better model generalization.

Comparing and Evaluating Models

Example: Compare the ROC curves on the validation data set for the two models that correspond to the model fit in Chapter 2 and the model fit in Chapter 4.

To get the validation performance, you need to score the validation data with the two models.

```
/* pmlr04d05.sas */

proc logistic data=train1 noprint;
   class res;
   model ins(event='1')=dda ddabal dep depamt checks res;
   score data=valid1 out=sco_validate(rename=(p_1=p_ch2));
run;

proc logistic data=train1 noprint;
   model ins(event='1')=&selected;
   score data=sco_validate out=sco_validate(rename=(p_1=p_sel));
run;
```

Using the ROC and ROCCONTRAST statements, you can create and compare the ROC curves for the two models.

```
ods select ROCOverlay ROCAssociation ROCContrastTest;
proc logistic data=sco_validate;
   model ins(event='1')=p_ch2 p_sel / nofit;
   roc "Chapter 2 Model" p_ch2;
   roc "Chapter 4 Model" p_sel;
   roccontrast "Comparing the Two Models";
   title "Validation Data Set Performance";
run;
```

Selected MODEL statement option:

NOFIT performs the global score test without fitting the model. This option is used so that only the models specified in the ROC statements are compared.

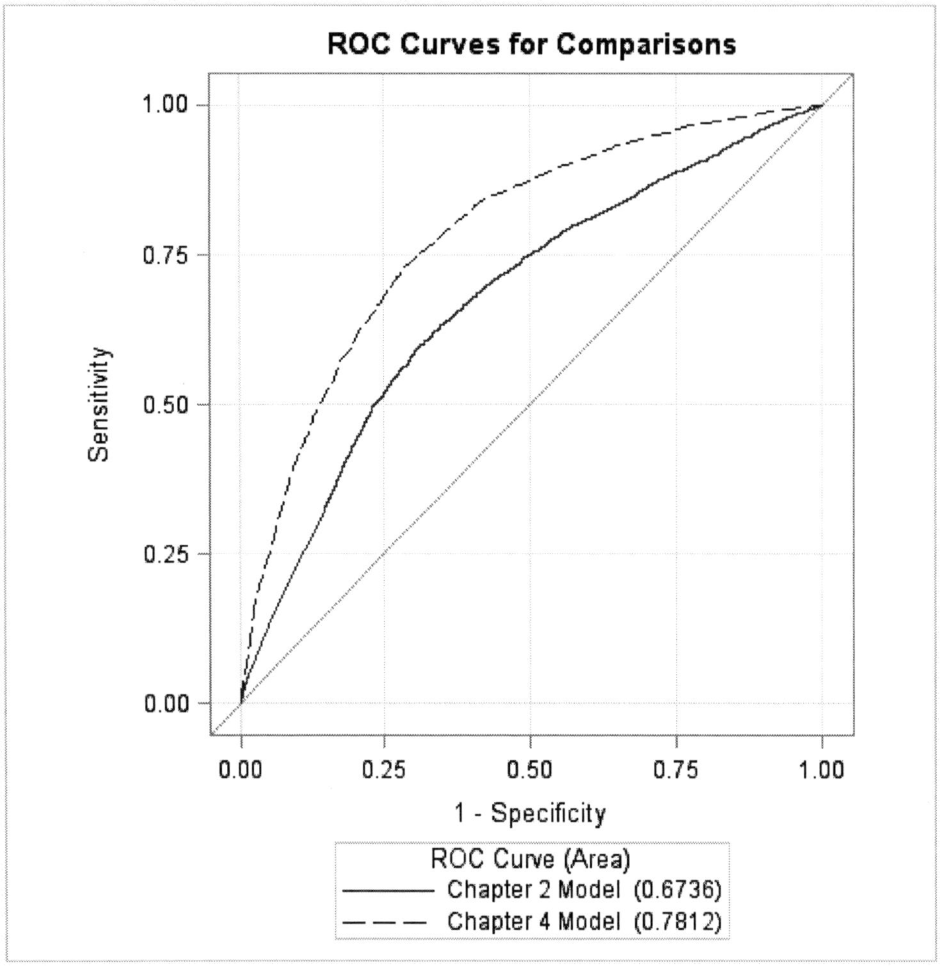

ROC Association Statistics

ROC Model	Mann-Whitney Area	Standard Error	95% Wald Confidence Limits		Somers' D (Gini)	Gamma	Tau-a
Chapter 2 Model	0.6736	0.00546	0.6630	0.6843	0.3473	0.3517	0.1573
Chapter 4 Model	0.7812	0.00460	0.7721	0.7902	0.5623	0.5623	0.2546

ROC Contrast Test Results

Contrast	DF	Chi-Square	Pr > ChiSq
Comparing the Two Models	1	508.9567	<.0001

The validation results show that the c statistic is much lower for the model fit in Chapter 2. However, because these inputs were selected arbitrarily, it would be highly unlikely that the model in Chapter 2 would outperform the model fit in Chapter 4.

Example: Use the ASSESS and FITANDSCORE macros to generate a series of models by best subsets logistic regression and compare them on the validation data set performance.

This demonstration uses the validation performance of many different models as a guide to selecting models that will generalize well. Hence, the validation data must be prepared in the same way as the training data. To this end, the data sets **train2** and **valid2**, which were created by imputing for all numeric variables on the **train** and **valid** data sets, are augmented with the modified **DDABal** and **SavBal** variables. Moreover, because the all subsets algorithm in PROC LOGISTIC cannot be used with the CLASS statement, the dummy variables for **res** are created on these data sets as well.

```
/* pmlr04d06.sas */

data train2;
   set train2;
   resr=(res="R");
   resu=(res="U");
   if not dda then ddabal = &mean;
   brclus1=(branch='B14');
   brclus2=(branch in ('B12','B5','B8',
                       'B3','B18','B19','B17',
                       'B4','B6','B10','B9',
                       'B1','B13'));
   brclus3=(branch in ('B15','B16'));
   %include rank;
   if savbal > 16000 then savbal=16000;
run;

data valid2;
   set valid2;
   resr=(res="R");
   resu=(res="U");
   if not dda then ddabal = &mean;
   brclus1=(branch='B14');
   brclus2=(branch in ('B12','B5','B8',
                       'B3','B18','B19','B17',
                       'B4','B6','B10','B9',
                       'B1','B13'));
   brclus3=(branch in ('B15','B16'));
   %include rank;
   if savbal > 16000 then savbal=16000;
run;
```

PROC LOGISTIC with SELECTION equal to SCORE is called. The number of models per complexity is specified by the BEST= option. The ODS output data set **score** contains the inputs used in at each complexity level. Setting BEST=2 will generate twice as many candidate models as BEST=1; this might prove useful in finding a model that fits the validation data, and hence the population, well.

```
ods html close;
ods output bestsubsets=score;

proc logistic data=train2;
   model ins(event='1')=&screened
   / selection=SCORE best=2;
run;

ods html;
```

Recall that the **screened** macro variable contains the list of inputs created by making missing indicators (**MIPhone**, and so on), clustering categorical input levels (**brclus1**, and so on), and then clustering variables and choosing representatives. The inputs deemed to have low correlation with the target according to the Spearman and Hoeffding measures have been excluded. All in all, this leaves 36 inputs.

The inputs placed in **score** by PROC LOGISTIC are transferred to macro variables using an SQL SELECT INTO function. The automatic macro variable **SQLOBS** gives the number of models produced overall.

```
proc sql noprint;
   select variablesinmodel into :inputs1 - :inputs99999
   from score;
   select NumberOfVariables into :ic1 - :ic99999
   from score;
quit;

%let lastindx = &SQLOBS;
```

Two macros will be compiled. One, %ASSESS, will assess the performance of a model on a particular data set, and append a record summarizing that model's performance to the **results** data set. The parameters for the macro are the data set's name, the number of parameters in the model in question, the list of parameters in the model, the unique index number for the model, the π_1 and ρ_1 values, the name of the target variable, and the profit matrix values. The %ASSESS macro is called in the %FITANDSCORE macro. The %FITANDSCORE macro will fit and score many different models; here, the series of models created by the all subsets algorithm. The macros are shown in an appendix.

```
%include "s:\workshop\pmlr04d06a.sas";

%include "s:\workshop\pmlr04d06b.sas";

%fitandscore(data_train=train2,data_validate=valid2,target=ins);
```

The result of the %FITANDSCORE macro is a **results** data set.

```
proc print data=results(obs=10);
   title "Model Performance Measures for Training and Validation "
         "Data Sets";
run;
```

Model Performance Measures for Training and Validation Data Sets

Obs	DATAROLE	INPUT_COUNT	TOTAL_PROFIT	OVERALL_AVG_PROFIT	ASE	C	index
1	TRAIN	1	21568.67	1.00316	0.32047	0.50975	1
2	VALID	1	10779.50	1.00307	0.32030	0.50341	1
3	TRAIN	1	23185.91	1.07838	0.32771	0.65604	2
4	VALID	1	11497.12	1.06985	0.32752	0.65324	2
5	TRAIN	2	25444.45	1.18342	0.31608	0.73248	3
6	VALID	2	12483.13	1.16160	0.31579	0.72680	3
7	TRAIN	2	21568.67	1.00316	0.31661	0.58425	4
8	VALID	2	10779.50	1.00307	0.31668	0.57216	4
9	TRAIN	3	25812.26	1.20053	0.31262	0.75293	5
10	VALID	3	12770.93	1.18838	0.31256	0.74437	5

The results data set has the c statistic, average overall profit, and the ASE or average squared error. ASE is related to MSE, mean squared error, but it has a different divisor.

Example: Generate a graph of the c statistics by model and a graph of the overall average profit by model. Separate the plots by the training and validation data sets and only show the model with an index over 12 (7 inputs or more).

```
proc sgplot data=results;
   where index > 12;
   series y=c x=index / group=datarole markerattrs=(symbol=circle)
                        markers;
   yaxis label="C Statistic" Values=(0.770 to 0.790 by 0.001);
   xaxis label="Model Number" Values=(15 to 70 by 5);
   title "C Statistics by Model";
run;
```

Selected SERIES statement options:

GROUP= specifies a variable that is used to group the data. A separate plot is created for each unique value of the grouping variable. The plot elements for each group value are automatically distinguished by different visual attributes.

MARKERS adds data point markers to the series plot data points.

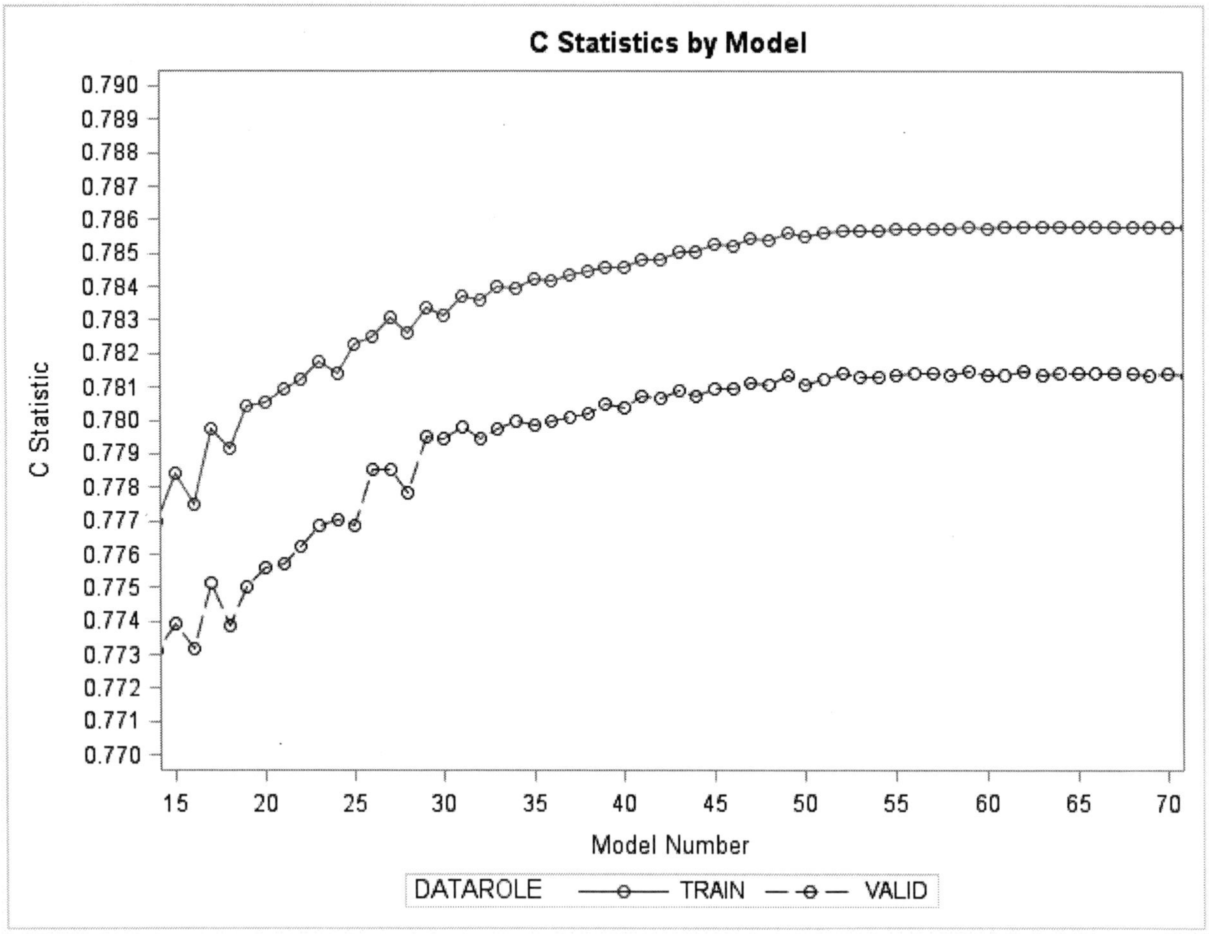

The plot seems to reach a plateau around index 45 or 50. Because the goal is to find a model that generalizes well, the simplest model that has good performance on the validation data is probably the best candidate.

Of course, it is difficult to quantify the trade-off between a slightly more complex model and a slightly higher c statistic. The trade-off might be easier to think about in terms of profit. What is it worth to the organization to use a more complex model? A plot of profit might help to visualize, and to quantify, this trade-off.

```
proc sgplot data=results;
   where index > 12;
   series y=overall_avg_profit x=index / group=datarole
           markerattrs=(symbol=plus) markers;
   yaxis label="Overall Average Profit"
         Values=(1.210 to 1.260 by 0.010);
   xaxis label="Model Number" Values=(15 to 70 by 5);
   title "Overall Average Profit by Model";
run;
```

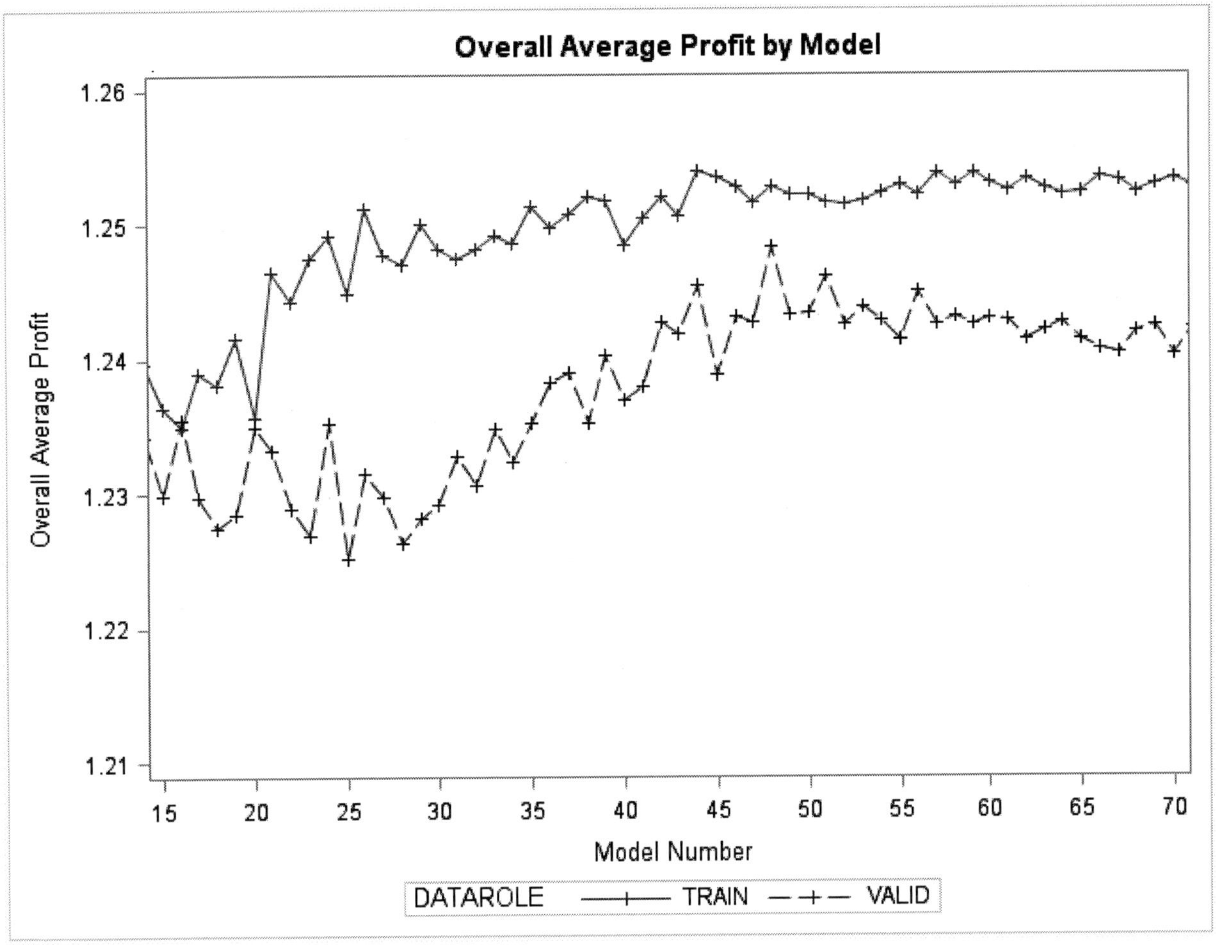

Again, the plot seems to show that the validation data performance peaks near index 50. Plotting the ASE will show similar results as well. Of course, you could use PROC MEANS or PROC SQL to find the model index associated with the highest validation profit, or c, or ASE. Because the highest validation performance is achieved by the model with index 48, that model is a good candidate.

Example: Show the results for model 48, which is the model with the highest profit on the validation data set. Score the validation data set and create an output data set with the results. Finally, compute a c statistic on the validation data set.

```
proc logistic data=train2;
   model ins(event='1')=&inputs48;
   score data=valid2 out=scoval2 fitstat;
   title "Logistic Model with Highest Profit";
run;
```

Logistic Model with Highest Profit

The LOGISTIC Procedure

Model Information	
Data Set	WORK.TRAIN2
Response Variable	Ins
Number of Response Levels	2
Model	binary logit
Optimization Technique	Fisher's scoring

Number of Observations Read	21512
Number of Observations Used	21512

Response Profile		
Ordered Value	Ins	Total Frequency
1	0	14061
2	1	7451

Probability modeled is Ins=1.

Model Convergence Status
Convergence criterion (GCONV=1E-8) satisfied.

Model Fit Statistics		
Criterion	Intercept Only	Intercept and Covariates
AIC	27759.675	22866.682
SC	27767.651	23066.092
-2 Log L	27757.675	22816.682

Testing Global Null Hypothesis: BETA=0			
Test	Chi-Square	DF	Pr > ChiSq
Likelihood Ratio	4940.9925	24	<.0001
Score	4674.1126	24	<.0001
Wald	3628.2749	24	<.0001

Analysis of Maximum Likelihood Estimates					
Parameter	DF	Estimate	Standard Error	Wald Chi-Square	Pr > ChiSq
Intercept	1	-1.9715	0.0581	1151.4808	<.0001
MIPhone	1	-0.3425	0.0623	30.2307	<.0001
Teller	1	0.0559	0.00808	47.8327	<.0001
MM	1	0.7747	0.0505	235.7065	<.0001
ILS	1	-0.2186	0.0810	7.2894	0.0069
LOC	1	-0.2760	0.0707	15.2462	<.0001
CD	1	0.9614	0.0473	412.6956	<.0001
CCPurc	1	0.0809	0.0400	4.0812	0.0434
ATMAmt	1	0.000027	5.567E-6	22.8649	<.0001
brclus2	1	0.2586	0.0366	49.8116	<.0001
Inv	1	0.5426	0.1015	28.6009	<.0001
Dep	1	-0.0725	0.0139	27.0357	<.0001
IRA	1	0.3152	0.0714	19.4742	<.0001
MIAcctAg	1	-0.2076	0.0671	9.5746	0.0020
MTGBal	1	-2.87E-6	8.771E-7	10.6979	0.0011
AcctAge	1	-0.0208	0.00271	58.9850	<.0001
SavBal	1	0.000130	4.964E-6	683.6868	<.0001
B_DDABal	1	0.0180	0.000633	811.5302	<.0001

Sav	1	0.2375	0.0396	36.0415	<.0001
Phone	1	-0.0642	0.0188	11.6484	0.0006
CCBal	1	2.834E-6	8.839E-7	10.2802	0.0013
MTG	1	-0.2637	0.0866	9.2753	0.0023
DirDep	1	-0.1728	0.0402	18.4607	<.0001
ATM	1	-0.1556	0.0405	14.7301	0.0001
brclus1	1	-0.3878	0.1171	10.9629	0.0009

Odds Ratio Estimates

Effect	Point Estimate	95% Wald Confidence Limits	
MIPhone	0.710	0.628	0.802
Teller	1.057	1.041	1.074
MM	2.170	1.966	2.396
ILS	0.804	0.686	0.942
LOC	0.759	0.661	0.872
CD	2.615	2.384	2.870
CCPurc	1.084	1.002	1.173
ATMAmt	1.000	1.000	1.000
brclus2	1.295	1.205	1.392
Inv	1.720	1.410	2.099
Dep	0.930	0.905	0.956
IRA	1.371	1.191	1.576
MIAcctAg	0.813	0.712	0.927
MTGBal	1.000	1.000	1.000
AcctAge	0.979	0.974	0.985
SavBal	1.000	1.000	1.000
B_DDABal	1.018	1.017	1.019

Sav	1.268	1.173	1.370
Phone	0.938	0.904	0.973
CCBal	1.000	1.000	1.000
MTG	0.768	0.648	0.910
DirDep	0.841	0.778	0.910
ATM	0.856	0.791	0.927
brclus1	0.679	0.539	0.854

Association of Predicted Probabilities and Observed Responses			
Percent Concordant	78.4	**Somers' D**	0.571
Percent Discordant	21.4	**Gamma**	0.572
Percent Tied	0.2	**Tau-a**	0.258
Pairs	104768511	**c**	0.785

Fit Statistics for SCORE Data

Data Set	Total Frequency	Log Likelihood	Error Rate	AIC	AICC	BIC	SC	R-Square	Max-Rescaled R-Square	AUC	Brier Score
WORK.VALID2	10752	-5751.1	0.2679	11552.13	11552.26	11734.21	11734.21	0.197926	0.27307	0.781097	0.178258

4.6 Chapter Summary

One of the most important steps in predictive modeling is to assess the performance of the model. To correct for the optimism bias, a common strategy is to holdout a portion of the development data for assessment. The LOGISTIC procedure can then be used to score the data set used for assessment. Statistics that measure the predictive accuracy of the model include sensitivity and positive predicted value. Graphics such as the ROC curve, the gains chart, and the lift chart can also be used to assess the performance of the model.

If the assessment data set was obtained by splitting oversampled data, then the assessment data set needs to be adjusted. This can be accomplished by using the sensitivity, specificity, and the prior probabilities.

In predictive modeling, the ultimate use of logistic regression is to allocate cases to classes. To determine the optimal cutoff probability, the plug-in Bayes rule can be used. The information that you need is the ratio
of the costs of false negatives to the cost of false positives. This optimal cutoff will minimize the total expected cost (or maximize the total expected profit).

The profit itself can be used as an assessment statistic, presuming that some reasonable estimate of the appropriate financial figures can be found.

When the target event is rare, the cost of a false negative is usually greater than the cost of a false positive. For example, the cost of not soliciting a responder is greater than the cost of sending a promotion to someone who does not respond. Such considerations dictate cutoffs that are usually much less than .50, the cutoff that maximizes accuracy.

A popular statistic that summarizes the performance of a model across a range of cutoffs is the Kolmogorov-Smirnov statistic. However, this statistic is not as powerful in detecting location differences as the Wilcoxon-Mann-Whitney test. Furthermore, the Wilcoxon-Mann-Whitney test statistic is equivalent to the area under the ROC curve (the c statistic). Thus, the c statistic should be used to assess the performance of a model across a range of cutoffs.

The output of a predictive model should be predictions that generalize well over time. Using the validation data set for honest assessment, a series of models can be compared according to their fitness to this task. Appropriate measures of fit and complexity might vary.

In the absence of profit information, the MSE (or, equivalently, ASE) can be used as a model fit metric to detect models with low bias, or lack-of-fit.

General form of PROC NPAR1WAY:

PROC NPAR1WAY DATA=*SAS-data-set <options>*;
    CLASS *variable*;
    VAR *variable*;
RUN;

4.7 Solutions

Solutions to Exercises

1. **Model Assessment**

   a. Use PROC SURVEYSELECT to split the imputed data set (**pva1**) into training and validation data sets. If **pva1** does not exist, submit programs **pmlr00d01.sas** and **pmlr03s01.sas**. Use 50% of the data for each data set role. Stratify on the target variable and use a seed of 27513.

An electronic copy of the solution program is in **pmlr04s01.sas**.

```
proc sort data=pva1 out=pva1;
   by target_b;
run;

proc surveyselect noprint data=pva1 samprate=.5 out=pva1 seed=27513
        outall;
   strata target_b;
run;

data pva_train pva_valid;
   set pva1;
   if selected then output pva_train;
   else output pva_valid;
run;
```

1) There are 9687 observations on the training data set.

   b. Fit a logistic regression model on the training data set using **TARGET_B** as the target variable and the macro variable **EX_SELECTED** as the input variables. Use the event= option to model the probability that **TARGET_B**=1. Use the SCORE statement to score the validation data set adjusting for oversampling. Use the OUTROC= option to create a data set and to create an ROC curve for the validation data set. Use the FITSTAT option to generate model fit statistics.

```
proc logistic data=pva_train;
   model target_b(event='1')=&ex_selected;
   score data=pva_valid priorevent=&ex_pi1 outroc=roc fitstat;
run;
```

Model Information	
Data Set	WORK.PVA_TRAIN
Response Variable	TARGET_B
Number of Response Levels	2
Model	binary logit
Optimization Technique	Fisher's scoring

Number of Observations Read	9687
Number of Observations Used	9687

Response Profile		
Ordered Value	**TARGET_B**	**Total Frequency**
1	0	7265
2	1	2422

Probability modeled is TARGET_B=1.

Model Convergence Status
Convergence criterion (GCONV=1E-8) satisfied.

Model Fit Statistics		
Criterion	**Intercept Only**	**Intercept and Covariates**
AIC	10897.230	10629.036
SC	10904.409	10715.179
-2 Log L	10895.230	10605.036

Testing Global Null Hypothesis: BETA=0			
Test	**Chi-Square**	**DF**	**Pr > ChiSq**
Likelihood Ratio	290.1942	11	<.0001
Score	290.9621	11	<.0001
Wald	279.7527	11	<.0001

Analysis of Maximum Likelihood Estimates					
Parameter	DF	Estimate	Standard Error	Wald Chi-Square	Pr > ChiSq
Intercept	1	-1.1835	0.1780	44.2130	<.0001
LIFETIME_CARD_PROM	1	0.0114	0.00327	12.2204	0.0005
PER_CAPITA_INCOME	1	7.48E-6	2.956E-6	6.4027	0.0114
RECENT_RESPONSE_PROP	1	1.6823	0.2401	49.1065	<.0001
ClusCdGrp3	1	-0.3146	0.0973	10.4505	0.0012
INCOME_GROUP	1	0.0587	0.0155	14.3721	0.0002
STATUS_ES	1	0.0857	0.0641	1.7870	0.1813
STATUS_FL	1	-0.2562	0.1041	6.0576	0.0138
ClusCdGrp1	1	0.1715	0.0884	3.7626	0.0524
MONTHS_SINCE_LAST_GI	1	-0.0376	0.00618	37.0493	<.0001
RECENT_AVG_GIFT_AMT	1	-0.0102	0.00285	12.7353	0.0004
ClusCdGrp2	1	0.0631	0.0576	1.1992	0.2735

Odds Ratio Estimates			
Effect	Point Estimate	95% Wald Confidence Limits	
LIFETIME_CARD_PROM	1.011	1.005	1.018
PER_CAPITA_INCOME	1.000	1.000	1.000
RECENT_RESPONSE_PROP	5.378	3.359	8.609
ClusCdGrp3	0.730	0.603	0.884
INCOME_GROUP	1.060	1.029	1.093
STATUS_ES	1.089	0.961	1.235
STATUS_FL	0.774	0.631	0.949
ClusCdGrp1	1.187	0.998	1.412
MONTHS_SINCE_LAST_GI	0.963	0.952	0.975
RECENT_AVG_GIFT_AMT	0.990	0.984	0.995
ClusCdGrp2	1.065	0.951	1.192

Association of Predicted Probabilities and Observed Responses			
Percent Concordant	61.0	Somers' D	0.221
Percent Discordant	39.0	Gamma	0.221
Percent Tied	0.0	Tau-a	0.083
Pairs	17595830	c	0.610

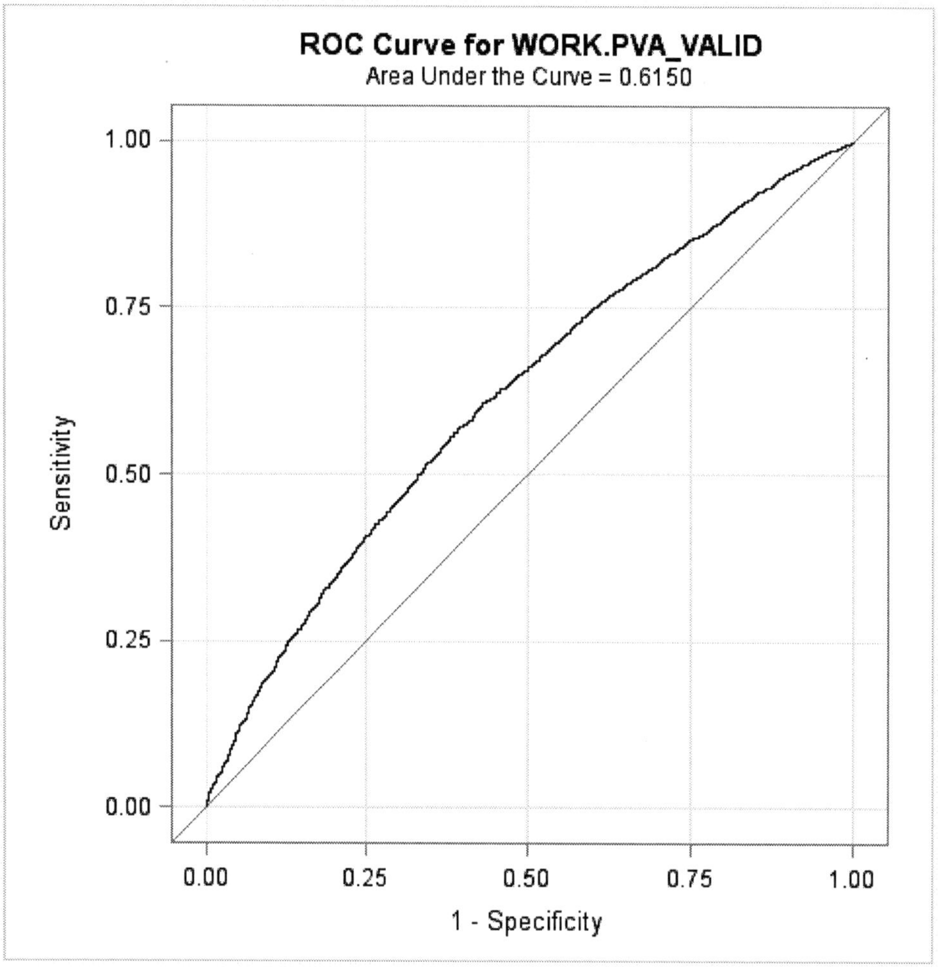

Fit Statistics for SCORE Data											
Data Set	Total Frequency	Log Likelihood	Error Rate	AIC	AICC	BIC	SC	R-Square	Max-Rescaled R-Square	AUC	Brier Score
WORK.PVA_VALID	9685	-7446.6	0.2500	14917.2	14917.23	15003.34	15003.34	-0.51157	-0.75763	0.614996	0.224036

1) The c statistic for the validation data set is 0.6150.

c. Using the OUTROC= data set, write a DATA step to compute the proportion of true positives, the proportion of false negatives, the proportion of true negatives, the proportion of false positives, the positive predicted value, the negative predicted value, the accuracy, the proportion allocated to class 1 (depth), and the lift. Then use PROC SGPLOT to create a lift chart. Add a reference line at a lift of 1 and restrict the focus to the region where depth is greater than 0.5% and less than 50%. Also restrict the Y-axis from 0 to 4 by 1.

```
data roc;
   set roc;
   cutoff=_PROB_;
   specif=1-_1MSPEC_;
   tp=&ex_pi1*_SENSIT_;
   fn=&ex_pi1*(1-_SENSIT_);
   tn=(1-&ex_pi1)*specif;
   fp=(1-&ex_pi1)*_1MSPEC_;
   depth=tp+fp;
   pospv=tp/depth;
   negpv=tn/(1-depth);
   acc=tp+tn;
   lift=pospv/&ex_pi1;
   keep cutoff tn fp fn tp
        _SENSIT_ _1MSPEC_ specif depth
        pospv negpv acc lift;
run;

proc sgplot data=roc;
   where 0.005 <= depth <= 0.50;
   title "Lift Chart for Validation Data";
   series y=lift x=depth;
   refline 1.0 / axis=y;
   yaxis values=(0 to 4 by 1);
run; quit;
```

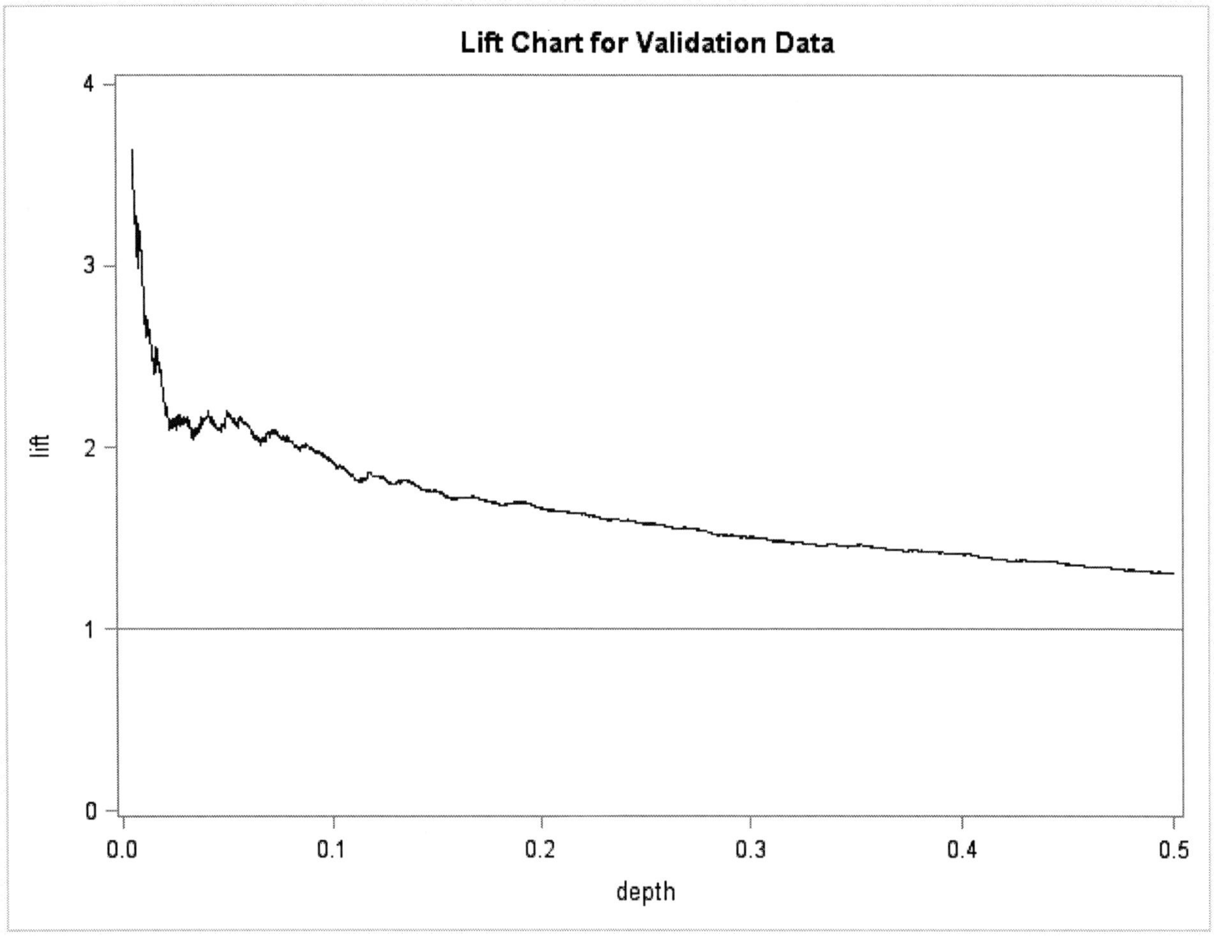

1) The lift at a depth of 10% is approximately 1.9.

Solutions to Student Activities (Polls/Quizzes)

4.02 Multiple Choice Poll – Correct Answer

What is the formula for sensitivity?

a. true positives / total actual positives (circled)
b. true positives / total predicted positives
c. true negatives / total actual negatives
d. true negatives / total predicted negatives

19

4.03 Multiple Choice Poll – Correct Answer

What is the lift at a depth of 10%?

a. 1.5
b. 1.9 (circled)
c. 2.3
d. 2.7

23

4.04 Multiple Choice Poll – Correct Answer

If the profit margin of true positives is 9 times higher than the loss margins of false positives, then according to Bayes rule what is the cutoff that maximizes the expected profit (assuming 0 profit and loss for true negatives and false negatives)?

a. 0.90
b. 0.09
c. 1/9
(d.) 0.10

33

4.05 Multiple Choice Poll – Correct Answer

Which of the following statements is false regarding the K-S statistic?

a. The test statistic, D, is the maximum vertical distance between the cumulative distributions.
b. An oversampled validation data set does not affect the test statistic D.
(c.) The K-S statistic is statistically equivalent to the area under the ROC curve.
d. The K-S statistic is not as powerful at detecting location differences as the Wilcoxon-Mann-Whitney test.

42

Appendix A References

A.1 References

Breiman, L., Friedman, J. H., Olshen, R. A., and Stone, C. J. (1984), *Classification and Regression Trees*, Chapman and Hall.

Cohen, A. (1991), "Dummy Variables in Stepwise Regression," *The American Statistician*, 45, 226-228.

Conover, W. J. (1980), *Practical Nonparametric Statistics*, New York: John Wiley & Sons.

Donner, A. (1982), "The Relative Effectiveness of Procedures Commonly Used in Multiple Regression Analysis for Dealing with Missing Values," *The American Statistician*, 36, 378-381.

Duffy, T. J. and Santner, D. E. (1989), *The Statistical Analysis of Discrete Data*, New York: Springer-Verlag.

Georges, J.E. (2004), *Advanced Predictive Modeling Using SAS® Enterprise Miner 5.1 Course Notes*, Cary, NC: SAS Institute Inc.

Greenacre, M. J. (1988), "Clustering Rows and Columns of a Contingency Table," *Journal of Classification*, 5, 39-51.

Greenacre, M. J. (1993), *Correspondence Analysis in Practice*, San Diego, CA: Academic Press.

Hand, D. J. (1997), *Construction and Assessment of Classification Rules*, New York: John Wiley & Sons.

Hand, D. J. and Henley, W. E. (1997), "Statistical Classification Methods in Consumer Credit Scoring: A Review," *Journal of the Royal Statistical Society A*, 160, 153-541.

Harrell, F. E. (1997), *Predicting Outcomes: Applied Survival Analysis and Logistic Regression*, Charlottesville Virginia: School of Medicine, University of Virginia.

Hastie, T. J. and Tibshirani, R. J. (1990), *Generalized Additive Models*, London: Chapman and Hall.

Huber, P. J. (1997), "From Large to Huge: A Statistician's Reactions to KDD & DM," *Proceedings of the Third International Conference on Knowledge Discovery and Data Mining*, Menlo Park, CA: AAAI Press.

Jackson, J. E. (1991), *A Users Guide to Principal Components*, New York: John Wiley & Sons.

Jones, M. P. (1996), "Indicator and Stratification Methods for Missing Explanatory Variables in Multiple Linear Regression," *Journal of the American Statistical Association*, 91, 222-230.

Lawless, J. F. and Singhal, K. (1978), "Efficient Screening of Nonnormal Regression Models," *Biometrics*, 34, 318-327.

Little, R. J. A. (1992), "Regression with Missing X's: A Review," *Journal of the American Statistical Association*, 87, 1227-1237.

Magee, L. (1998), "Nonlocal Behavior in Polynomial Regressions," *The American Statistician*, 52, 20-22.

Mantel, N. (1970), "Why Stepdown Procedures in Variable Selection," *Technometrics*, 12, 621-625.

McLachlan, G. J. (1992), *Discriminant Analysis and Statistical Pattern Recognition*, New York: John Wiley & Sons.

Nelson, R. W. (1997), *Credit Card Risk Management*, Warren Taylor Publications.

Prentice, R. L. and Pike, R. (1979), "Logistic Disease Incidence Models and Case-Control Studies," *Biometrika*, 66, 403-411.

Ripley, B. D. (1996), *Pattern Recognition and Neural Networks*, Cambridge University Press.

Sarle, W. S. (1994), "Neural Networks and Statistical Models, " *Proceedings of the 19th Annual SUGI*, Cary, NC: SAS Institute Inc.

SAS Institute Inc., *SAS® 9.1 Language Reference: Concepts, Third Edition,* Cary, NC: SAS Institute Inc., 2005.

SAS Institute Inc., *Base SAS® 9.1Procedures Guide, Second Edition,* Cary, NC: SAS Institute Inc., 2006.

SAS Institute Inc., *SAS/STAT® 9.1 Users Guide,* Cary, NC: SAS Institute Inc., 2004.

SAS Institute Inc., *Logistic Regression Examples Using the SAS System, Version 6, First Edition,* Cary, NC: SAS Institute Inc., 1995.

Scott, A. J. and Wild, C. J. (1986), "Fitting Logistic Regression Models under Case-Control or Choice Based Sampling, " *Journal of the Royal Statistical Society B*, 48, 170-182.

Scott, A. J. and Wild, C. J. (1997), "Fitting Regression Models to Case-Control Data by Maximum Likelihood," *Biometrika*, 84, 57-71.

Appendix B Additional Resources

B.1 Automatic Score Code Generation

The Output Delivery System is an easy way to save results that are typically displayed as output into a data set. The data set **betas2** contains the output listed under the heading "Analysis of Maximum Likelihood Estimates" in the PROC LOGISTIC output.

```
ods output parameterEstimates = betas2;
proc logistic data=develop des;
   model ins=dda ddabal dep depamt cashbk checks;
run;

proc print data=betas2;
   var variable estimate;
run;
```

Obs	Variable	Estimate
1	Intercept	0.1259
2	DDA	-0.9705
3	DDABal	0.000072
4	Dep	-0.0715
5	DepAmt	0.000018
6	CashBk	-0.5618
7	Checks	-0.00400

The code to generate score code from the **betas2** data set follows. This code creates a file that contains the code to create the linear predictor. The macro variable **target** is used in the name and label of the predicted probability variable. The code handles categorical inputs as well, even though there are none in this example. Categorical inputs should be numerically coded using reference cell coding. The code essentially automates the tedious task of cutting and pasting parameter estimates from logistic regression results into DATA step code.

```
%let target=INS;

filename scorecd 'c:\temp\logistic score code.sas';

data _null_;
   attrib PREDNAME length=$32
          TARGNAME length=$32
          LastParm length=$32
          ;
   file scorecd;
   set betas2 end=last;
   retain TARGNAME PREDNAME LastParm ' ';
   if (Variable="Intercept") then do;
      TARGNAME=compress("&target");
      PREDNAME="P_"||compress(TARGNAME);
      put "*********************************************;";
      put "*** begin scoring code for Logistic Regression;";
      put "*********************************************;";

      put "length " PREDNAME "8;";
      put "label " PREDNAME "= 'Predicted: " TARGNAME +(-1) "';";

      put "*** accumulate XBETA;";
      put "XBETA = " Estimate best20. ";";
   end;
   else if (ClassVal0=' ') then do;
      put "XBETA = XBETA + (" Estimate best20. ") * " Variable ";";
   end;
   else if (compress(Variable)=compress(LastParm)) then do;
      put "else if (" Variable "='" ClassVal0 +(-1) "') then do;";
      put "   XBETA = XBETA + (" Estimate best20. ");";
      put "end;";
   end;
   else do;
      put "if (" Variable "='" ClassVal0 +(-1) "') then do;";
      put "   XBETA = XBETA + (" Estimate best20. ");";
      put "end;";
   end;
   LastParm=Variable;
   if last then do;
      put PREDNAME "= 1/(1+exp(-XBETA));";
   end;
run;
```

The output of the code generator is DATA step code to score a new data set.

```
*********************************************;
*** begin scoring code for Logistic Regression;
*********************************************;
length P_INS 8;
label P_INS = 'Predicted: INS';
*** accumulate XBETA;
XBETA =       0.12592268473366;
XBETA = XBETA + (   -0.97052008343956) * DDA ;
XBETA = XBETA + (    0.00007181904404) * DDABal ;
XBETA = XBETA + (   -0.07153101800749) * Dep ;
XBETA = XBETA + (     0.0000178287498) * DepAmt ;
XBETA = XBETA + (   -0.56175142056463) * CashBk ;
XBETA = XBETA + (   -0.00399923596541) * Checks ;
P_INS = 1/(1+exp(-XBETA));
```

The %INCLUDE statement brings a SAS programming statement, data lines, or both, into a current SAS program. Using the SOURCE2 option after a slash treats the code as if it were pasted into the Program Editor - the text appears in the log. The %INCLUDE statement can use an explicit filename (C:\Temp\logistic score code.sas) or a fileref (scorecd).

```
data scored;
   set pmlr.new;
   %include "c:\temp\logistic score code.sas" /source2;
run;
```

The above code generates the same results as the following code:

```
data scored;
   set pmlr.new;
   %include scorecd /source2;
run;
```

The results are equivalent to the earlier two techniques.

```
proc print data=scored(obs=20);
   var p_ins xbeta dda ddabal dep depamt cashbk checks;
run;
```

Obs	P_INS	XBETA	DDA	DDABal	Dep	DepAmt	Cash Bk	Checks
1	0.27476	-0.97058	1	56.29	2	955.51	0	1
2	0.32343	-0.73807	1	3292.17	2	961.60	0	1
3	0.30275	-0.83426	1	1723.86	2	2108.65	0	2
4	0.53144	0.12592	0	0.00	0	0.00	0	0
5	0.27180	-0.98552	1	67.91	2	519.24	0	3
6	0.32482	-0.73172	1	2554.58	1	501.36	0	2
7	0.27205	-0.98425	1	0.00	2	2883.08	0	12
8	0.30558	-0.82087	1	2641.33	3	4521.61	0	8
9	0.53144	0.12592	0	0.00	0	0.00	0	0
10	0.28679	-0.91103	1	52.22	1	75.59	0	0
11	0.37131	-0.52659	1	6163.29	2	2603.56	0	7
12	0.18001	-1.51631	1	431.12	2	568.43	1	2
13	0.53144	0.12592	0	0.00	0	0.00	0	0
14	0.20217	-1.37280	1	112.82	8	2688.75	0	3
15	0.31330	-0.78473	1	1146.61	3	11224.20	0	2
16	0.53144	0.12592	0	0.00	0	0.00	0	0
17	0.27549	-0.96694	1	1241.38	3	3538.14	0	15
18	0.30509	-0.82318	1	298.23	0	0.00	0	0
19	0.28299	-0.92966	1	367.04	2	4242.22	0	11
20	0.26508	-1.01975	1	1229.47	4	3514.57	0	10

In order to use the model, you must create scoring code. This method automatically creates a DATA step that you could use to score new cases, without running the SCORE procedure or having to cut and paste parameter estimates into code by hand.

B.2 Correcting the Intercept in the Score Code Generator

Because the correction for oversampling is simply an adjustment to the intercept, you could build that correction into the score code generator. The following code is similar to the initial score code generator, but the intercept term is corrected by the amount of the offset.

```
%let pi1=.02;

proc SQL noprint;
  select mean(INS) into :rho1 from develop;
quit;

ods output parameterEstimates=betas2;
proc logistic data=develop des;
   model ins=dda ddabal dep depamt cashbk checks;
run;

%let target=INS;
filename scorecd 'c:\temp\logistic score code.sas';
```

```
data _null_;
   attrib PREDNAME length=$32
          TARGNAME length=$32
          LastParm length=$32
          ;
   file scorecd;
   set betas2 end=last;
   retain TARGNAME PREDNAME LastParm ' ';
   if (Variable="Intercept") then do;
      TARGNAME=compress("&target");
      PREDNAME="P_"||compress(TARGNAME);
      put "**********************************************;";
      put "*** begin scoring code for Logistic Regression;";
      put "**********************************************;";

      put "length " PREDNAME "8;";
      put "label " PREDNAME "= 'Predicted: " TARGNAME +(-1) "';";

      put "*** accumulate XBETA;";
      Estimate + (-log(((1-&pi1)*&rho1)/(&pi1*(1-&rho1))));
      put "XBETA = " Estimate best20. ";";
   end;
   else if (ClassVal0=' ') then do;
      put "XBETA = XBETA + (" Estimate best20. ") * " Variable ";";
   end;
   else if (compress(Variable)=compress(LastParm)) then do;
      put "else if (" Variable "='" ClassVal0 +(-1) "') then do;";
      put "   XBETA = XBETA + (" Estimate best20. ");";
      put "end;";
   end;
   else do;
      put "if (" Variable "='" ClassVal0 +(-1) "') then do;";
      put "   XBETA = XBETA + (" Estimate best20. ");";
      put "end;";
   end;
   LastParm=Variable;
   if last then do;
      put PREDNAME "= 1/(1+exp(-XBETA));";
   end;
run;
```

The score code follows. Note the change in the intercept term, which was 0.12592268473366 before.

```
*********************************************;
*** begin scoring code for Logistic Regression;
*********************************************;
length P_INS 8;
label P_INS = 'Predicted: INS';
*** accumulate XBETA;
XBETA =     -3.13082398583352;
XBETA = XBETA + (   -0.97052008343956) * DDA ;
XBETA = XBETA + (    0.00007181904404) * DDABal ;
XBETA = XBETA + (   -0.07153101800749) * Dep ;
XBETA = XBETA + (     0.0000178287498) * DepAmt ;
XBETA = XBETA + (   -0.56175142056463) * CashBk ;
XBETA = XBETA + (   -0.00399923596541) * Checks ;
P_INS = 1/(1+exp(-XBETA));
```

Again, you can use the %INCLUDE statement to score data with this code.

```
data scored;
   set pmlr.new;
   %include scorecd /source2;
run;

proc print data=scored(obs=20);
   var p_ins dda ddabal dep depamt cashbk checks;
run;
```

The output is the same as the results of the PRIOREVENT=&pi1 correction, above.

Obs	P_INS	DDA	DDABal	Dep	DepAmt	Cash Bk	Checks
1	0.014381	1	56.29	2	955.51	0	1
2	0.018078	1	3292.17	2	961.60	0	1
3	0.016447	1	1723.86	2	2108.65	0	2
4	0.041854	0	0.00	0	0.00	0	0
5	0.014171	1	67.91	2	519.24	0	3
6	0.018191	1	2554.58	1	501.36	0	2
7	0.014189	1	0.00	2	2883.08	0	12
8	0.016665	1	2641.33	3	4521.61	0	8
9	0.041854	0	0.00	0	0.00	0	0
10	0.015250	1	52.22	1	75.59	0	0
11	0.022241	1	6163.29	2	2603.56	0	7
12	0.008384	1	431.12	2	568.43	1	2
13	0.041854	0	0.00	0	0.00	0	0
14	0.009665	1	112.82	8	2688.75	0	3
15	0.017268	1	1146.61	3	11224.20	0	2
16	0.041854	0	0.00	0	0.00	0	0
17	0.014433	1	1241.38	3	3538.14	0	15
18	0.016628	1	298.23	0	0.00	0	0
19	0.014973	1	367.04	2	4242.22	0	11
20	0.013701	1	1229.47	4	3514.57	0	10

B.3 Sampling Weights

$$weight_i = \begin{cases} \dfrac{\pi_1}{\rho_1} & \text{if } y_i = 1 \\ \dfrac{\pi_0}{\rho_0} & \text{if } y_i = 0 \end{cases}$$

Another method for adjusting for oversampling is to incorporate sampling weights. Sampling weights adjust the data so that it better represents the true population. When a rare target event has been oversampled, class 0 is under-represented in the sample. Consequently, a class-0 case should actually count more in the analysis than a class-1 case. The predicted values will be properly corrected by using weights that are inversely proportional to selection probabilities (for each class, the number of cases in the sample divided by the number of cases in the population). It is convenient to use the normalized sample weights because they sum to the original sample size

$$\sum_{i=1}^{n} weight_i = n_0 \frac{\pi_0}{\rho_0} + n_1 \frac{\pi_1}{\rho_1} = n\pi_0 + n\pi_1 = n$$

The weights adjust the number of cases in the sample to be $n\pi_0$ and $n\pi_1$, in class 0 and 1 respectively. The classes now are in the same proportion in the adjusted sample as they are in the population. The normalization causes less distortion in standard errors and *p*-values. While statistical inference is not the goal of the analysis, *p*-values are used as tuning parameters in variable selection algorithms.

The offset method and the weighted method are not statistically equivalent. The parameter estimates are not exactly the same, but they have the same large-sample statistical properties. When the linear-logistic model is correctly specified, the offset method (unweighted) analysis is considered superior. However, when the logistic model is merely an approximation to some nonlinear model, weighted analysis has advantages (Scott and Wild 1986).

$$\text{Sampling Weight} = \begin{cases} \dfrac{0.02}{0.35} = 0.58 \text{ if Ins} = 1 \\ \dfrac{0.98}{0.65} = 1.46 \text{ if Ins} = 0 \end{cases}$$

Sampling Weights

Example: Add sampling weights to the data set **develop**. The weights are .058 (.02/.346) for class 1 and 1.5 (.98/.654) for class 0. Then use the WEIGHT statement in PROC LOGISTIC to weight each observation in the input data set by the value of the WEIGHT variable.

The sampling weights could have been assigned manually without having to reference macro variables. The logical expressions **(Ins=1)** and **(Ins=0)** in the assignment statement return the value one when true and zero when false. Consequently, this syntax is a more compact way of expressing a conditional.

```
%let pi1 = 0.02;

proc sql noprint;
   select mean(ins) into :rho1 from pmlr.develop;
quit;

data develop;
   set pmlr.develop;
   sampwt=((1-&pi1)/(1-&rho1))*(ins=0)+(&pi1/&rho1)*(ins=1);
run;

proc logistic data=develop des;
   weight sampwt;
   model ins = dda ddabal dep depamt cashbk checks / stb;
   score data=pmlr.new out=scored;
run;
```

```
                         The LOGISTIC Procedure

                           Model Information

              Data Set                      WORK.DEVELOP
              Response Variable             Ins
              Number of Response Levels     2
              Weight Variable               sampwt
              Model                         binary logit
              Optimization Technique        Fisher's scoring


                 Number of Observations Read         32264
                 Number of Observations Used         32264
                 Sum of Weights Read              32263.99
                 Sum of Weights Used              32263.99
```

Response Profile

Ordered Value	Ins	Total Frequency	Total Weight
1	1	11175	645.281
2	0	21089	31618.707

Probability modeled is Ins=1.

The results show that the response profile table has a new column named **Total Weight**. The figures in the column represent the sample sizes adjusted to the population proportions. Note that the Sum of the Weights equals the total sample size.

Model Convergence Status

Convergence criterion (GCONV=1E-8) satisfied.

Model Fit Statistics

Criterion	Intercept Only	Intercept and Covariates
AIC	6328.271	6194.870
SC	6336.653	6253.542
-2 Log L	6326.271	6180.870

Testing Global Null Hypothesis: BETA=0

Test	Chi-Square	DF	Pr > ChiSq
Likelihood Ratio	145.4014	6	<.0001
Score	230.9722	6	<.0001
Wald	156.2504	6	<.0001

The LOGISTIC Procedure

Analysis of Maximum Likelihood Estimates

Parameter	DF	Estimate	Standard Error	Wald Chi-Square	Pr > ChiSq	Standardized Estimate
Intercept	1	-3.1308	0.0756	1714.2522	<.0001	
DDA	1	-0.8398	0.1207	48.4361	<.0001	-0.1583
DDABal	1	0.000024	4.241E-6	32.6018	<.0001	0.0669
Dep	1	-0.0756	0.0376	4.0510	0.0441	-0.0718
DepAmt	1	2.807E-6	6.199E-6	0.2050	0.6507	0.00814
CashBk	1	-0.5691	0.4240	1.8016	0.1795	-0.0461
Checks	1	0.00479	0.0105	0.2080	0.6484	0.0139

```
                         Odds Ratio Estimates

                         Point          95% Wald
          Effect      Estimate      Confidence Limits

          DDA            0.432       0.341       0.547
          DDABal         1.000       1.000       1.000
          Dep            0.927       0.861       0.998
          DepAmt         1.000       1.000       1.000
          CashBk         0.566       0.247       1.299
          Checks         1.005       0.984       1.026

     Association of Predicted Probabilities and Observed Responses

          Percent Concordant          53.6    Somers' D    0.282
          Percent Discordant          25.3    Gamma        0.358
          Percent Tied                21.1    Tau-a        0.128
          Pairs                  235669575    c            0.641
```

```
proc print data=scored(obs=20);
   var p_1 dda ddabal dep depamt cashbk checks;
run;
```

Obs	P_1	DDA	DDABal	Dep	DepAmt	Cash Bk	Checks
1	0.016095	1	56.29	2	955.51	0	1
2	0.017385	1	3292.17	2	961.60	0	1
3	0.016880	1	1723.86	2	2108.65	0	2
4	0.041854	0	0.00	0	0.00	0	0
5	0.016233	1	67.91	2	519.24	0	3
6	0.018463	1	2554.58	1	501.36	0	2
7	0.017019	1	0.00	2	2883.08	0	12
8	0.016586	1	2641.33	3	4521.61	0	8
9	0.041854	0	0.00	0	0.00	0	0
10	0.017213	1	52.22	1	75.59	0	0
11	0.019232	1	6163.29	2	2603.56	0	7
12	0.009292	1	431.12	2	568.43	1	2
13	0.041854	0	0.00	0	0.00	0	0
14	0.010447	1	112.82	8	2688.75	0	3
15	0.015850	1	1146.61	3	11224.20	0	2
16	0.041854	0	0.00	0	0.00	0	0
17	0.016535	1	1241.38	3	3538.14	0	15
18	0.018644	1	298.23	0	0.00	0	0
19	0.017152	1	367.04	2	4242.22	0	11
20	0.014986	1	1229.47	4	3514.57	0	10

The probabilities from the weighted analysis are similar but not equivalent to the probabilities estimated by the offset method (pseudo model).

B.4 Cluster Imputation Using the FASTCLUS Procedure

PROC FASTCLUS can be used to replace the missing values with the cluster means from the training data set. First, the data set is split into the training and validation data sets. Then PROC FASTCLUS is used to compute the cluster means on the training data set and save the cluster means on an output data set.

```
proc fastclus data=train impute outiter outseed=seed out=train1
              maxclusters=5;
   var &inputs;
run;
```

Selected PROC FASTCLUS statement options:

IMPUTE	requests imputation of missing values after the final assignment of observations to clusters. If an observation that is assigned (or would have been assigned) to a cluster has a missing value for variables used in the cluster analysis, the missing value is replaced by the corresponding value in the cluster seed to which the observation is assigned (or would have been assigned). If the observation cannot be assigned to a cluster, missing value replacement depends on whether the NOMISS option is specified. If NOMISS is not specified, missing values are replaced by the mean of all observations in the DATA= data set having a value for that variable. If NOMISS is specified, missing values are replaced by the mean of only observations used in the analysis. (A weighted mean is used if a variable is specified in the WEIGHT statement.) If you specify the IMPUTE option, the imputed values are not used in computing cluster statistics. If you also request an OUT= data set, it contains the imputed values.
OUTITER	outputs information from the iteration history to the OUTSEED= data set, including the cluster seeds at each iteration.
OUTSEED=	is another name for the MEAN= data set, provided because the data set can contain location estimates other than means.
MAXCLUSTERS=	specifies the maximum number of clusters permitted. If you omit the MAXCLUSTERS= option, a value of 100 is assumed.

PROC FASTCLUS is then used to replace the missing values from the validation data set with the cluster means from the training data set computed at the first iteration.

```
proc fastclus data=valid impute seed=seed(where=(_iter_=1))
              replace=none maxclusters=5 out=validate1 maxiter=0;
   var &inputs;
run;
```

Selected PROC FASTCLUS statement options:

SEED=	specifies an input data set from which initial cluster seeds are to be selected. If you do not specify the SEED= option, initial seeds are selected from the DATA= data set. The SEED= data set must contain the same variables that are used in the data analysis.
REPLACE=	specifies how seed replacement is performed. NONE suppresses the seed replacement.
MAXITER=	specifies the maximum number of iterations for recomputing cluster seeds.

B.5 %ASSESS Macro

The %ASSESS macro simplifies the assessment of each of the models found by the best subsets procedure. Data for assessment are assumed stored in a data set named SCORE&DATA, where DATA is a macro parameter with anticipated values TRAIN, VALID, and potentially TEST. The INPUTCOUNT= macro parameter points to the number of parameters in the model in question. The INPUTSINMODEL= macro parameter points to the list of parameters in the model. The INDEX= macro parameter is a unique index for each model in the series. This enables you to have more than one model with, say, 16 inputs.

```
%macro assess(data=,inputcount=,inputsinmodel=,index=,pi1=,rho1=,
target=,profit11=,profit01=,profit10=,profit00=);
```

The variables π_1, ρ_1, π_0, and ρ_0 are necessary to calculate sampling weights. π_1 must be known a priori, and ρ_1 was calculated earlier in PROC MEANS. To simplify the code, macro variables are created to house π_0 and ρ_0 as well. The %SYSEVALF function takes the text string in its argument and performs the calculation. For example, %SYSEVALF(1-**&pi1**) will resolve to 0.98 in this instance.

```
%let rho0 = %sysevalf(1-&rho1);
%let pi0 = %sysevalf(1-&pi1);
```

The assessment data are sorted by descending posterior probability. This sorting allows the calculation of a c statistic by the **ASSESS** DATA step below.

```
proc sort data=scored&data;
  by descending p_1;
run;
```

The main assessment DATA step begins. The **DATAROLE** variable is defined to contain the type of assessment (for example, VALID). A two-by-two temporary array, **n**, is defined and initialized to all zeros. The **n** array will contain the confusion matrix based on the profit matrix specified by decision processing.

A two-by-one temporary array, **w**, is defined and initialized to the ratio of the population and sample marginal averages (π_0/ρ_0) and (π_1/ρ_1). The **w** array will be used to adjust the model posterior probabilities as well as to calculate total profit and the confusion matrix.

```
/* create assessment data set */
data assess;
  attrib DATAROLE length=$5;
  retain sse 0 csum 0 DATAROLE "&data";

  /* 2 x 2 count array, or count matrix */
  array n[0:1,0:1] _temporary_ (0 0 0 0);
  /* sample weights array */
  array w[0:1] _temporary_
    (%sysevalf(&pi0/&rho0) %sysevalf(&pi1/&rho1));
  keep DATAROLE INPUT_COUNT INDEX
       TOTAL_PROFIT OVERALL_AVG_PROFIT ASE C;
```

An observation is read from the assessment data.

```
set scored&data end=last;
```

Assuming that the LOGISTIC call that generates the scored data sets will correct for oversampling, you can use the predicted probabilities. If the probabilities are biased due to oversampling, and you do not correct for this before the assessment, you could do that here.

Profits for each decision alternative are calculated, based on the user-specified decision data.

```
d1=&Profit11*p_1+&Profit01*p_0;
d0=&Profit10*p_1+&Profit00*p_0;
```

Variable **t** equals 1 if the target equals the primary target value and zero otherwise. That is, **t** is a flag for response. Variable **d** equals 1 if the profit for decision 1 exceeds the profit for decision 0. That is, **d** is the profit maximizing decision. The STRIP function removes trailing and leading blanks. Contrast this with the default behavior of the COMPRESS function, which removes all blanks in a field.

These variables might be defined differently in the presence of different decision rules or different values for the target classes; for example a different profit matrix or a Y/N target instead of a 1/0 target.

```
/* T is a flag for response */
  t=(strip(&target)="1");
/* D is the decision, based on profit. */
  d=(d1>d0);
```

The appropriate cell of the confusion matrix array **n** is incremented by the appropriate element of the weight vector. The sum of squared error, **sse**, is incremented. The sum used to calculate the c statistic, **csum**, is incremented. The increment will be positive only when the target value is zero. This is in effect a Riemann sum of the Receiver Operating Characteristic (ROC) curve.

```
/* update the count matrix, sse, and c */
  n[t,d] + w[t];
  sse + (&target-p_1)**2;
  csum + ((n[1,1]+n[1,0])*(1-t)*w[0]);
```

On the last time through the DATA step, finalize the fit statistics and output. To finalize the ASE, divide the sum of squared errors by the sample size. Total profit is the product of the sample sizes in each cell of **n** with the appropriate profit amount. The c statistic is based on the sum of the area of rectangles that approximate the ROC curve, but those areas are based on the sample size. To restrict this area to be between 0 and 1, the range of the c statistic, divide through by the product of n_1 and n_0.

```
  if last then do;
    INPUT_COUNT=&inputcount;
    TOTAL_PROFIT = sum(&Profit11*n[1,1],&Profit10*n[1,0],
                       &Profit01*n[0,1],&Profit00*n[0,0]);
    OVERALL_AVG_PROFIT =
TOTAL_PROFIT/sum(n[0,0],n[1,0],n[0,1],n[1,1]);
    ASE = sse/sum(n[0,0],n[1,0],n[0,1],n[1,1]);
    C = csum/(sum(n[0,0],n[0,1])*sum(n[1,0],n[1,1]));
    index=&index;
    output;
  end;
run;
```

Update the **Results** data set with this data's assessment results.

```
proc append base=results data=assess force;
run;
```

End the %ASSESS macro.

```
%mend assess;
```

B.6 %FITANDSCORE Macro

The %FITANDSCORE macro will refit the series of logistic regression models, and create the scored data sets that the %ASSESS macro needs.

```
%macro fitandscore(data_train=,data_validate=,target=);
```

Any previous version of the **Results** data set is removed using PROC DATASETS.

```
proc datasets
   library=work
   nodetails
   nolist;
   delete results;
run;
```

A loop begins over all models fit by the original PROC LOGISTIC. The macro variable **IM** is set equal to the inputs in the **MODEL_INDX** model. **IC** is set equal to the number of inputs in the **MODEL_INDX** model.

```
%do model_indx=1 %to &lastindx;

%let im=&&inputs&model_indx;
%let ic=&&ic&model_indx;
```

The macro variable **LASTINDX** was created in the program **pmlr04d07.sas**. It points to the total number of models in the series of models to be considered.

PROC LOGISTIC refits the model with inputs specified in **IM**. The SCORE option is used to score the training and validation data sets and place the result in **ScoredTrain** and **ScoredValid**, respectively. Only the target value and posterior probabilities are kept. The PRIOREVENT= option corrects the predicted probabilities for oversampling. If you have many models, or if you are not interested in the output, you can use the Output Delivery System to eliminate the printed listing of the PROC LOGISTIC results.

```
proc logistic data=&data_train;
   model &target(event='1')=&im;
   score data=&data_train
         out=scoredtrain(keep=ins p_1 p_0)
         priorevent=&pi1;
   score data=&data_validate
         out=scoredvalid(keep=ins p_1 p_0)
         priorevent=&pi1;
run;
```

The %ASSESS macro is called for each of the scored data sets. The values of the parameters in the call (DATA=, INPUTCOUNT=, INPUTSINMODEL=, ND index=) become macro variables in the %ASSESS macro.

```
%assess(data=TRAIN,inputcount=&ic,inputsinmodel=&im,index=&model_indx,
        pi1=0.02,rho1=0.346,target=ins,profit11=99,profit01=-1,
        profit10=0,profit00=0);
%assess(data=VALID,inputcount=&ic,inputsinmodel=&im,index=&model_indx,
        pi1=0.02,rho1=0.346,target=ins,profit11=99,profit01=-1,
        profit10=0,profit00=0);
```

The loop over all models fit by the LOGISTIC procedure with the SCORE option ends.

```
%end;
```

The %FITANDSCORE macro definition ends.

```
%mend fitandscore;
```

Recommended SAS® Titles

Predictive Modeling Using Logistic Regression

	Title	Price (U.S. Dollars)
	SAS® Press	
978-1-59994-298-8	*Analyzing Receiver Operating Characteristic Curves with SAS®*	$31.95
978-1-59994-641-2	*Logistic Regression Using SAS®: Theory and Application, Second Edition*	$49.95
978-1-59994-660-3	*Output Delivery System: The Basics and Beyond*	$55.95
978-1-60764-800-0	*SAS® Statistics by Example*	$34.95
978-1-58025-725-1	*SAS® System for Regression, Third Edition*	$43.95
978-1-60764-485-9	*Statistical Graphics in SAS®: An Introduction to the Graph Template Language and the Statistical Graphics Procedures*	$37.95
978-1-59994-656-6	*Statistical Programming in SAS®*	$64.95
	SAS® Documentation	
978-1-61290-076-6	*SAS® 9.3 ODS Graphics: Procedures Guide, Second Edition*	$63.95

Notes

- Prices are subject to change without notice.
- To order, please visit **support.sas.com/bookstore**.
- SAS documentation is available to search, browse, or print **free** online at: **support.sas.com/documentation**.